If Only These Walls Could Speak

If Only These Walls Could Speak

An Orphanage Diary

Alan Hamblin

Blenheim Press Limited
Codicote

Published in 2010
by
Blenheim Press Ltd
Codicote Innovation Centre
St Albans Road
Codicote
Herts SG4 8WH
www.blenheimpressltd.co.uk

ISBN 978-1-906302-21-4

Typeset by TW Typesetting, Plymouth, Devon
Set in 11 point Janson

Printed and bound by CPI Antony Rowe, Eastbourne

To:

MILDRED, my mother, and MARGARET, my sister

And to the countless thousands of children and staff,
both living and dead, for whom these words speak.

CONTENTS

FOREWORD

'Gone are the days of dark brown and dark green paint and the smell of stale cabbage,' was how a Barnardo's advertisement described its new image in the 1980s.

The truth is there was a lot more to an orphanage than the colour of paint or the smell of food! Within these pages are personal recollections from the first part of the last century which tell the real human story.

This is the story of two orphanages, the RAO and the PAO – the Royal Albert Orphanage in Worcester and the Princess Alice Orphanage in Birmingham. Both had royal patronage, the Royal Albert in 1868 and the Princess Alice in 1882.

Since those times until the 1960s the children of the poor and destitute were sent to institutions such as these – whereas the rich and royal of the land were, and still are, sent to boarding schools for a good disciplined Christian religious education.

For children, whether from poor or from rich parents, loneliness and loss of love was and is still the same.

The following quotes are a sad indictment of the English: Alistair Cooke in his *Letter from America* said that the English criticise the Americans for their racism, whereas the Americans think the English inhuman for sending their children to boarding schools.

A former landlady of mine who came to England from France after the second world war said, 'English people love their pets more than they love their children!'

ACKNOWLEDGEMENTS

Judy Hamblin
Muriel McKie
G.H. Bishop
Alex Bowen
Bowen Dawes Wagstaff & Co
Ilma Broadbent
Scott Carroll
Philip & Karen Demonte
Sidney R. Doran
Susan Ford
Mike Grundy
H. W. Gwilliam
Betty Humphries
K. Lambourne
Tom & Valerie Libby
Gleadah Little
Malcolm Potts
Kath Power
Reg Rudd
Tony Smith
John Wagstaff
Marjorie Wheeler
Worcester Evening News
Marion Zagar
and to the contributors who made the Royal Albert Orphanage, Worcester live.

PART ONE

Royal Albert Orphanage
Worcester

INTRODUCTION

MY MOTHER'S DEATH

My mother was dying but we didn't realise this at the time. We had come down to visit her in hospital at Worcester.

Over those few days our thoughts turned to the past and the subject of the Royal Albert Orphanage came up in conversation. My sister and I might have gone there in 1942 as the orphanage was only five to ten minutes walk from where we lived. Instead my mother took us 26 miles to the Princess Alice Orphanage in Birmingham, an institution belonging to the National Children's Home and Orphanage now known as Action For Children. My mother was a Methodist and this was the reason why we were sent further away from home.

One night after hospital visiting, my sister said, 'Would you like to see the Royal Albert Orphanage?' To my surprise my wife said, 'I've never seen it.' As my brother-in-law drove up it was all lit up in the moonlight and my wife cried out, 'What an awful place!'

THE SEARCH FOR THE ROYAL ALBERT

I had first seen the Royal Albert Orphanage in the late 1940s and I remember standing back aghast and thinking, 'The poor little devils.'

After my experience at Birmingham at the Princess Alice Orphanage my sympathy went out to the children within those walls.

It looked like a military academy; the building was large and three storeys high with towers and pinnacles like a small St Pancras station. The hedge was as straight as a knife and the grass like a bowling green. There was a high flagpole where the Union Jack was flying. The steps up to the entrance were painted white. Running what seemed the length of the building between the two main gates was a huge sign which read 'THE ROYAL ALBERT ORPHANAGE' in very large letters. The drive was in the shape of a half-moon around the grass.

I wish I had had the nerve to knock at the door and ask to look around. I am sure that then the orphanage would have been scrubbed clean, the kitchens and bathrooms sparkling with the sweat of elbow grease and Vim, the taps brightly polished and everything spick and span where not a bit of dust would have dared to be seen!

But I did not go in.

IF ONLY THESE WALLS COULD SPEAK

Now in the late 1980s the four of us stood looking up at the building in the daylight. I turned to my wife and said: 'If only these walls could speak, what stories would they tell?'

Then we went up the steps through the main door, along the corridor into the dining hall where sat a number of elderly men eating their lunch, for now the orphanage was the property of the YMCA.

One of the men took us on a tour of the building with its narrow stairways and huge dormitories now boarded over and made into separate bedrooms for the men. He had been a coalman and remembered the boys of the orphanage helping him carry the sacks of coal off his wagon and up the stairs into the orphanage.

We left the Royal Albert and visited the local St John's library where we found one book by the local Worcester historian H. W. Gwilliam. Within its pages was a short history of the orphanage. Now well on into his eighties, Mr Gwilliam said that he knew a man, George Poole, whom he had played cricket with for over sixty years who had been brought up at the Royal Albert Orphanage. He suggested I contact George who had been a good friend and would be most helpful in my quest.

I wrote to George Poole, and this was his reply:

> It seems you followed the same pattern as I did. Yours was during the Second World War and mine in the 1914–1918 war. Looking back, therefore, we both had the hardships of rationing of food that would have been a good excuse if we had been in a position to complain like Oliver Twist.
>
> My parents lived in Coventry and had three sons, William, Leslie and me. We went into the children's homes together. My mother had been left to bring us up from 1916 which was quite a hardship during those war years and her health got worse and worse. We were then living in Warwick and it was there that one afternoon out of the blue she was taken away to hospital and died six months

afterwards. Because we had no relations in Warwick the local council put brother William in a children's home in Warwick and Leslie and I went to a children's home at Binley which was in the country. You can understand how we felt when our family was separated and the way the matron just said, 'Don't get upset, but your mother died in hospital today.'

We made a request: could our brother William come and live with us? The matron traced my grandmother in Birmingham and we were all sent to a children's home in Coventry; and this is where the cruelty and hardship and strong discipline started.

This was a home for thirty boys, ranging from three years of age to fourteen years. The staff consisted of one matron and two helpers. We used to get up early each morning and do certain tasks such as make our own beds the uniform way, to clean or scrub floors. Then we had to get ourselves washed for school and parade for inspection. If any of these duties were not performed correctly punishment was given, such as the birch or belt across the bare bottom or the hairbrush on the back of the hand. The worst example was when a boy of three years old soiled his trousers: the matron paraded all us boys in the yard to witness her throwing a cold bucket of water over him naked. I know what the hairbrush punishment was like. She gave it to me for something I didn't do which still sticks in my memory. It left lumps on my hands for a month.

When my grandmother visited us and saw my hands she contacted the matron and said that she would do the same to her if that happened again. So you can understand that we were moved from this home to the cottage homes in Stourbridge.

This was a much bigger place consisting of five homes: two for boys, two for girls, and one for boys and girls. There were eighteen children in each home looked after by a mother with a separate house for the master and matron. Here again hardship and discipline were carried out but all punishment was carried out by the master. He was a big stout man who lived on the fat of the land but his wife, the matron, was a kind and gentle lady. The mother in our home was a frustrated spinster who used to dish out her own punishments – she used to be a nurse – and therefore she exercised her own discipline. We had to memorise a collect from the prayer book every Sunday and say it to her before we went to church. If we failed, we had no pudding.

The master punished a boy with the belt which he wore round his fat belly, and then told the lad to roll the lawns. The lad reported to the master that he had finished, but the master said, 'Carry on till you roll yourself flat!'

The food we had consisted of the following:

Breakfast: Plate of thick porridge with salt on.
One round of dry bread. Mug of tea.

Dinner: Potatoes and meat – more fat than meat!
Pudding on Sunday only.

Tea: *Older boys*
2 rounds of bread with butter, jam or treacle.
Middle aged boys
1 ½ rounds of bread with butter, jam or treacle.
Younger boys
1 round of bread with butter, jam or treacle.

There was no tea for any boy who wet the bed. There were no special treats at Christmas. We didn't know what an egg tasted like!

We used to walk two miles to school each morning and dinner time to Coventry or Stourbridge. When at Coventry we went to the church which was the Cathedral, bombed during the last war.

When my eldest brother William became fourteen years old the Ministry of Pensions decided to move all three of us to Worcester to be fostered by a very nice lady. There we all joined the Scouts and that is when I first met Bill Gwilliam.

I have mentioned lots of the hardships during childhood. Now what of the good things? We had a nice clean bed to sleep in, clean bodies, clean clothes. Discipline taught good manners and respect for our elders and I think you will agree that is what some children want, then some of the crimes would be less.

When I started work it was my ambition if I had any children to try and give them a better start than I had.

What was amusing was that George Poole was not an old Royal Albertian after all! I then decided to put an advertisement in the local paper. This is what appeared in the *Worcester Evening News*:

ORPHANAGE. I am doing research on the Royal Albert Orphanage, Henwick Road, Worcester which closed in the 1950s and would be grateful if any readers could supply details of staff, events or background information. ALAN HAMBLIN.

It is because of the response that I write this book.

THE ROYAL ALBERT DISCOVERED

The Royal Albert was not, as my sister and I had always thought, a branch or home belonging to the Church of England – The Waifs and Strays, now known as the Children's Society – but an independent institution set up by the businessmen of Worcester. In our days of great cynicism we might conclude that this was the work of Victorian businessmen bent on one huge ego-trip. I believe this would be missing the mark, for many of the folk of that era were great idealists whose only thought was of doing good.

Some of the names of those who were to form the Committee that ran the orphanage were: Richard Padmore; T. Rowley-Hill; J. Parrott Lett; Lea & Perrins; Fownes Brothers, William Stallard; Walter Wood; George Goodwin; Harry Day & Co.; Albert Webb; Waiter Holland; Speckley Brothers. Other patrons included the Earl and Countess of Dudley, Lady Lechmere and Lady Huntingdon.

The Committee met once a month from its inception. The children whose names had been put forward to enter the orphanage were chosen by the votes of the patrons. The number of votes depended on the amount of financial patronage they gave.

1

THE VICTORIAN AND EDWARDIAN ERA

The orphanage began in 1862 in a house in St John's, Worcester which is still in use as a doctor's practice. This was possible through the generous donation of a Mr J. Wheeley. The Institute then moved to the mansion in Henwick Road, built in 1868, the date engraved in the brickwork over the main entrance, a year after St Pancras Station in London. Richard Padmore gave £4,000 to build this fine Gothic edifice, with its turrets, towers and fine iron work.

The first fifty-seven children to enter the Royal Albert were all girls.

The following pages are based on records taken from the minutes and the admission and discharge book of the orphanage in the Victorian and Edwardian era.

IN THE ORPHANAGE UNTIL 16

The document a parent would have to sign when placing their child in the Royal Albert reads as follows:

> In consideration of the benefits to be conferred by the Orphan Asylum Committee upon my child . . . . by being maintained and educated in the asylum I hereby undertake and agree with the said committee that (he or she) shall remain in the said asylum under the rules and regulations thereof until the age of 16 years and that I will not remove or attempt to remove (him or her) from the said asylum until (he or she) has attained that age without the previous consent of the said committee.

Sixteen years of age seems rather extreme as the school leaving age at the time was thirteen (ten in special family circumstances) but the minutes of 7 August 1889 state that the decision was unanimous.

It must have resulted in a harrowing time for parents. As one of several cases it states in the minutes of 7 October 1903, 'A request from Mrs Weaver for permission to return her daughter Edith from the orphanage before she was 16 years of age was considered, but that Mrs Weaver's request to remove her daughter Edith be refused.'

In March 1901, 'The application of Miss Parks, Aunt of Lilian Widdows to take the child out of the orphanage be declined.' However, the following November when Lilian reached sixteen she was apprenticed to her aunt who was a milliner at Stourbridge: 'Premium £10. Five pounds on being bound and the remainder at the end of two years.'

In March 1903, 'The master was instructed to see Mrs Cross of Summer Lane, Birmingham who has applied to remove her child and ask her in the interest of the child to reconsider the matter.' The following month, 'The master reported that he had seen Mrs Cross who wished to remove her boy and Mrs Cross was still very desirous that the boy should now go with her. It was resolved that in view of the fact that Mrs Cross assented in 1899 to the request of the committee for her boy to remain in the orphanage for a further period of 2 years and that period having expired. John Cross be now permitted to return to his home. The usual outfit to be provided.' John was fourteen and his discharge read, 'Taken out by mother who was in a position to maintain him.'

The committee turned down the request of a Mrs Willer in July 1889 asking for the withdrawal of her daughter Agnes. The request was declined on the grounds that it would not be in the child's interest to have her removed at present. In another case, in July 1904, a mother was refused permission to visit her son: 'That the mother of Arthur Barnett having misconducted herself be not allowed to visit her boy at the orphanage and that the boy be not permitted to go home without the sanction of the committee.' In May 1906 Arthur Barnett emigrated to Canada aboard the SS *Tunissian* but was killed in action in 1917 in the Great War.

The letter of the law was adhered to in the case of Mrs Key in February 1905 who asked the committee 'to remove her boy from the orphanage in order that she could apprentice him to Mr Howard, Foregate Street, Worcester, Hairdresser.' Their answer was, 'That as Henry Key is only 14 years of age the committee are unable to accede to the request of his mother.'

When a parent remarried it was the rule that their child should be discharged from the orphanage. This was true in the case of Eleanor Wall who left in 1906 because her father had remarried, and was in service as a coachman at a salary of £1 per week and had three children dependent on him. He was requested to remove his child from the institution, the usual half outfit to be provided!

GIRLS DISCHARGED FOR SERVICE

On being discharged at sixteen years of age the majority of girls went into service as kitchenmaids, dairymaids, housemaids, nurserymaids, undermaids, under-nurses and between-maids.

Hermia Rose however went from one asylum to another. After remaining in the service of Dr Bird for 12 months in 1887, she obtained a situation in Powick Asylum – the local mental hospital – as attendant. Emma Franklin left in 1878 to be thoroughly taught dressmaking. One girl also found employment as a laundress near Tenbury, one in mantlemaking in London and one in the needle factory at Redditch.

Salaries rose in nearly twenty years at the end of the nineteenth century. Alice Dovey was employed as general servant at £5 per annum in 1893 whereas Rhoda Fowler entered service as a maid in 1909 for £9 per year.

Some girls were employed by the very top drawer! In October 1895 Jane Wood entered the service of Lady Ampthill of 109 Park Street, London with a salary of £6 per annum.

The CV of Dorothy Nicholas who was employed as a kitchenmaid is paradoxical: 'Conduct good – sulky, rather slow.'

BOYS DISCHARGED FOR WORK

Some boys went into service but not so many as the girls. Their duties ranged from general servant to page, house-boy, under-gardener or ploughboy.

James Middleton entered the service of Mr Dee of Woolas Hill near Pershore in 1892, his salary to commence at £5 per annum. 'His duties chiefly to look after pony and trap, do garden work and clean knives and forks, boots and shoes and to make himself generally useful in the house. Good home and to live indoors.'

At a Committee meeting in December 1882 an application was received for Leonard Warman, aged thirteen, to be allowed to leave the institution, and the secretary was instructed to write to the mother and inform her that the Committee did not think it advisable to grant the request for at least another year. Why the request was not granted is not given. However the boy was discharged the following June and apprenticed for seven years at Baylis Lewis and Co., Printers in New Street, Worcester. Other boys found openings in printing in Worcester at the *Printing Times*, *Herald* office and the *Echo* and *Chronicle*.

Most boys were going into industry and commerce, as builders, grocers, drapers, blacksmiths, photographers, carpenters, plumbers and house decorators, engineers, butchers, jewellers, boot and shoe makers, carriage builders, wheelwright and coach builders and saddler and harness makers. Some boys found employment in the famous firms of Worcester, at Dent & Co., Fownes Gloves Manufacturers, the Royal Porcelain Works and Nicholson & Co., Organ Builders. Victor Rhodes joined the Great Western Railway in 1907 at Shrubhill Station as an engine cleaner with wages to commence at 1*s.* 6*d.* per day.

These were the days when it was common to pay for an apprenticeship. Edwin Lee was apprenticed to a baking firm at Hallow. The premium was paid by the boy's mother. Harry Goode was more fortunate. He was apprenticed to a bookbinder for six years and his wages were for the first year 4*s.* 6*d.* per week, for the second 5*s.* 6*d.*, the third 6*s.* 6*d.*, the fourth 7*s.* 6*d.*, the fifth 8*s.* 6*d.* and for the sixth 11 shillings.

Some boys didn't always fit the bill, like Thomas Kilminster who in 1889 was apprenticed to a chemist at St Johns. On account of the boy being so careless and indolent Mr Silk refused to keep him. He then entered the service of a fishmonger in Foregate Street, but what became of him later is not known.

The orphanage staff kept an interest in their children once they had left. It was reported in December 1889 that Sydney Hoggins had absconded from his situation, the boy alleging ill treatment by his employer. Since the January of that year he had been apprenticed to a saddler and harness maker in Malvern Link.

TAKEN OUT BY THEIR MOTHERS

During the Victorian and Edwardian era some five hundred children had entered the Royal Albert but many were to leave prematurely before the age of sixteen. This was because their mother or father had remarried. The ratio is a large one: 54 mothers to 3 fathers. Others were taken out by sisters, grandparents and friends.

On leaving the orphanage at sixteen, the girls who went home rather than into service have these entries against their names:

> Went home to live with her mother.
> Went home to assist her mother.
> Went home to live with her mother who was in a position to maintain her.

Elsie Davis, aged 16, was 'Taken out by mother. Mother required her help to do the work at home.' Edith Cook, aged 15, was 'Taken out by grandmother who was in a weak state of health and required her grand-daughter to wait on her.'

It seems that to live in an orphanage or be in service one had to be tough. These weaker mortals went home!

Jessie Fitzer, aged 16, 'Taken out by mother, the girl was very slow and not at all bright or in any way fitted for domestic service.' Fanny Bough, aged 12, 'Taken out to live with her mother. The girl was not very strong and was subject to St Vitus Dance. The mother in a position to maintain her.' Gertrude Davis, aged 13, 'Taken out by mother. The Committee granted the mother £5 in lieu of the usual outfit. The girl was never strong, as she was continually having operations on her leg.' Mary Reynolds, aged 11, 'Taken out by mother on her remarrying. A small ricketty child.' Esther Blundell, aged 16, 'Taken out by mother who is a dressmaker and is anxious to teach her daughter the trade too. The girl is not suitable for service as she is subject to tetanoid convulsions and acute rheumatism.'

Eleanor Wall left in 1906, because her father remarried and was in service as a coachman at a salary of £1 per week and had three children dependent on him. He was requested to remove his child from the institution, the usual half outfit to be provided.

Whether a boy's unhappiness in the home appears to be the reason for him being taken out by his mother is contained in the words, 'In consequence of the reported discontent of the boy William Smith it has been the decision of the Committee to remove him.' This was written on 20 November 1889 and by 8 December of that year he left with his mother. William was thirteen.

Agnes Willer, aged 11, after spending some two years in the Royal Albert was 'taken away from Asylum by her mother without the sanction of the Committee.' However mother and daughter presumably continued to live happily together in Malvern Link.

ABSCONDING AND DISMISSAL

As in most orphanages absconding was quite a normal occurrence and the Royal Albert was no exception.

This issue came to a head at a meeting of the Committee in 1883 over the report of the absconding boy, Alfred Rammell. The boy and his grandmother attended the meeting of the Committee when Rammell stated that his reasons for running away were that he had a pain in his shoulder and side, and complained of this to the master who still made him work in the garden; that he only had 4 oz of bread given him for breakfast instead of 7 oz: and that the master beat him with a cane till his back was blue. He denied that he broke open or opened the wardrobe to get his best suit of clothes out. The Committee questioned the master, the cook and several of the boys and after thoroughly investigating the charges came to the conclusion that the statements made by Rammell were unfounded. It was therefore resolved that he be dismissed forthwith from the institution and further that the master be instructed to take from him his best suit of clothes and boots and send him away in his working clothes!

Alfred Wilson was 'expelled for immoral conduct' on 1 January 1890 but by then he was only nine days away from his sixteenth birthday! Alfred was taken out by his mother by order of the Committee and afterwards entered the service of a Mr Wisher who was a farmer in Malvern Link.

Eight other boys were dismissed over this period. The reasons given were misconduct, insubordination, insolence, repeated petty thefts, untruthfulness and absconding from the asylum.

Frederick Bateman, aged fourteen, was expelled in 1894 and the reason given was, 'Dismissed by the Committee as his general conduct for several years had been very unsatisfactory. He had also absconded four times during the last four years.' Thomas Blake was an orphanage boy criticised by the Committee for his ingratitude! Thomas left the Royal Albert in 1884 to enter the service of Rev. S. S. Foster at the Blind College, Worcester at £4 per annum and livery. The objection of the Orphanage Committee was because his mother had taken Thomas from the Blind College and the secretary was instructed, 'to write to his mother as to the ingratitude of her boy after the benefits he has received in the Institution.' The reasons why his mother took Thomas away from the Blind College are not stated!

Sixteen-year-old Annie Guise who had gone into service in Stockton near Rugby was dismissed after six months in 1882. In a letter her employer stated that she had dismissed Annie Guise in consequence of having missed half a pound of sugar. Both Annie and the cook had been dismissed. A letter was also read from Annie denying having stolen the sugar. The orphanage committee in their desire to help Annie, 'were going to see her employer and try to get Annie restored to her situation but if this failed to try and get them to give Annie a character [reference].'

When Fanny Griffiths left, the entry simply reads 'Transferred to the Princess Mary's Village Homes, Addlestone, Surrey. Conduct while in The Asylum very indifferent.' The facts are that Fanny had been repeatedly guilty of theft and now confessed to having stolen a shilling on 22 October. After some consideration it was resolved that the child should be dismissed from the asylum and should be taken at once before the magistrates with the view to her being sent to an industrial school. The dean reported that Fanny would be admitted to the Princess Mary's Village Homes on 21 December 1885 for two years on payment of £12 per annum. Fanny was just over thirteen years of age. The months passed by, then on 4 May 1887 the orphanage committee received a letter from the lady superintendent of the Village Homes: 'Fanny Griffiths is much improved of late, but as she has only given up pilfering for a few months we think a longer training necessary to establish her principles.' A further letter was received in July of that year expressing an unfavourable account of Fanny and on 3 August 1887, the orphanage and Mrs Griffiths attended the meeting. The chairman informed her of her daughter's bad conduct at the Home and said that the committee were willing to keep Fanny there for the present if they received good reports of her conduct but if another bad report were received she would be dismissed. Finally in December 1887 a letter was received stating that Fanny Griffiths had of late shown an improvement in her conduct but that at present it was considered undesirable to let her take a situation and asking the committee if they would permit her to go home on 21 December for a holiday. The committee turned down the Lady Superintendent's request because of the great expense to which the institution had been put, in consequence of this girl's bad conduct.

However the orphanage did forgive three boys who ran away! On 4 June 1902 'It was resolved that three boys George Coomby, Frederick Lowe and Victor Rhodes who left the institution on 17th instant without permission be reprimanded and forgiven.' A few years later George and Frederick emigrated to Canada, whereas Victor worked for the railway at Shrubhill Station in Worcester.

The same Christian charity was not shown on 6 August 1902: 'That the boy Thomas Lewis who left the orphanage on the morning of the 5th inst without permission and did not return until 7 p.m, be whipped.'

Insubordination reared its ugly head in December 1889, the guilty parties being William Glassbrook and George Smart who were reprimanded but both boys expressed contrition. As this was nearly Christmas we can assume Christian charity and goodwill had the final say!

DEATH OF AN INFANT

For the staff and children of the orphanage the saddest time of all was when a child died. A total of nine children died in this era, one girl from an accident on the Malvern Hills in 1876, others from peritonitis, endocarditis, and syncope, diphtheria and meningitis.

Martha Roberts was one of the first girls to enter the orphanage on 1 December 1862. She died on 20 September – the year is not given. The cause of her death and her age is not given. Against her name is the simple entry: 'Died in the asylum.'

It seems that some of the children entered the asylum in a very weak state. Henry Barnett was such a boy who arrived at the orphanage on 15 December 1897 aged eight. His obituary reads, 'Died in the orphanage after six days illness from diphtheria and meningitis. This boy when admitted was in a very weak state and was exceptionally thin. Conduct of boy very good. Died 10.25 p.m. on 13 February 1898.'

There is no doubt that the staff and doctors did their very best for the children as in the case of William Lewis. 'Died almost suddenly of endocarditis and syncope. He had been ill only a few days and seemed to be improving until 12 o'clock on Sunday midnight where he was taken seriously ill and died at 2.40 p.m. 6 January 1896. He was attended by Mr Crowe, Mr Budd and Mr Polson.'

Violet Brooks was admitted to the Royal Albert on 18 April 1900 and this was Dr Crowe's report: 'I have today made a careful examination of this child and can find no evidence of disease. Of course, owing to her family history she would be more likely to contact consumption if exposed to infection than another child whose parents were not consumptive.' Violet was to live for only another ten months; she died on 8 February 1901. A poignant tribute is made to her. 'Died at 2.30 p.m. Cause of death phthisis (consumption) certified by J. R. Polson, St John's. A very dear little girl, most patient under her severe illness and deeply grateful for all that was done for her up to the last moment.' Violet was only eight.

HOLIDAYS

In the May of 1883 the subject of children going out for a holiday was discussed, and it was resolved that those wishing to go home should be allowed one day and those at a distance two days, but that no child should be allowed to go out unless they had been in the institution over six months, except under special circumstances, and that they should not be allowed to go home more than twice a year.

Staff holidays were much better than those of the children as stated in August 1901: 'That in future, officers' annual holidays be extended to four weeks providing they are not absent more than three weeks at any one time.'

In June 1900 leave of absence was given for Mrs Wormington's thirteen-year-old daughter Beatrice to go to Manchester to visit her mother. In July 1901 however Beatrice was unable to go on holiday with her mother. The committee decreed 'that Mrs Wormington's application for her daughter to go to London on holiday be refused'. No details are given. Beatrice left the orphanage at sixteen and entered the service of Rev. Canon Hennessey, Dean's Yard, Westminster, as kitchenmaid on a salary of £12 per annum.

Permission was given to Elsie Davis and Florence Loader to visit their relatives at Redditch for three days during the Christmas week of 1889. Ethel Cook, who in the winter of 1902 underwent an operation on her knees, was granted a week's holiday!

NEARLY FINISHED UP IN THE WORKHOUSE

In 1907 Emily Smith nearly finished up in the workhouse! Her father already resided in one, as is clear from the minutes of October 1902: 'The medical and other papers were considered satisfactory and the nominations were accepted subject to enquiry being made as to the state of the health of the father of Emily Smith, now in the Kingswinford Workhouse Infirmary.'

Emily was admitted to the orphanage on 3 December 1902 but a few years later she nearly finished up in the workhouse. In February 1907, 'The master reported that a complaint had been made by some of the girls in the institution that they had missed money from time to time, that a purse containing *2s. 6d* was found in the trash bin and that Emily Smith, a girl fourteen years of age, had confessed to stealing the money. After carefully considering the matter and questioning the girl it was resolved that Emily Smith be excluded from the institution and that Mr Melvin be required to arrange for her removal forthwith.'

The following month, 'The secretary reported that he had been in correspondence with Mr Melvin respecting this girl. Her aunt declined to receive her and therefore he asked that she should be sent to the Worcester Union Workhouse.' However, 'The Ladies committee reported that they had carefully considered the case and were of the opinion that if sent to the workhouse it would probably mean the girl's ruin.' She was 14½ years old and the Ladies pleaded that she might be sent to a Home for Young Girls in Birmingham, 'where for a payment of 5/- a week she would be thoroughly well cared for and in due course a situation would be found for her.'

The committee decided that 'Emily Smith be sent to the home and that a payment at the rate of 5/- per week be made by the institution in respect of her maintenance at such home, until she shall reach the age of 16 years, or shall be discharged, whichever may happen first.'

In the discharge book it says: 'Transferred to the Ladies' Association for the protection of Young Girls, 101 Newhall Street, Birmingham. Conduct of girl not very satisfactory.'

Emily left the orphanage on 11 March 1907.

THE CASE OF THE FISH DINNERS

The fish dinner saga went on for some seven years!

In August 1883, 'The subject of giving the children a fish diet once a week was discussed and the secretary was instructed to request Dr Strange to consult with the other medical men and report to the committee.

On 5 September that year, 'It was reported that the children had a fish dinner on Friday last and it was resolved that Dr Strange be requested to alter the diet table.' However on 2 July 1884, 'The master made a complaint that the children did not like their fish dinners and asked that it should be discontinued. It was resolved that the fish dinners be continued.'

The trouble brewed up again four years later on 14 December 1889. 'The unpopularity of the fish dinners was discussed, and it was arranged that with a view to making the meal more palatable some cheap sauce be provided, and that as an alternative, an allowance of bread and cheese, the quantity of which is to be fixed by one of the medical officers, be substituted.'

Four days later it was decided that 'owing to the fact that 52 of the children prefer bread and cheese to fish it was arranged that the supply of fish should be reduced from 56 lbs to 30 lbs.'

Finally on 5 February 1890 'It was resolved that the fish dinner be discontinued forthwith and that Dr Strange be requested to advise a substitute.' One month later, 'Dr Strange reported that he had considered the dietary table, and recommended that the dinner on Thursday should consist of pea-soup and four ounces of bread and on Friday should be mutton pie. Two ounces of meat for each child, potatoes, onions and crust over, also two ounces of bread.'

But all this had been too much for Dr Strange as was recorded ten months later on 7 January 1891: 'We extend sympathy to his family on the death of Dr Strange for the valuable services rendered by him to this institution for so many years both as a member of the committee and as honorary consulting physician.'

ILLNESS: A COMMON OCCURRENCE

Illness was a common problem in the orphanage where disease among children spread like wildfire. It seems that whenever an epidemic broke out at the Royal Albert the dormitories were always whitewashed and coloured. No doubt that was thought to kill off the germs from the ceilings and walls!

On 4 July 1883 it was brought to 'the attention of the medical staff that "Ring Worm" had existed in the institution for nearly twelve months and request them to present a report with any suggestions to prevent the spread of it and cure the children now suffering from it.' The following month the secretary was 'instructed to have the dormitories coloured and the water pipes repaired and also to ascertain the cost of self-acting water taps similar to those in use at Powick Lunatic Asylum'.

It was reported on 20 April 1904 that 'Lucy Weaver had a ringworm on her forehead and it was decided not to admit the child until cured'. But on 4 May, Lucy was admitted to the orphanage. Presumably her ringworm had gone!

On 6 February 1889 'A letter was read from Dr Crowe stating that the illness of Eliza Warman was the result of hereditary syphilis and that she is progressing favourably, and to ask him whether to accept the offer made by Mrs Lea to send Eliza to Margate Sanatorium would be beneficial to the girl.' Whether or not this offer was taken up is not stated but Eliza left the orphanage in September that year, aged sixteen, and entered the service of a Mrs Moses Jones at No. 1 Bath Road, Worcester.

Because of the death of his brother in the orphanage that February the committee seemed rather on the defensive for admitting Arthur Barnett, who was nearly seven. In a letter of 26 October 1898 from Dr Crowe, 'I have today examined Arthur Barnett and can find nothing wrong with him but an enlarged gland in one side of the neck. He is not very strong physically and the family history as the committee are aware is distinctly bad.' In a letter of 2 November 1898 to Mrs Barnett, 'Although the committee admit your child, it is somewhat doubtful whether they will be able to retain him in the institution if his health does not improve.' However Arthur was admitted eight days later and lived at the orphanage for over seven years. In May 1906, he emigrated to Canada with other orphanage children aboard the SS *Tunissian* but was killed in action in 1917 during the Great War.

Scarlatina broke out in 1892. In June 'The master was authorised to have the cottage whitewashed and thoroughly cleansed when free from scarlatina.' In July 'The medical officers were to confer with Dr Mabyn Read with the view to ascertaining the cause and outbreak of scarlatina if possible and also forward two examples of the milk supplied to the institution to Dr Bostok Hill for analysis and report.' As with all epidemics at the Royal Albert, visiting by parents was cancelled and so were the children's outings. At this time the Band of Hope requested to be allowed to use the field adjoining Cromer Road for members of the Sabrina Band of Hope. The orphanage stated, 'Permission would have been granted were it not for the outbreak of scarlatina.' In May 1902 scarlatina broke out again and 'monthly visits of children's friends to be discontinued until further notice'. Again in February 1903 there was a further outbreak and the 'medical officers reported that Edith Gwilliam had an attack of scarlatina. The girl had been sent to the fever hospital.' Six weeks later 'Edith was permitted to visit her mother at Evesham for a period not exceeding fourteen days on leaving the isolation hospital, and a month later journeyed to Stoke Prier to be with her aunt.

Scarlet fever reared its ugly head in 1892 and on 16 November, 'it was decreed that children's holidays be suspended during the prevalence of scarlet fever.' There was another 'downer' in October 1901, when 'a third case of scarlet fever was reported and it was upon the recommendation of the medical officer that no visitors be admitted to the institution until further notice.' In May 1902 'Susie Lewes who has been exposed to scarlet fever at the Worcester Royal Infirmary be removed from the orphanage and placed in the isolation hospital for seven days.' Censorship was exacted in October 1902: 'That owing to the prevalence of scarlet fever in the neighbourhood, visits to the institution be suspended until further notice. That the children be not allowed to visit their friends for the present,' and again in November 1902, 'Owing to the prevalence of scarlet fever it was decided to postpone the admission of the children recently elected,' and again on 17 December 1902, 'Letters from Dr Crowe and Dr Polson stating that it was not desirable to permit visiting at present and therefore the committee could not give permission for visiting to be resumed.'

Measles broke out in November 1886 and 'The master reported the removal of three more cases of measles to the asylum infirmary making six cases in all.' In February 1893 measles caused disappointment: 'The invitation of the Worcester Amateur Operatic Society for the officers and children to attend a performance at the theatre was declined owing to the epidemic of measles.' Another disappointment came in December 1893: 'The action of the master in prohibiting the usual monthly visit of the parents and friends owing to the prevalence of measles was approved,' and again in February 1905, 'There were two cases of measles, one boy and one girl. The master was instructed to take the advice of the medical officer as to the desirability of closing the house to visitors.'

An outbreak of typhoid fever was reported in 1894, when it was stated 'that Dr Crowe be requested to furnish a special report with regard to the case of typhoid fever now in the institution.' A day later on 4 January a letter from Dr Crowe was read stating that he is 'unable to ascertain the cause of the outbreak of typhoid fever' but that he is 'in communication with the medical officer of health upon the subject'. One other case was referred to on 18 January 1899 when it was requested 'that Fanny Cope be sent to the fever hospital if her illness is typhoid fever'.

Smallpox appears not to have entered the inner sanctums of the orphanage but there evidently was an outbreak of smallpox in Worcester in 1894. The minutes of 2 May read: 'Owing to the prevalence of smallpox in the city it was decided that Dr Crowe be instructed to vaccinate such of the children as he may deem desirable.' Then on 20 June came a further sanction: 'Owing to the prevalence of smallpox it was arranged that the visiting of parents and friends be suspended for another month.' On 4 July as a final precaution against germ warfare: 'The master was authorised to get the necessary painting, colouring and whitewashing of the dormitories done and was empowered to engage such assistance as may be necessary.' As an extra back-up: 'The master was instructed to obtain a supply of Sanitas and have it regularly used in the closets every morning.' As a further backup: 'Two weeks later it was decided that the visiting of parents and friends should be suspended for another month.'

Mumps is only reported once in January 1896 when 'The master reported an outbreak of mumps and instructions were given for the cases to be isolated in the hospital and a nurse engaged.'

Three girls with three different illnesses are mentioned in November 1896. 'It was decided that Laura Jones who is suffering from chronic heart disease and Florence Selby suffering from chronic rheumatism and Edith Griffiths suffering from whooping cough be removed to the hospital and that a suitable nurse be engaged to attend them as a temporary expedient. Dr Crowe was to report specially on the suitability of the arm extension exercise in the case of Laura Jones.'

Laura Jones, a girl of only eleven years of age, was in a very weak condition. In August of 1896, 'It was decided to send Laura Jones to the West of England Sanatorium, Weston-Super-Mare, for one month. Mr T. Rowley Hill will supply ticket. Railway expenses to be paid by the institution.' Whether Laura went to Weston-Super-Mare is not known. In December it was considered whether to send Laura to the Midland Home for Incurables, Leamington or to the Byfleet Home near Woking once admission and terms were agreed. In January 1897 her case was again considered by the committee. 'In the case of Laura Jones letters were read from secretaries of the Homes for Incurables at Leamington, Byfleet and 2 Maida Vale, London, from which it appeared that the latter would probably receive the child upon payment of 7/- per week and a subscription of £1. 1*s.* 0*d.* per annum' and on 9 February 1897 Laura Jones was transferred there.

On 6 April 1899, over two years after Laura Jones left the orphanage, a letter was sent to Maida Vale. 'The secretary was requested to obtain a report from the Home for Incurable Children, Maida Vale, London as to the present health of Laura Jones and the medical officer's opinion as to whether she is likely to be fitted for light employment.' The answer came six days later. 'In reply to yours of 6 April I beg to enclose a report from our medical officer on Laura Jones. The matron tells me she is being instructed in fancy work – bent iron work and also does a fair amount of sewing. Laura Jones is in fair health at present but her heart trouble is not greatly improved and any extra exertion is prejudicial. I cannot advise that she should be employed even in light work requiring bodily exertion.' Two years later on 17 July 1901 the orphanage made a decision after a request from Laura's father: 'That Mr Jones's application for the removal of his daughter Laura from the Home for Incurables be acceded to.' The following month on 4 August the orphanage changed their minds: 'The decision of the house committee to allow the father of Laura Jones to take her home from the Home for the Incurables was with their consent cancelled and the secretary was directed to communicate this decision to the matron of the Home. The master was also instructed to see Rev. J. Devenport of Wickenford Vicarage and ask him to explain the circumstances to the father.' The next we hear of Laura is in a letter from Maida Vale on 15 January 1902: 'Recommendations were received from the matron of the Home for Incurables, 2 Maida Vale, London with a view to getting Laura Jones into another home when her time expires in February.' The final happy chapter on Laura's life ends with the minutes of 5 February 1902: 'A letter from Rev. J. Devenport intimating that the girl's father insists upon his daughter's return home to live with him when her time expires at the Home for Incurables in London. The master was authorised to arrange safe conduct of the girl from London when she leaves that institution.' On 23 February 1902 Laura became sixteen and it is to be hoped that she spent a happy birthday with her father in their home.

The other two girls, Florence Selby and Edith Griffiths, were older and much more fortunate than Laura. Florence left two years later and went into service and Edith was at the orphanage another three years before being apprenticed to a dressmaker at a premium of £20. The committee paid £10 and the sisters £10. The length of apprenticeship was two years with assistance in general housework.

It was considered good for the patient in the 1890s to bathe and some children were sent to Droitwich Baths. One girl, Phoebe Osborne, was sent much further away to the Margate Sea Bathing Infirmary with a subscription of £2. *2s.* *0d.* Four months later 'a letter from the superintendent of Margate Sea Bathing Infirmary was read recommending that Phoebe Osborne should remain for four weeks longer in the Infirmary and the secretary reported that he had remitted the necessary fee of £1.' Whether Phoebe did have an operation is not stated but in May 1895 the master reported that the medical officer Dr Budd had ordered Leonard Grundy and Phoebe Osborne to go into the infirmary to undergo operations, the former for a growth in the nose and the latter for enlarged glands. Four years later Phoebe left the orphanage and her records state, 'entered the service of a Mrs Foster at the Post Office, London Road, Worcester on a salary of £6 per annum. Conduct of girl in the orphanage satisfactory. Health of girl not good. Suffered from enlarged glands.'

In the last century children would try and 'put it on' as in this report of January 1897 by Dr Crowe: 'I have examined this girl on two occasions and have come to the conclusion that she has been shamming lameness and pain. I can now find nothing wrong with her.'

Not even the medical staff were immune from orphanage criticism. 'We find that serious inconvenience is occasionally found in consequence of the distance at which both the medical officers reside from the orphanage, and we are of the opinion that it is necessary and desirable in the interests of the orphans that one of them should live nearer to the orphanage. We therefore recommend that Dr Budd as the junior officer, be informed fully of these views and be requested to relinquish his appointment at midsummer and that a medical officer be appointed in St John's as near to the orphanage as possible.' Two months later the orphanage backed down! 'The recommendation of the meeting held on 3 March 1897, be rescinded. That Dr Budd and Dr Crowe and Dr Polson remain and they are hereby appointed joint medical officers as and from midsummer next with an honorarium of £10 each and that the ordinary visits to the orphanage be made in rotation.'

The doctors seem to have had differing opinions about hereditary illnesses. Note Dr Crowe's word 'it' in reference to either a boy or girl! In a letter dated February 1895, he says, 'I have examined Francis Farley and can find no evidence of any disease. I do not think the fact of a child's father or mother having died of consumption ought in itself to disqualify it for admission to the asylum. There are many children of consumptive parents who never develop the disease. If both parents were consumptive and there were a history of consumption in other members of the family I think there would then be some reason to hesitate before admitting the child. I think it would be a good plan if a book were kept for each child after its admission with the medical history previous to admission and spaces where subsequent illness with dates, might be entered by the medical officer. There would then be a complete medical history of the child's life when leaving the asylum for good.'

Two months later Dr Crowe's idea was thrown out. 'That the committee consider a medical case book for entry, health history of each child in the asylum recommended by Dr Crowe in his letter of 25 February is unsuitable in this institution. Four voted for the resolution and four against and it was carried by the casting vote of the Chairman.' Four years later on 15 November 1899 it was decided that 'Francis Farley be sent to the Birmingham Ophthalmic Institution. Mr A. C. Cherry kindly promised to furnish him with an out-patients ticket.' In December it was also agreed 'that an in-patient's ticket be purchased for Francis Farley to be sent to the Birmingham Eye Hospital to have an operation performed subject to the consent of his mother.' Francis left the orphanage on 3 November 1901, aged sixteen. His records state: 'Went home to live with his mother with a view to obtaining work in Cheltenham as a carpenter. Full outfit granted him. Conduct of boy in the orphanage exceptionally good. Good worker and good mannered.'

Dr Budd's views on hereditary illness seem to differ from those of his colleague Dr Crowe. In his letter of May 1896 Dr Budd states: 'With reference to the illness amongst several of the children over the last few months, it is to be traced directly to their family history, that is their parents died of phthisis [consumption] or scrofula [chronic swellings of the glands especially in the neck] or cancer and affections of the lungs. Of course there is no possibility of guarding against these illnesses unless the committee take steps to prevent any orphans being admitted whose parent or parents died of any of the diseases mentioned above.'

Diphtheria struck the orphanage in 1898. 'Dr Crowe reported that 14 boys and 3 girls were suffering from diphtheric throats and had been isolated. He advised that any child complaining of the throat should be bacterially examined and isolated. It was resolved (a) That the cottage hospital be disinfected and used for suspicious cases after today. (b) That two nurses be engaged for the two dormitories, the medical staff to have discretion to engage further help if necessary. (c) That decisive cases be confined to the top dormitories. (d) That one of the medical officers shall attend the institution daily. (e) That the master be instructed to question all the children each day and to at once isolate any child complaining of the throat. (f) That all milk be boiled before being used. (g) That the drainage operations be deferred. (h) That instructions be given to the matron to abstain from visiting the top dormitories. (i) That the master be authorised to purchase two washable coats for use in the infected wards. (j) That the master be authorised to engage a man to assist him with the boys but not to sleep in the house. (k) That if necessary the dormitory over the carpenter's shop be used as a convalescent room for boys.' Two months later the committee decided that the 'sum of £5. 5*s*. 0*d*. was voted to be given to the master and the matron and £1 to the cook for their services in connection with the last outbreak of diphtheria.' That same month: 'The master reported that the infected dormitory had been disinfected and he was authorised to have it thoroughly scraped and coloured by Messrs Hancock Bros.'

In June 1898 there was a case of lupus. The records state: 'That Dr Crowe be requested to advise as to the boy Leonard Grundy now suffering from Lupus, being sent to some home or institution.' Dr Cowe recommended Leonard going to the Royal Bathing Infirmary, Margate but whether he ever went is not stated. It was not considered suitable to send him to the Children's Hospital for incurable children in Maida Vale, London. In fact later that year Leonard left to work at Woodhall Farm, near Clifton-on-Teme, with wages 2/- per week with board, lodging and washing. His duties were ordinary farmwork and housework. His conduct during his last year at the orphanage is stated as 'not satisfactory'. At the time when Leonard Grundy was suffering with lupus, the committee had instructed 'Messrs Stokes Bros Builders to whitewash the ceiling of the girls' bedroom, two boys' dormitories, staircase and passage and colour the walls with Duresko'. The following month it was recommended by the three doctors that the committee have the drainage and ventilators overhauled and that they should remove outside drains and water closets to make the house sanitary.

The only mention of tonsils was on 21 August 1901: 'That sanction be given for Susie Lewes to go into the Worcester Royal Infirmary for the removal of her tonsils in accordance with the doctor's recommendations.' Nine-year-old Susie had only been in the orphanage a few months, having been admitted on 17 April 1901. If she had the operation it was successful for she left the orphanage in 1908, aged sixteen, to go into service as nursemaid to the Holt Fleet Hotel, Holt Fleet.

One girl was destined for a serious operation as is recorded on 4 December 1901: 'That the recommendation of the medical officer and subject to the consent of the mother that Ethel Cook be sent to the infirmary to undergo an operation on her knees.' Ethel underwent the operation and when she left the orphanage two years later she entered the service of Col. Marsden of Cedar Court, Farnham on a wage of £10 per annum.

On 6 February 1907 'A letter from the house surgeon at the Worcester Royal Infirmary was read in which he stated that the two children Troughton and Warren were both very ill and it was doubtful if the boy would recover.' The girl was Edith Troughton who in the May of 1907 was 'In the Royal Infirmary for appendicitis and complications – this operation had been performed on her. She would be much benefitted by a change of air. Permission granted to go to the Sanatorium at Rhyl. Mr. F. J. Forrest undertook to procure a ticket of admission.' The boy was Arthur Warren who 'Died in Worcester Infirmary on 13 September 1907 after having his left leg amputated. He had been in the above institution for 10 months before his death.' Arthur would have been twelve a month later on 13 October.

There was the strange case of eleven-year-old Emily Osborne who on 17 June 1903 'Had the misfortune to run a needle into her arm. She was sent to the Royal Worcester Infirmary and an operation performed but the needle was not located. Another operation would be necessary.' Whether Emily had another operation or not is not known but five years later she left the orphanage to become a maid in Milverton Lodge, Leamington at £10 per annum.

Illnesses in those days were of a great variety as reported in August 1903 when 'several cases of sickness were reported including one scarlet fever, one pleurisy and one eczema. The girl suffering from scarlet fever had been removed to the fever hospital and was progressing satisfactorily.'

May Bollen was only thirteen when she 'had met with an accident to her eye, which has resulted in her being sent to Birmingham, where the medical authorities found it necessary to remove the eye.' The cause of the unfortunate accident of May is not given. Two years later, 'The medical officer suggested that May should go to the Birmingham and Midland Eye Hospital and have her eye attended to.' Two weeks later, 'The master reported that he had taken May to Birmingham. The girl had been measured for a new eye but an in-patients letter was required.' He also stated that the maker of artificial eyes to the Birmingham Eye Hospital had suggested that if a 'suellen' eye was recommended the committee would be willing to pay the extra guinea. A month later 'The master reported that a "suellen" eye had been recommended for May Bollen and therefore the extra guinea had been paid. The master was instructed to have the "shell" eye re-enamelled.' On 21 October the committee stated 'that permission be given to May Bollen to visit her father from Thursday morning until Sunday evening'. The following June of 1904, May 'entered the service of Rev. G. H. Poole, Himbledon Vicarage. House Parlourmaid. Salary £8 per annum.'

The orphanage still kept in touch with May as it was reported the following February 1905, 'The Ladies Committee reported that May Bollen now in the service of Rev. Gordon Poole Himbledon had had trouble with her eye and it was necessary for her to go to the Birmingham Eye Hospital again and suggested that the committee might help her. It was resolved that an outpatients ticket to Birmingham Eye Hospital be given to May Bollen and that the committee pay her return railway fare to Birmingham.'

Sometimes the orphanage rejected children because of uncleanliness presumably because of the risk of infection to children already in the orphanage, as happened in April 1905. 'In the cases of the girls Dorothy Nicholas and Edith Hinton, the medical officers stated that their heads were not clean. Admission was therefore declined. The parents were asked to have the children thoroughly cleaned and present them again on Wednesday 3 May. Three boys OK.' A month later Edith Hinton was presented for admission on 3 May 1905, and admitted. Dorothy Nicholas was admitted a few days later on 17 May.

The decision to reject the child of a 'lunatic parent' was made in June 1906. 'A letter was read from the secretary of a charity organisation [it doesn't say which one] asking if a boy whose father was an inmate of Powick Lunatic Asylum was eligible for nomination to the orphanage. The secretary was instructed to reply that under the rules the committee had no power to accept such nomination.' Who the boy was is not stated. Let us hope he found a happy place.

It seems that in the early part of the twentieth century hospitals were looked up to as in the following case of 3 February 1904. 'It was reported that Harriet Hunt was suffering from lung trouble and the medical officers advised her removal to Knightwick Sanatorium. The secretary was instructed to make enquiries and ascertain if the girl could be received at Knightwick. The chairman undertook to communicate with Archbishop Walters and enquire the position of the father of the girl.' The following month it was stated 'that Harriet Hunt had been removed from Bromsgrove Workhouse Infirmary and that the boy Powell had been taken from the Isolation Hospital to Malvern for a period of 14 days before returning to the orphanage.'

As early as 1896 it appears that vaccination was used at the Royal Albert. In May of that year 'in view of the recent illness amongst the girls, the secretary was directed to request medical officers to make a special report and state if in their opinion there is a cause for this which can be remedied, and the secretary was instructed to request the medical officers to examine the children and re-vaccinate any they may think necessary together with the staff of the institution.'

Gertrude Davis was eight when she was admitted to the orphanage in October 1888. In June 1891 it is recorded that her mother objected to her daughter having an operation although later her mother gave her consent. But in December 1893 Gertrude was to leave the Royal Albert early, aged thirteen. The reason given: 'Taken out by mother. The committee granted the mother £5 in lieu of the usual outfit. The girl was never strong as she was continually having operations on her neck.'

The committee were always generous regarding the health of a child. Eliza Warman was sent to the Worcester Ophthalmic Institute for examination in July 1889 and the committee sent one guinea to pay for the visit. If further examinations were necessary at the Birmingham Institution a Mr Jacobs kindly offered to pay the cost of them.

In August 1895 'the secretary was directed to call the attention of the authorities at the Worcester Royal Infirmary to the fact that Edith Cook one of the inmates of the orphanage was sent to the infirmary with a dislocated elbow on 29 July at 6 p.m. and that the injury was not thoroughly attended to until the following morning at 11 o'clock – and to ask for an explanation.' The following month an answer was received from the House Surgeon of the Worcester Infirmary but his comments were not listed!

In the minutes of October 1895 'the mother of James Tolley wrote explaining that the child was suffering from a violent cold and unfit to leave home and the master was instructed to admit him on the production of the usual certificates and other papers.' James was admitted into the Royal Albert on 26 October but was taken out by his mother on 11 February 1899 just before his thirteenth birthday.

In many ways the Victorians and Edwardians were ahead of their time in advocating the best environment for a child's recovery as in the case of fourteen-year-old 'Edith Gwilliam suffering from purpurea. Suggested change of air would do her good. Some responsible person in Malvern or Broadheath.' The following month in July 1902 the records state: 'This girl, boarded out at Mrs Camwell, Stoke Prior, was much better and decided to send her to a convalescent home at Weston-Super-Mare or Blackwell. Mr F. J. A. Wood kindly promised to give a ticket for whichever home was selected. Mrs Camwell to be paid the sum of 12/- weekly for Edith Gwilliam's board etc.' A fortnight later we read, 'Girl much better. The mother asked if Edith could go to her at Evesham but it wouldn't be convenient until 29 July. It was necessary to ascertain if the girl should go in a convalescent home or remain with Mrs Camwell, then go to the mother for a week on the 29th, then return to the orphanage.' As stated earlier in this chapter Edith was to go down with scarlatina the following year. Finally on 22 September 1904 Edith left the orphanage, aged sixteen, and 'entered the service of Rev. Deeke, Burlingham, near Defford at a salary commencing at £9 per annum. Conduct of girl in the orphanage very good.'

A further case of a change of environment as a help to cure was decided for Harriet Coleman in July 1906. 'It was suggested that this girl who had had a severe attack of pneumonia would benefit from a change of air. It was resolved that if the medical officer approves, Harriet Coleman be sent to Malvern for two or three weeks, if suitable arrangements can be made for the girl to be taken care of.' Malvern is after all the most beautiful place in all England but whether Harriet went there is not known!

VISITING

Children were allowed to be visited once a month. Sanctions were imposed on parents and friends of the children regarding food. In the minutes of the orphanage committee of January 1884: 'It was resolved that no provisions or food with the exception of fruit be allowed to be brought into the Asylum by the parents or friends of the children and no fruit without the sanction of the master.'

Even the monthly visits sometimes stretched into one visit every two or three months because of illness. On 18 July 1894: 'It was decided that the visiting of parents and friends should be suspended for another month.' Visiting had already been cancelled on 20 June because of an outbreak of smallpox.

Visiting was suspended in March 1895. 'It was resolved that the visits of parents and friends of the children be suspended for the present.' The reason seems to have been that one boy, Francis Farley, had consumption.

In the November of 1895: 'Permission was given to Mrs Caldwell to visit her children now in the Institution once, upon a day and time to be arranged by the Master.' Her daughter Blanche had entered the orphanage four years previously and was now twelve. Her son Samuel was admitted the following year, and was a year younger than Blanche. Samuel emigrated to Canada in the SS *Dominion* in 1899.

'No visiting be allowed until further notice' was proposed by the orphanage committee in December 1897. The reason was an outbreak of scarlet fever in the October.

The same month Queen Victoria died in February 1901, illness again prevented visiting: 'That in consequence of the continued illness at the Orphanage the visits of parents and friends be suspended until further orders.'

The doctors in December 1902 put a stop to visiting: 'Letters from Dr Crowe and Dr Polson stating that it was not desirable to permit visiting at present and therefore the committee could not give permission for visiting to be resumed.' The reason again was because of an outbreak of scarlet fever in the October and November. There appears to have been a reluctance by the doctors for visiting presumably to prevent spread of the disease.

On 18 March 1903: 'The secretary was instructed to write to the medical officers and ask why visiting should not be resumed and if they raised no objection, the master was authorised to allow the children to be visited by their friends.' On 1 April: 'Letters from Dr Crowe and Dr Polson were read repeating the question of visiting. They stated that they could not recommend it at present except in a modified form and it was decided to adjourn the consideration of the matter for a month.' Finally on 6 May it was agreed: 'That friends, adults only be permitted to visit the children this day week.'

ENTERTAINMENTS

The orphanage children were invited to certain outside functions and entertainments. For varying reasons sometimes they were allowed to go and sometimes they were refused.

In October 1887, whether in celebration of Queen Victoria's Golden Jubilee is not stated, 'The master reported that the mayoress of Worcester, Mrs Holland had invited the inmates of the orphanage to a tea-and-entertainment at the Guildhall on 6 October 1887. The secretary was instructed to convey to Mrs Holland the thanks of the committee for her kindness.'

Literature which through time has proved one of the greatest sources of entertainment was selected for the children. In October 1888: 'It was arranged that the *Gardeners Chronicle* and one other periodical should be purchased for the use of the boys, and two weekly papers for the use of the girls, and Rev. H. R. Cleaver was requested to select them.' In March

1891 the Rev. W. Thorn presented to the orphanage a gift of the *Illustrated London News* and further magazines were offered children years later. In December 1905 it is stated: 'That the master is hereby authorised to purchase magazines for the use of the children as follows: two copies of the *Boy's Own Paper* and *Girl's Own Paper*. One copy each of *Farm Life* and *Farm and Garden* and one paper for the infants.' In January 1907 it was decided that 'the master purchase two dozen magazines monthly for boys and a similar number for the girls'. But it doesn't state which magazines!

Before the movie camera, the greatest invention of the twentieth century, came to be established, the children were able to enjoy the next best thing. In October 1888: 'The secretary was desired to convey the best thanks of the committee to Sergeant Norman for his kindness in exhibiting a Magic Lantern at the orphanage. Also to Mr G. Martin, Manager of the Tramway Company for placing a tramcar at the disposal of the officers and girls of the institution.' (The staff and teachers of the orphanage in those times were sometimes called officers.)

The wonders of the Magic Lantern were enjoyed by the children as recorded in October 1904, 'It is resolved that Mr Brian's offer to give a lecture illustrated by Lantern Slides on "Living Ants" at a cost of 10/6*d* be accepted and that the master be authorised to purchase a case of Living Ants at a cost of 21/-.'

Presumably Edison's Animated Pictures was the link between the Magic Lantern and the movie camera. The children were entertained by this new medium in January 1903. 'The secretary was instructed to accept an offer for the children to see Edison's Animated Pictures at the Public Hall on Saturday afternoon January 10th.'

Madame Nicolo and what she did is possibly lost to history for the orphanage minutes unfortunately do not say what she did, only that on 3 July 1889 'A letter from Madame Nicolo was read offering entertainment at the orphanage for a fee of three guineas. Declined.'

'The entertainment proposed to be held on 25 January 1889 was ordered to be postponed for three months on account of the unsatisfactory conduct of the boys' but what the entertainment was is not stated!

When it came to the possibility of extra revenue the orphanage committee were always pleased to oblige, as in the case when in July 1890, 'The Sabrina Band of Hope asked permission to use the field adjoining the orphanage on some day in this month. Agreed.' The use of this field was also granted to the Worcester Rugby Football Club on 19 and 26 December 1891.

Good advice on football sportsmanship was given to the boys in October 1890: 'It was resolved that the boys be permitted to play football subject to the master undertaking to prevent dangerous mode of play.' The girls were not left out. In February 1890, 'The recommendation from the Ladies Committee to purchase skipping ropes for the use of the girls was approved and Mrs Carr was requested to obtain them.'

The Ladies Committee voted themselves the use of the orphanage for their hockey! In August 1901, 'that application of "Ladies" through Mrs Cherry and Miss Bramwell for the use of the field to play hockey during the winter months at a rental of £4 per annum be granted.'

Tea and entertainment at the Guildhall was again offered to the children and staff by Mrs Walter Holland on 13 January 1892.

One of the delights for orphanage children was to be asked out for the day. The only drawback was having to go back afterwards! Such a request was made for an outing in August 1892: 'In a letter Miss Milward asks permission to be allowed to take six children into the city for the day. The master pointed out, if the request was accepted, it would in all probability create dissatisfaction amongst the other children.'

In July 1891 the orphanage received an 'invitation to Halt Fleet upon the steamer *Lady Alwyne* from Messrs Everton and Co.' The *Lady Alwyne* steamed up the Severn between Worcester and Holt. The minutes do not say whether the children went on the trip, but a year later we do know that though the invitation was offered again, this time the children definitely didn't go. The records for September 1892: 'Decided to decline Mr Everton's offer to take children upon his steamer to Holt on the grounds of the lateness of the season and the unsatisfactory conduct of the boys.' At some later date however children from the Royal Albert did go on the steamer up the Severn. I have photographs to prove this!

In May 1894: 'The secretary was requested to convey the best thanks of the committee to Mr & Mrs Cock for entertaining the children at their residence and to Mr H. Gale, manager of the Worcester Tram Company for conveying them there.' The minutes do not tell us what entertainment went on at the Cocks' residence! The same thanks were expressed a year later to the manager of the Worcester Tramway Company for kindly giving the children a ride. Thanks were expressed in May 1985 to Mr Summerhayes 'for entertaining the boys on his Hobby Horses'.

Fêtes may come and go but 'the master was instructed to decline the invitation to the children to attend the Foresters' Fête' in May 1894. The reason is not stated. One fête the children did go to was at Perdiswell in

July 1901. 'Thanks to Mr Martin Curtler for his kindness in treating the children to the Fete at Perdiswell on 18 July and to Mr Foster for providing brakes for their conveyance.'

However, the girls were more fortunate in August 1894 when it is recorded that 'a vote of thanks be given to Mrs H. Temple Bowne for her kindness in entertaining the girls at Sebright Lawn.' The records do not state whether the kind Mrs Temple Bowne gave the girls tea and cake, or something more.

The children did occasionally visit country houses in the local area. In August 1896 'permission was given for the boys to go to Hallow Park on the invitation of Mr J. A. Wood.' Whether or not the children went to Hallow Park again is not known but in April 1898: 'The master authorised to let the children go out of the institution in the direction of Hallow and Broad Heath subject to the sanction of the medical officers.' The more famous Madresfield Court was also visited by the children from the Royal Albert. In August 1896: 'Permission was given for the children to accompany St John's Sunday School Party to Madresfield Court on Tuesday the 25th instant.' One assumes the children went each year, but it is not recorded again until eight years later when 'permission be given to children to go with St John's Sunday School children to Madresfield Court on 2 July on the invitation of the Earl and Countess Beauchamp.'

'The Rhydd', the home of Lady Lechmere was also visited by the children in September 1899. The record states 'that Katherine Lady Lechmere's invitation to the children to visit "The Rhydd" be accepted. The institution to pay half the conveyance.' What wonders must have gone through those children's minds after living in an orphanage with all its disciplines and then to encounter what is really heaven on earth – a visit to an English country house and estate.

One concert in November 1897 the children were able to go to was subject to the medical officers: 'An invitation from the RAO Buffaloes for the children to attend a concert on 26th inst. was accepted subject to the medical officers certifying that they would not be running any kind of conveying infection.' It appears that children have in all times been the biggest means of spreading disease!

The Bijou Minstrels seem to have been very unlucky or were not thought suitable for the children as they were rejected on successive years. In December 1897: 'An invitation for the children to attend the performance of the Bijou minstrels was declined with thanks.' In December 1898 again the invitation was turned down and in December 1899: 'Again the boys' visit to the Bijou Minstrels be declined.' The persistence of the Minstrels in wanting to bring joy to children at Christmas is to be applauded, even if their efforts went unrewarded.

The Mayor's invitation however was possibly considered more suitable, perhaps because the children didn't leave the orphanage! In December 1898 it was agreed: 'That the Mayor's invitation to a Christmas entertainment at the orphanage be accepted with thanks.'

Whatever were the merits of the Worcester Art Gallery over the Worcester Amateur Operatic Society is unknown but this was the case in December 1901: 'That the invitation of the Amateur Operatic Society for children to attend the rehearsal be declined. That the invitation of the secretary to the Art Gallery for the children to view the pictures be accepted.' The children may have missed out on the opera but they did visit the circus in April 1902: 'That the mayor's invitation for the children to visit the circus be accepted with thanks.'

No reason is given for why the children were refused the invitation to the Christmas pantomime in January 1905. The statement simply reads: 'That the invitation of Mrs Carlton for the children to witness the pantomime at the Theatre on Thursday afternoon 5 January be declined.' However, the same day that this rejection was made on 21 December 1904 it was agreed for the children to be entertained by students! 'That permission be given for an entertainment to be performed at the orphanage by the students at the Victoria Institute.'

A request on 17 July 1901 'That permission be given for Mr Williams to exhibit his Graphophone to the children on Saturday next' was put before the Committee but whether this took place is not stated.

In May 1901 it was recommended that 'The invitation of Mr Mayglothing for the children to attend the Sansome Walk Baptist Chapel be declined.' The reason possibly for this was that the Royal Albert had links with the Church of England at St John's and later St Clement's, and in those days the Church of England and the non-conformists were poles apart.

The children may have missed out on certain entertainments by Madame Nicolo, the Bijou Minstrels, the Foresters' Fete, the Amateur Operatics, the Christmas Pantomime, and a visit to the Baptist Chapel but one thing they must have enjoyed to the full was their Christmas dinner as recorded on 7 December 1904. 'That the grateful thanks of this committee be, and they are hereby accorded, to Lady Northwick for her gift of venison and to Mr E. H. Hill for his kind gifts of pheasants.'

EMIGRATION

The emigration of orphanage children which has been such a talking point of recent years has a very long history and with the Royal Albert Orphanage this was no exception.

The following letter of 20 March 1887 by the Rev. Walter R. Carr was read to the committee:

> Rev. and Mrs R. Wallace of Marchment Hall, Belleville, Ontario, in company with Mr Phipps of Buckenhill, Bromyard, who takes great interest in Dr Barnardo's Homes visited the Royal Albert Orphanage on Thursday 10 March 1887 and were shown by me over the Orphan Asylum. They were just returning to Canada to carry on the work in which they have been engaged for the past 15 years, during which time nearly 5,000 children between the ages of 4 and 15 have passed through their hands. They have no connection with Dr Barnardo's Homes preferring to deal with smaller numbers so that they may retain greater supervision over the children whom they plant out in the various Canadian Homes. They receive children from the following:
>
> 1. Mr William Quarrier, Orphan Home, Glasgow.
> 2. Mr Leonard Shaw, Home for Destitute Children, Manchester.
> 3. Mr Campbell, Douglas, Isle of Man.
> 4. Mr D. Blackie, Edinburgh.
>
> also a few from
>
> 5. Mrs Wenryss, Washwell House, Painswick, Gloucester, a small private home where children who have lost both parents are taken and others of a similar kind.
>
> Children are generally sent out about March (this is the best time), under the charge of one of the officers from these homes. They do not care to receive any children above the age of 15 and they prefer not to have them above 12. The only charge over and above the expense of the journey is £3 a head. Mr & Mrs Wallace receive the children at Marchment Hall and as quickly as possible (generally within a few days) plant them out in various homes. They have a constant demand for them and exercise the greatest care in the selection of places – they allow no child to go to a place without they are satisfied by a reference from the clergyman of the district that the house is suitable. They enter into an agreement with the

> master or mistress under which they reserve the right at any time to remove the child if he or she is not happy or not receiving proper treatment. They require the child shall attend school during the four winter months and shall regularly attend a place of worship. They constantly visit all the homes to see how the children are prospering and allow the children at any time to return to the home. As a rule the boys go on to the farms where they receive board, clothing and education and after they are 13 small wages. Younger children are very often adopted into families and the girls taken for domestic service. No child may be sent away or removed to another home or situation without the consent of Rev. and Mrs R. Wallace. I was very much struck with the intelligence and good sense and devotion to the cause of both Mr & Mrs Wallace and feel sure that children placed under their charge would have every attention and consideration. They were much pleased with the Asylum and the children and desired me to assure the Committee how gladly they would co-operate with us if at any time we desired to promote the cause of emigration of children to Canada.

Rev. Carr was thanked for his 500-word memorandum. The subject of emigration was discussed but no resolution passed on that important meeting of the committee of 6 April 1887 which was in future to affect the lives of many of the children under their care.

Things lay dormant for six months but at the meeting of 5 October 1887 the Rev. Walter Carr was requested to draw up a circular for parents in relation to emigration. Upon a suggestion of a Mr Curtler, the secretary was instructed to write to Dr Barnardo for particulars as to the conditions under which boys are sent abroad by him and a circular letter was received from Dr Barnardo in relation to emigration a few days later.

At the committee meeting of 5 December 1988 the master reported that the following boys had expressed a desire to emigrate to Canada and that in each case the consent of the surviving parent had been obtained:

William Henry Teague aged 15 years.
Edwin Bund aged 15 years.
William George Ward aged 14 years.

The secretary was instructed to write to the Rev. R. Wallace of Belleville, Ontario, Canada, asking him to make arrangements for the reception of these boys during the following March.

William Henry Teague emigrated to Canada on 20 March 1889 under the supervision of Mr Wallace in SS *Vancouver*, arriving safely at Marchment House, Belleville, Ontario. He obtained a good situation in a farm at Hawley, Canada. Henry left behind in England his thirteen-year-old sister Beatrice who left the orphanage two years later and went into service at Bowling Green Terrace, Worcester.

Edwin Bund sailed in the same ship as Henry Teague and ultimately obtained a situation with a Mr James Hodgins in Shawville, Quebec, Canada. Edwin's elder brother Benjamin remained in England. He had left the orphanage two years previously to enter the service of Dr Greensill, Great Witley, Stourport on a salary of £5 per annum. William George Ward also sailed with Edwin Bund and Henry Teague and after arriving in Canada he obtained a good situation in a large printing establishment in Montreal.

Another boy who sailed with Henry, Edwin and George was Charles Monk, eleven days short of his sixteenth birthday. It seems he had a job for a while but shortly afterwards was taken ill. A letter arrived in England on 18 September 'dated 26 ultimo from Rev. R. Wallace, Canada, stating that Charles Monk was seriously ill with consumption.' Charles died after a lingering illness on 4 December 1889, in Marchment House. The records state that 'every attention was paid to him'. What must have been comforting to Charles as he lay dying was that his fourteen-year-old sister Eliza was with him in that strange land. Eliza had emigrated to Canada two months after Charles with Miss Weym's party on 16 May 1889.

For the record, the cost of taking a child to Canada was £8. 9*s*. 9*d*. The fare from Worcester to Halifax was £3. 14*s*. 0*d*., from Halifax to the Marchment Home £1. 7*s*. 9*d*., the 'diet' 8 shillings and the Home fee three pounds.

The Committee agreed that the money standing credit of each child in the Savings Bank together with a sum of 5/- each be handed to Mr Wallace and be placed in the Savings Bank of Canada.

A letter from Lady Georgina Vernon of 3 April 1889 stated the opportunity of sending a girl to Canada and enquiring if there was one in the Orphanage willing to go. As Emily West expressed a desire to go to Canada it was arranged that subject to the consent of her surviving parent, she should be offered to Lady Georgina Vernon.

A letter of 14 May from the Canadian Shipping Company Ltd stated that Mr Middlemore of Birmingham was sending a party of children by SS *Lake Winnipeg* to Canada on 31 May. It was arranged that Emily be sent by this vessel and if possible under the management of Mr

Middlemore, who was instructed to communicate with Lady Georgina Vernon, with the view that the girl was met on her arrival at Quebec. However, a postcard was received on 13 July from the Secretary of the Woman's Protective Immigration Society, Montreal, Canada stating that Emily West had arrived safely, but without funds for her inland journey and that Lady Georgina Vernon's instructions could not therefore be carried out. A cheque for £2. 9*s*. 4*d*. was sent to Canada with the best thanks of the committee to the officials of the society for their great kindness in taking charge of the girl.

After arriving in Canada, sixteen-year-old Emily entered the service of Mr G. Pain of Maple Grove, Pigeon Lake, Manitoba and her younger brother George joined her two years later when he emigrated to Canada under the supervision of Mr Wallace aboard the liner SS *Sarnia*.

Frank George Dyer was the first boy from the Royal Albert Orphanage to emigrate to Canada on 25 April 1888 with Miss Weym's party aboard the SS *Sarmatian*. He was only 13½ years old. After arriving in Canada he was apprenticed in printing with Smith and Gowan Equity Office, Shawville, Quebec. Ten years later on 6 July 1898 a letter was received from Rev. R. Wallace with the sad news that Frank had died of consumption at Shawville in Canada. He was only twenty-four.

William Davis little realised what the future had in store for him when he boarded the SS *Dominion* to Canada on 13 April 1899. Two years later a letter was received from him which remains in the orphanage minutes of 7 August 1901 stating that William Davis, a former inmate of the institution, who emigrated to Canada two years earlier, was complaining of the people in whose employment he now was. That is the last we hear of William.

Some of the letters must have been different from that of William Davis according to Canon Carr, who in March 1904 said he had 'sometimes pressed the Board of Guardians to send children to Canada, but they seemed to think it was almost cruelty to send children out of this country. If they could only see the letters from boys whom the committee had sent out they would see that there was in Canada a field second to none for boys from this over-crowded country.'

A letter dated 2 December 1898 from the Children's Emigration Homes was read stating that George Henry Griffiths who emigrated under their auspices in June the previous year was in a comfortable situation but received no salary! Whether another George wanted to go to Canada and his father didn't want him to, is not clear but the minutes of 18 February 1903 say: 'The master reported that the father of George Henry Coomby objected to the boy being sent to Canada. Mr Wood undertook to enquire if it was possible to persuade the father to change his mind and allow the boy to go.' He obviously changed the mind of George's father as George Henry Coomby emigrated to Canada a year later on 14 April 1904.

On 18 March 1903 permission was given for Charles Wood to go home three days prior to his departure to Canada. Charles left England on 2 April under the supervision of Mr Checker aboard the ship SS *Tunissian*. He was nearly fourteen.

For those interested in ships the following were used to transport the children to Canada between 1888 and 1910: SS *Vancouver*, SS *Lake Winnipeg*, SS *Sarnia*, SS *Sarmatian*, SS *Dominion*, SS *Tunissian* and SS *Ionian*. It is presumed they all sailed from Liverpool. We know that the SS *Dominion* sailed from the Prince's Landing Stage, Liverpool at 5 p.m. on 11 April 1901.

Forty-eight children emigrated to Canada from the Royal Albert orphanage in the Victorian and Edwardian era. Of those only three were girls. They were mostly aged between thirteen and sixteen years old; only two were younger: George Browning was one month and George Smart two months short of their thirteenth birthdays. All the children arrived safely and all this of course took place some years before the fatal maiden voyage of the RMS *Titanic*.

Two boys, Arthur Barnett who sailed on 3 May 1906, and Harry Waterman Dowling the following April little realised that they were not to spend the rest of their lives in Canada. Ten years later they were to return to Europe to fight for King and Empire in the Great War. Harry was killed in action in 1916 and Arthur suffered the same fate the next year.

Archer John Moon, whose patron Lady Lechmere had brought him into the orphanage, was to travel much further afield. Fourteen-year-old Archer emigrated to New Zealand aboard SS *Ruaphen* on 20 March 1889 and he arrived safely after only seven weeks. He found a job in Dunedin as a printer.

A further seventeen children emigrated before the outbreak of the Great War, the last one on 14 April 1914. After the War only six children were to make the long Atlantic voyage between 12 April 1921 and 23 February 1923. Louis Mitchell who emigrated to Canada in 1923 aged 16 left behind his brothers Edgar aged 13 and Charlie aged 11. Sadly Charlie wasn't to see Louis again.

PARENTS REMARRIED

It was part of the committee's policy to be aware of the changing circumstances of a child's parent as was stated at a meeting in November 1887: 'It was resolved that in the case of the marriage of a parent of an inmate, the master to be requested to inform the committee at the next meeting.' One wonders whether the Royal Albert were ahead of their day in suggesting that with a remarriage it was preferable for the children to leave the orphanage and go and live with their mother or father and their new spouse.

The committee felt at their meeting on 2 November 1887 that in the case of Jessie Fitzer, emigration to Canada should be recommended and the secretary was instructed to ascertain whether the mother of the girl would consent to this. The reason presumably for their decision was that Jessie's mother had remarried to a Mr G. Price, a greengrocer of Birdport, Worcester. She had five children before her second marriage and her second husband had six of his own. Later that month the mother of Jessie Fitzer rejected the committee's recommendation by saying that she was unwilling for her daughter to emigrate.

The mother of Mabel Emmeline Munn married a man named Hill who worked at McNaught and Co. She had four children of her own (one in service) and three of her husband's. Mr Hill's wages when on full time was £1 per week. Though Mabel's mother had remarried in 1887, Mabel was to stay in the orphanage for another six years, the maximum time until sixteen, before going into service at Melford House, Battenhall, Worcester on a salary of £6 per annum as a parlour maid.

'The father of Lucy Carwardine married a Mrs Allen who is a good laundress and earns a great deal of money weekly. The father is a hop dryer who also earns a good wage.' Though Mr Carwardine had remarried, Lucy was to stay in the orphanage for another eighteen months, after which she left aged 10½ to live with her father and stepmother in Powick, near Worcester.

'The mother of Marianne Elizabeth Jones married a Mr Griffiths who is a coachman at Alfrick. They have two children dependent on them.' Perhaps because of this Marianne stayed on in the orphanage for a further six years until she went into service aged sixteen.

'The mother of Alice and Rose Lee married a man named Frickling who is employed in the Vulcan works.' The mother had four children before her second marriage and two in the Asylum. They married in 1887 but by that time Rose was already fifteen, having spent a fortnight at a convalescent home in the West of England Sanatorium, Weston-Super-

Mare owing to poor health. Rose left the following year and entered the service of Mrs Jones, Board Schools, Rushwood, Droitwich, but after living in this situation for a few weeks Rose was to leave on account of ill health, only to go into service again with a Mrs Clarke in Lansdown Crescent, Malvern. Her sister remained in the orphanage for a further three years, then left, aged fifteen, to be a general servant in Brougham House, Malvern.

George Gale's mother married a Mr Davis, a wheelwright, of Fernhill Heath. Since her marriage they had for some time lived apart. The mother who went out charring and washing had one boy dependent on her. George left the orphanage the following year but by that time he was well over sixteen. He was apprenticed to a Mr Edwards, a blacksmith at Copcut, near Droitwich. Edwin Merrill according to the orphanage records was of a rather indolent nature and was taken out of the orphanage by his mother who had remarried. A 'partial' outfit was to be provided at an approximate cost of £2. 10*s*. 0*d*. Leaving outfits seemed to range from 30/- to 50/- which was a lot of money in 1897.

Mrs Gwilliam, mother of William and Alice Selina, now in the orphanage stated that her husband was not in a position to maintain them. The Committee also felt that William and Selina should not go home to their mother with these words: 'The Committee feel bound to express their condemnation of the immoral state of life in which the mother of the children is living and do not feel they can send away the children to re-enter such an improper home. That Mrs Gwilliam be never allowed to enter the Asylum nor the children to visit her, but that the eldest sister be allowed occasionally to visit the children here.' Four years later William emigrated to Canada on 10 April 1902 aboard SS *Ionia*. His sister left two years later to live with her mother locally in Worcester.

What the reason was for the verbal abuse which Mrs Allcock vomited forth over the Orphanage Committee is not known. However some days later a letter was received from Mrs Allcock expressing her regret for using improper language reflecting upon the management of the institution and the apology was received. That her outburst was over her son's career is a possibility as David Allcock started an apprenticeship with Fownes glove manufacturers in June 1890 aged 14½, whereas it was the policy of the orphanage for the children to stay on until sixteen years of age to work on the farm and gardens.

MUSIC

Music which must have been the greatest blessing to a boy or girl brought up in the Orphanage is mentioned very little in the records.

A letter of 16 November 1887 addressed to Mr T. R. Hill by the schoolmaster (Mr Barrow) was read asking the sanction of the Committee for the boys to be allowed to join the Total Abstinence Society and suggesting the desirability of providing a harmonium for class singing. The subject was fully discussed but in the opinion of the Committee it was deemed inadvisable to sanction the proposal though it was resolved to recommend the purchase of a harmonium for the use of the school. The following month a letter was read from a Mr Sparks stating that he had sent a more expensive harmonium than the one selected, but that he did not propose to alter the price originally quoted. The minutes state that a harmonium (No. 1025) be purchased from Mr Sparks for the sum of £5. *2s .6d*. Whether this was the more expensive instrument is not stated.

Cathedral music must be the finest music in the world. I'm sure this was the view of the Rev. H. Clifford who sent this report from The College, Worcester to the orphanage on 25 May 1888: 'Dear Sir, By the rules of the orphanage would it be possible for the members of the voluntary choir of the Cathedral on the payment of £15 or £16 which it costs annually to maintain a boy there to have the right of nominating a boy, subject of course to the Governors or the Committee?'

Sadly, 'the secretary was instructed to inform Rev. H. Clifford that the rules did not provide for the adoption of his suggestion.' Perhaps the orphanage committee declined because it would favour one boy more than the others!

Arguably the greatest English composer is Sir Edward Elgar. His father's music shop was situated in the centre of Worcester not far from the Cathedral. In a minute dated 3 July 1889, 'It was arranged that the necessary repairs to the piano should be done by Messrs Elgar Bros.' One wonders if the great man was there the day the piano was delivered. Perhaps the piano never turned up at Elgar Bros. but eighteen years later on 3 July 1907: 'The Ladies Committee stated that the piano in the school room was worn out and Mrs Sparks offered to allow £4 for it in exchange for a new instrument. He also offered a good pianoforte for £18. It was resolved that a Mr Street Chignell be asked to inspect the instrument' but whether the Royal Albert paid out the £18 is not known!

One thing the orphanage did splash out on were some eighty-four hymn books on 19 February 1902. It is written 'that the Master be authorised to purchase seven dozen hymn books at *6d.* each'. As the orphanage children went to either one of two Anglican churches, St Clement's and St John's, was it 'Ancient and Modern' that was chosen?

A suggestion for apprenticeship of Cecil Willoughby Crook to Messrs Nicholson & Co. Organ Builders was considered and it was decided that the Chairman should see Messrs Nicholson to endeavour to arrange for a higher rate of wages during the final three years. A month later Cecil did leave the orphanage on 27 May 1903 to start his apprenticeship as an organ builder but one wonders if he obtained higher wages!

ROYAL EVENTS

The Royal events of our own time are rather special: the Coronation of Queen Elizabeth II in 1953; the investiture of the Prince of Wales in 1969; the fairy-tale wedding of Prince Charles and Lady Diana Spencer in 1981. Who can forget the pathos as Lady Diana guided her ailing father up the long aisle of St Paul's Cathedral, possibly the most memorable event ever seen on a television screen. Then in 1997 came the surprising and incredible public reaction to the death of Princess Diana, remembered with the burning of candles and the gifts of flowers. The funeral of Princess Diana must have been London's greatest procession since Sir Winston Churchill's State Funeral in 1965.

The Victorians and Edwardians were very much the same as us, and the staff and children in the Royal Albert Orphanage celebrated the events as much as 'the outsiders' – the civilian population.

Queen Victoria's Golden Jubilee was celebrated by both staff and children. The record of 1 June 1887 reads: 'Queen's Jubilee rejoicings. A letter from the Secretary of the county of Worcester Queen's Jubilee Committee was received in which it was stated that the Jubilee Committee had provided the sum of £5. 5*s.* 0*d.* towards the cost of feasting the inmates and staff of the Orphan Asylum on 21 June, in celebration of the Queen's Jubilee, also that a supply of medals would be forwarded for distribution amongst the inmates and staff and a £5. 5*s.* 0*d.* case of fireworks. The offer of the County Jubilee Committee was accepted with thanks. It was referred to the sub-committee to make arrangements for the rejoicing at the orphanage and it was resolved that a Post Office Savings Bank Book with the sum of 1/- deposited therein should be presented to each of the children as a memorial of her Majesty's Jubilee.'

The Jubilee arrangements were discussed again on 15 June 1887. 'It was resolved that the children should be allowed to join the Jubilee Procession to Pitchcroft on Tuesday 21 June and that the contribution from the County Jubilee Committee be expended in providing a dinner for the children consisting of roast beef, plum pudding, tarts and ginger beer, bon bons and crackers. The secretary was instructed to invite all the members of the Committee to be present on the occasion and to insert a paragraph in the newspapers calling attention to the dinner and saying that the Committee will be pleased to see any of the subscribers present.'

The Royal Wedding of Prince George to Princess Mary of Teck received very little mention. The entry for 7 June 1893 reads: 'Royal Wedding Buns. The Master was authorised to provide buns etc. for the children's tea on Thursday 6 July in commemoration of the Royal Wedding.' One wonder what the 'etc.' provided consisted of!

A far more memorable occasion than the wedding of the future King George V and Queen Mary was celebrated four years later in 1897, the Diamond Jubilee of Queen Victoria. The minutes of 19 May 1897 read: 'Jubilee Cup. A letter dated 13th instant from Messrs Mann & Sons, High Street, Worcester offering to present a Jubilee Cup to each of the children in the orphanage was read and the secretary was directed to accept their offer and convey the thanks of the committee for their gift.'

On 2 June 1897, 'A letter from the Town Clerk was read announcing that the Jubilee Committee had unanimously granted the sum of 8*d*. per head for the children's tea, the number not to exceed 89. The Secretary was requested to convey the best thanks of the Committee for the grant. It was decided that there should be a special celebration of the Jubilee at the orphanage and the Chairman undertook to confer with Rev. W. R. Carr and bring the matter before the House Committee who were authorised to make the necessary arrangements.' On 16 June 1897, 'Sanction was given for the schoolmaster and schoolmistress to take a half week's extra holiday this year in consideration of the Jubilee, subject to satisfactory arrangements being made for the discharge of their duties.'

'Thursday 24 June 1897 was fixed for the Children's Sports and Evening Entertainment and the programme of the entertainment was submitted and approved.' One wonders what the entertainment entailed.

The records on the Diamond Jubilee close on 7 July 1897. 'Jubilee. Secretary directed to convey best thanks of the Committee to Mrs Forrest and Mrs Knott for their kindness in inviting the children to view the boat procession and fireworks on 21 and 22 June.' The River Severn has probably never seen such a glorious event as happened on these two nights in 1897.

The death of Queen Victoria was certainly the end of an era and the Institute on 6 February 1901 wrote: '. . . unanimously that the Committee of the Royal Albert Orphan Asylum desire to record their deep sense of the irreparable loss which the nation has sustained through the death of their revered Queen and their respectful condolence with the Royal Family in their bereavement.'

The Coronation of King Edward VII was suitably marked on 4 June 1902:

(a) That the children be provided with a Special Dinner and Sports on Coronation Day. 30/- to be given for the prizes.
(b) That permission be given for the children to attend a tea at St John's School on 27 June and also to march with St John's School children to Pitchcroft to receive the Coronation Medals.
(c) That the House Committee be authorised to purchase china or other suitable presents for the staff on the occasion of the Coronation.
(d) That the Master be authorised to purchase such timber as he may think necessary to erect swings for the children on the occasion of the Coronation.

On 18 June 1902 a letter was read from Mr Lord, the schoolmaster, asking for an additional holiday on the occasion of the Coronation. The Committee however, 'resolved that Mr Lord be informed that the Committee regret they are unable on this occasion to accede to his request.' The Committee decided however to give presents to the staff on the occasion of the Coronation of King Edward VII. It was decided to purchase a pair of vases for the Master and Matron at a cost of thirty shillings; a cup and saucer each for the schoolmistress and needlewomen at a cost of 7*s.* 6*d.* each; and some suitable present to be selected by Mr Cherry at a cost not exceeding 7*s.* 6*d.* for the schoolmaster.

Finally, to a great benefactress of the orphanage the Committee expressed best thanks to Mrs Wheeley-Lea for her kind present to the children of books and cards in commemoration of the Coronation of King Edward VII, and also to Mr White of Birmingham for his gift of Coronation badges for the distribution among the children.

THE SWIMMING POOL

The minutes for 15 July 1890 read: 'The boys had at present no facilities for learning swimming and suggested that the master should consider the best means of effecting this object.'

The subject for a swimming bath was mentioned the following November: 'A letter from Messrs I. S. Wood & Sons enclosing plan for the proposed new swimming bath was read, the cost of which he estimated would be £400 exclusive of water supply and heating apparatus. It was considered to provide a covered bath.'

An estimate in June 1891 from Messrs I. S. Wood & Sons for providing heating apparatus came to a cost of £96. 12*s*. 9*d*. However, the erection of an open air swimming bath at a cost of £215 was accepted by the Committee. Excavation work was to commence in about six weeks' time, but by September nothing had started.

In February 1892 a plan and specification of the proposed swimming bath from another builder, Mr Lewis Sheppard, was submitted at a cost of about £230! Then in March 1892, a further estimate was received for the proposed swimming bath from Messrs. I. S. Wood & Sons for £297. 10*s*. 0*d*. subject to the work being completed within two months from the date of contract. The swimming bath was to be lined with brown salt glazed bricks at an additional cost of £10.

The following July the Corporation offered to supply water for use in the swimming bath at a charge of eight shillings per 26,000 gallons. In June 1893 upon the suggestion of a Mr Curtler it was decided to fix barbed wire on the walls of the swimming pool. It took many years however before it was built. Finally, it was dug out by hand by the boys of the orphanage and erected at the rear of the institution. It was open air and not heated. The boys had to clean the pool with wire brushes working eight abreast. There was no filtering system and no proper changing rooms, just two small sheds!

PRICES

Provisions

Although substantially cheaper than today, prices altered very little through the Victorian and Edwardian era as the minutes from the Royal Albert Orphanage show.

The following tenders for supplies were accepted on 6 December 1882:

MEAT	James Smith	@8 ½*d.* per lb
BREAD	J. Ward	@5 ½*d.* per 4 lb
SALT BUTTER	A. Higgins	@1/0 ½ per lb
MILK	A. Gardiner	@11*d.* per gallon.

Tenders for 14 July 1883:

BUTCHER'S MEAT	E. Tillat	@8*d.* per lb
BREAD	C. C. Wall	@4*d.* per 4lb
MILK	W. Collins	@11*d.* per gallon
COAL	Cannock Chase	@10/- per ton

Groceries for December 1887 were from T. K. Goodwin. The cheapest quote was always accepted!

BLACK TEA	@1/6 per lb
RAW SUGAR	@15*s* 6*d.* per cwt
SOAP (TALLOW CROWN)	@20*s.* 6*d.* per cwt
COFFEE (GROUND)	@1*s.* 3*d.* per lb
CHICORY (GROUND)	@3 ¾*d.* per lb.
GOLDEN SYRUP	@2*s.* per lb
BOOTS (BOX) Girls	@5/- per pair
Boys	@6/- per pair

Land

The question of purchasing additional land was discussed in July 1883. It was reported that the Ecclesiastical Commissioners were prepared to sell to the Asylum a square piece of land about six acres which would extend the orphanage boundaries in the same shape as at present right out to Comer Lane at £420 per acre.

Cowshed

The following tenders for the erection of a cowshed were received on 7 April 1887:

Mr J. H. Beard	£130
Mr Stokes	£135
Mr Haden	£132

It was unanimously resolved that the tender of Mr Beard be accepted. As usual it was the cheapest quote!

Pigs and cow

18 January 1893. The purchase of twelve store pigs and one milking cow.

Potatoes

16 December 1903. To purchase two tons of potatoes from Mr Green at £4 per ton.

Lightning conductors

A letter from H. Rowe and Son of 7 November 1883 was read enclosing an estimate from Joseph Blackburn of Nottingham to erect three lightning conductors at the Asylum at 2/- per foot.

Washing machines

An illustrated price list of washing machines was submitted on 3 December 1890 and the secretary was authorised to order one machine after the master had inspected those in use at the Powick Lunatic Asylum. I wonder what the cost was?

Printing machine

As in Dr Barnardo's and the National Children's Home and Orphanage, the master was instructed to purchase new type for a printing machine at an estimated cost of £9 on 21 January 1903.

Outside painting

On 23 May 1894 it was decided to accept the lowest estimate from Messrs Heath & Sons of £22. 3*s*. 0*d*.

Whitewashing

The following tenders for inside painting, whitewashing etc. were submitted on 15 April 1896. Stokes Bros. £49. Heath & Son £47. Tomlinson £30. As expected that of Messrs Tomlinson & Son was accepted!

Boys' clothing

It was resolved to order 46 suits from Messrs Russell & Dorrell, as per sample, at 24/- per suit on 17 February 1886.

Furnishings

These were purchased from Mr W. H. Hughes, The Cross, Worcester in February 1886.

10 Iron Bedsteads	at 8/- each
10 Straw Palliasses	at 5*s.* 6*d.* each
10 Wool Mattresses	at 10/- each
10 Feather Bolsters	at 3*s.* 7*d.* each

Serge

The Ladies Committee of 1 May 1889 gladly accepted the allowance of £2 made by Messrs. Scott & Crane in respect of the serge purchased for the girls' frocks.

Rugs

In December 1890, with the view to adding to the comfort of the children during the winter months, the secretary was authorised to purchase an Austrian wool rug for each of their beds.

Boys' capes

The master was authorised in December 1891 to have boys' capes relined if it appeared to worth doing, and to purchase the requisite number of new ones from Russell & Dorrells.

Bedsteads

December 1891. To purchase two new iron bedsteads and bedding from Messrs. W. & F. Webb.

Carpet

In April 1895 the Committee decided to purchase a new carpet for the boardroom. A month later a Brussels carpet was purchased for the boardroom from Messrs. W. F. Webb at a cost of about £4. 10*s.* 0*d.* and Anglo-Indian carpets were purchased for the master's and school-mistresses' sitting rooms at a cost of £3. 7*s.* 0*d.* and £2. 5*s.* 4*d.* respectively.

Tapestry curtains

On 1 May 1895 a pair of tapestry curtains were purchased for the master's sittingroom at a cost of about 25/-.

Blinds

The master was authorised to obtain outside blinds for the dining hall windows at a cost not exceeding 40/-.

Prizes for the annual examination

These were purchased in January 1885. Eight books at 2/- each were to be given to the child in each class who did best in the annual examination and 25 rewards at *6d.* each were given as prizes to each of the rest of the children for passes in reading, writing and arithmetic.

In December 1887 the following prizes were given under the Wheeler Lea benefaction.

GIRLS:	1st prize	Sewer	value 5/-
	2nd prize	Knitter	value 5/-
	2nd prize	Laundry maid	value 5/-
BOYS:	1st prize	Printer	value 10/-
	2nd prize	Carpenter	value 5/-
	2nd prize	Gardener	value 5/-

A lot of money for those days!

Bonus

A bonus was paid to boys and girls from 3 September 1890:

2*d.* per week for boy who milks cows.
2*d.* per week for girl who attends the dairy.

Haircutting

A letter dated 2 December 1891 from Mr H. W. Harrison was read applying for an increase in the amount paid for haircutting and suggesting that he should attend twice a quarter instead of once as at present. It was resolved that the sum of 15/- be paid for each attendance (subject to Mr Harrison and his apprentice completing the work in one day) and that the children's hair be in future cut twice in every three months. Quite an undertaking for nearly a hundred children!

Pigs

The master was instructed in December 1890 to sell the nine fat pigs at not less than 8/- per score!

TELEPHONE AND ELECTRIC LIGHT

The question of discontinuance of the telephone was raised in January 1897 and the secretary was instructed to produce a copy of the agreement with the National Telephone Company. When the agreement was produced it was decided that six months notice be given to terminate the existing contract in October next. No reason was given but on 1 December 1897 it was decided to renew the annual subscription! However, in February 1898 an estimate from the National Telephone Company amounting to £7. 10*s*. 0*d*. for the telephone connecting the hospital with the master's room was not accepted. Perhaps the Institution couldn't afford this amount. They did however have an electric bell fixed by a Mr Santonna.

On 17 May 1899 the orphanage received a letter from Messrs. Lewis Sheppard & Son, 51 Foregate Street, Worcester: 'We have considered the matter of lighting the Institution by electricity and are of the opinion that 147 lamps will be necessary and these should be controlled by 114 switches, arranged so that many of the lamps may be cut out without leaving the several rooms in darkness. Also each floor could be controlled by a main switch fixed near to the masters' rooms. We are of the opinion that complete installation with all necessary pendants and other fittings and lamps of best kind would not exceed in the cost the sum of £120. To this however must be added the cost of the builders' work in preparing for and making good after the electrical engineer. Probably £20 or £30 would be ample provision.'

The following month it was decided by the Committee to accept this quotation and the work was to be completed by the end of 1899.

THE BOER WAR

This war in South Africa came right at the end of the Victoria era and the start of Edward VII's reign.

On 1 November 1899, 'the secretary was directed to write to the secretary of each district of the Soldiers and Sailors Families Association in Worcestershire with a view to the nomination of any eligible children of soldiers or sailors who may be killed in the South African War.'

A rule was made by the Committee on 7 March 1900: 'Provided that in addition to the children elected in the ordinary way, it shall be lawful for the Committee to admit into the Institution children between the ages of seven and eleven, whose father has lost his life while on active service for his country, or has died from wounds or disease contracted whilst so serving, such father being a native of the county or city of Worcester or belonging to one of the territorial regiments of the county, or having been married to a native of the city or county who is the mother of the child so admitted but so that there shall not be in the Institution at any one time more than six children who have been so admitted.'

On 24 July 1900, Harriet Coleman, whose father had died in South Africa, was admitted to the Royal Albert. The secretary was instructed to make application to the War Office for an allowance towards the maintenance of Harriet. On 18 September a letter was received from Frank T. Marzials, Accountant General of the Army: 'I am directed by the Secretary of State for War to acknowledge the receipt of your letter of the 6th ultimo and to inform you that the Station Paymaster, Worcester has been instructed to issue the allowance of 1/6*d* a week, awarded to Harriet Coleman, daughter of Private P. Coleman, 1st Worcester Regiment, to you quarterly in arrears, in respect of her maintenance in the Royal Albert Orphan Asylum and application for payment should be made to the above named officer in due course.'

The Rev. Canon Carr, in a letter of 7 August 1901, 'Reported the case of May Alice Hams of Copenhagen Street, Worcester whose father had joined the army for active service but was invalided at Aldershot before starting for South Africa and died in Worcester Infirmary. I ask that the Committee consider that May Alice Harris may be properly admitted to the Institution under the special rule recently passed providing that the parents or one of them belonged to the city or county of Worcester or that the father belonged to one of the Territorial regiments.'

May Alice Harris was admitted to the orphanage on 6 September, aged ten, and lived there for six years before being discharged on 27 July 1907 to enter the service of Mrs Bromley Martin, St Cloud, near Worcester at a salary of £8 per annum.

THE BENEFACTRESS

Mrs C. Wheeley Lea donated over a period of time a great deal of money to the Royal Albert Orphanage. The annual school prize was named after her. Children from the orphanage went to stay with her in her home at Malvern.

At a Committee meeting on 29 March 1900 it was decided to make a presentation of a plaque to Mrs C. Wheeley Lea, with the 'Thanks of the meeting for not only her pecuniary munificence but for the amount of thoughtfulness she has gone to in successfully planning out the improvements and that a tablet be placed in a conspicuous place in the entrance hall as a memorial to her generosity.'

However, Mrs Wheeley Lea was not so generous a few months later as the following statement of 1 August 1900 reads: 'Mr Sheppard has at our request sent in a separate account for £135. 8*s*. 6*d*. being for work extra to the contract ordered by Mrs Wheeley Lea and originally charged to her but which she has declined to recognise and desired shall be transferred to the orphanage account. We have specially conferred with Mr Sheppard upon this matter and although we are quite satisfied from his statement that Mrs Wheeley Lea is legally liable to pay the amount, still, having regard to the large extent of her benefactions to the Asylum we have no hesitation in recommending the Committee under the peculiar circumstances to take upon themselves the payment of the amount of the Orphan Asylum Funds.'

However, the plaque or tablet for Mrs C. Wheeley Lea remained firmly screwed inside the entrance hall until the orphanage closed!

THE STAFF

So much is written about the children that it would be interesting to recount what the committee wrote about the staff!

9 June 1883. The report of the master on the conduct of Mrs Green, the cook, was read and the following children, Susan Baker, Alice Bowen and Mary Anne Berry were examined by the committee. After hearing their statements and the written statement of the master the committee informed Mrs Green that she must leave at once and the secretary was instructed to pay her wages to the 24th instant of £5. 8*s*. 6*d*. Beer money 15/-. Railway fare 2*s*. 4*d*. It does not unfortunately inform us of the nature of her misdemeanour!

8 April 1885. It was agreed that it was necessary to obtain the services of an Experienced Female Servant whose duties should be 'to sleep on the top floor, to assist in cutting out and instructing in needlework under the superintendence of the matron, to assist in the laundry, to wait upon the children in sickness and to perform all other such duties as the matron may require at a salary at the rate of £18 per annum without beer.'

4 May 1885. The Ladies Committee reported that the cook had given notice to leave.

10 June 1885. The secretary was instructed to have an advertisement for a schoolmaster inserted in the *School Guardian* and the *Schoolmaster* newspapers.

20 July 1887. It was ordered that the cook be granted two weeks' leave of absence upon the return of the needlewoman, and subject to the master's convenience.

6 August 1887. The Ladies Committee recommended that Miss Timms of Stanford Bridge, Worcester be appointed Schoolmistress, for a trial period of three months at a salary of £35 a year all found, except beer. Her duties were to begin on 1 September 1887.

3 August 1887. The master and matron's salary should be raised from £105 to £120 per annum.

15 August 1887. A cheque for £3 for Miss Breeden, temporary schoolmistress, was signed in accordance with the resolution passed at the last meeting.

17 August 1887. It was ordered that the schoolmaster be granted his annual holiday in accordance with the regulations of the institution and subject to the master's convenience.

7 December 1887. It was resolved that the following advertisement be inserted once in the *Echo*, the *Daily Times* and the *Worcester Advertiser*:

> WANTED, a thorough Needlewoman capable of cutting out etc. and willing to make herself generally useful under the matron's instructions. Wages £16 per annum. All found except beer. Preference will be given to one who has had experience in nursing.

17 October 1888. The Ladies Committee were to appoint Mrs Robinson as cook at wages commencing at £18 per annum and also Mrs Heath to assist in the laundry at wages 5/- per week.

5 December 1888. 'Mrs Richens has informed the committee that the use of finer materials will interfere with the ordinary work of the institution so much that it would be needful either to purchase garments heretofore made in the Asylum or to employ a needlewoman.'

2 January 1889. 'The salary of the schoolmistress, Miss E. Timms, is hereby increased to £40 per annum as from Christmas last.'

6 March 1889. The Ladies Committee approves raising the salary of Mrs Gwilliam, Needlewoman, to £20 per annum.

20 March 1889. A letter from Mr Wallace was read stating Mr Barrow had been in communication with him as to emigrating to Canada. A further letter from Mr G. H. Barrow resigning his position as schoolmaster was accepted. The committee was pleased to give him a testimonial.

17 April 1889. Applications for the appointment of schoolmaster were submitted and it was decided to interview the following:

George Hamlet (Eccleshall, Staffs.)
Thomas Hall (Hampton, Middlesex)
Edward Verse (Alfrick, Worcester)

The secretary was requested to invite each to attend a special meeting of the house committee at his office on Saturday next at 2 o'clock and to inform them that the committee would pay their 3rd class railway fares to and from Worcester.

20 April 1889. Resolved unanimously that Thomas W. Hall, assistant master of the English School, Hampton, Middlesex be appointed schoolmaster at a salary of £35 per annum. Allowance of £3 per annum in lieu of beer.

5 June 1889. The committee agreed that the sum of £3 be given to Miss Timms to enable her to go to Weston-Super-Mare for three weeks and that Mrs Richens should arrange discharge of the duties of schoolmistress during her absence.

12 January 1890. With a view to a more effective supervision in the dormitories at night the committee were recommended to fix clear glass into the panels of one door in every dormitory on both sides of the institution and that a gas jet should be kept burning all night, and that a monitor or monitress be appointed not only to help in the school, but to take some responsibility in the general supervision of the other children and that he or she be paid a small salary.

5 March 1890. Salary increase to Mrs Robinson to £20 per annum.

7 May 1890. 'The needlewoman's [Mrs Gwilliam] salary to be increased to £22 per annum from Lady Day last.'

8 September 1890. The master was authorised to engage a temporary schoolmaster at a salary of 15/- a week:

> WANTED immediately, schoolmaster for the above institution. Certificate not essential, but National School training preferred. Will be required to assist in the industrial training and the recreation of the boys (48 in number). Salary £40 per annum with board, lodging and washing.

This advertisement appeared in the *Schoolmaster* and the *School Guardian.*

15 October 1890. Mr W. Charles Riley appointed schoolmaster.

7 January 1891. 'An allowance for beer of £2. 10*s.* 0*d.* per annum has been granted to the needlewoman and cook.'

3 June 1891. 'That Mr Edward Vorse be accepted as schoolmaster at a salary of £40 per annum. £3 beer per annum.' Salary for master and matron to be increased to £150 per annum as from Midsummer next.

7 October 1891. 'Miss Wells has been appointed needlewoman at a salary of £20 per annum.'

6 January 1892. 'An estimate from Messrs Ward & Sons for providing and fixing two of the Officer's sitting rooms improved box coils for the sum of £14 be accepted, subject to a guarantee being given that the temperature will be maintained at 60 degrees.'

7 June 1893. 'A letter of the 16th instant from Mr C. F. Roach was read withdrawing his application for the position of schoolmaster on the grounds that his acceptance of the position would debar him sitting an examination. Resolved unanimously that Mr A. Rowley be appointed schoolmaster at £40 per annum with board, lodging and washing, together with an allowance in lieu of beer at the rate of £3 per annum.'

17 January 1894. 'A letter dated 17th instant from Miss Bendall, resigning her position as schoolmistress.'

7 March 1894. Miss A. E. Baker appointed schoolmistress at a salary of £35 per annum with 3 months notice to commence on 17 April. Mr

Rowley resigned his position as schoolmaster. He had only been there nine months!

4 April 1894. Ten applications had been received in reply to the advertisement in the *Schoolmaster*.

2 May 1894. 'The needlewoman, Miss Butcher is on leave of absence. Mr I. Pittard appointed schoolmaster £40 per annum with board, lodging and washing. Together with an allowance in lieu of beer at the rate of £3 per annum.'

6 June 1894. The needlewoman Miss Butcher's salary increase from £20 to £22 per annum is approved by the Ladies Committee. Obviously her leave of absence the previous month had paid dividends!

1 August 1894. 'The schoolmaster Mr I. Pittard has given instructions for his salary to be paid each month though he is still on three months notice.'

7 November 1894. 'That the schoolteacher Mr Pittard be suspended and refused permission to enter the institution and that he be informed that the members of the committee now present are willing to grant him an interview at the secretary's office for the purpose of considering a statement he may desire to make. That the house committee be and are vested with plenary powers to deal with the matter and if necessary to appoint a successor.'

21 November 1894. 'It was resolved that Mr Pittard having refused to meet the committee at the secretary's office as proposed with reference to the charges brought against him, he is hereby dismissed from the post of schoolmaster to this institution.' The charges are not mentioned! An advertisement for a new schoolteacher was placed in the *Schoolmaster*, candidates to be between 23 and 33 years of age.

5. December 1894. A letter from Mr I. Pittard was read giving three months notice of resignation of his post as schoolmaster. The secretary was instructed to inform him that in view of his previous conduct he was dismissed and notice could not be entertained. The reason for Mr Pittard's dismissal is still not given!

28 December 1894. Mr G. E. Lord was appointed schoolmaster at £40 per annum with board, lodging and washing together with an allowance in lieu of beer at the rate of £3 per annum.

3 April 1895. It was decided to purchase a new carpet for the boardroom and the secretary was requested to ask the Ladies Committee to select it.

1 May 1895. 'That a Brussels carpet be purchased for the boardroom from Messrs. W. F. Webb at a cost of about £4. 10*s*. 0*d*.' That Anglo-Indian carpets be purchased for the master and schoolmistress's sitting rooms at a cost of £3. 7*s*. 0*d*. and £2. 5*s*. 4*d*. respectively and a pair of tapestry curtains for the master's sitting room at a cost of about 25/-.'

17 July 1895. A fortnight's holiday was granted to the schoolmistress and needlewoman to be taken alternately subject to satisfactory arrangements being made for the discharge of their duties. Sanction was given for the needlewoman's bedroom to be papered and whitewashed and for the ceiling of the entrance hall to be whitewashed.

Authority was given for the cook, Alice Lee, to go to Mrs Reeve, at Margate and an allowance of 10/- per week was directed to be paid to Mrs Reeve and 1/- to the hospital for a period of three weeks together with travelling expenses.

7 August 1895. Permission was given for the cook, Alice Lee, to remain at Margate for another week.

23 August 1895. Leave of absence was granted to the matron for four or five days subject to satisfactory arrangements being made for the discharge of her duties.

4 September 1895. It was resolved that Alice Lee, the cook, be sent to Margate as recommended by the Ladies Committee and that matron arrange for Lizzie Price to undertake the cook's duties during her absence.

2 October 1895. Leave of absence for 14 days was granted to Mr G. E. Lord, schoolmaster, subject to satisfactory arrangements being made for the discharge of his duties.

5 February 1896. 'The salary of the schoolmaster be increased to £47 per annum as from Christmas last and that a further increase of £5 be given him at the expiration of another year.'

1 April 1896. A letter from the governess, Miss A. E. Baker, was read applying for an increase in salary and it was resolved that her salary be increased from £35 to £40 per annum from this date.

6 May 1896. 'The master authorised to obtain a supply of porter and beer for the cook, Alice Lee, in such quantity as may be ordered by the medical officers and to report to the next meeting of the committee.' It seems the committee valued the work of Alice Lee, their cook!

1 July 1896. A letter from the needlewoman, Miss Butcher, was read applying for an increase of salary and it was referred to the Ladies Committee for consideration and report.

5 August 1896. The arrangement made with Miss Butcher to receive £2 gratuity in lieu of an advance of salary was approved.

16 September 1896. Five days leave of absence to the cook, Miss Alice Lee, subject to satisfactory arrangements being made for the discharge of her duties.

2 December 1896. The Ladies recommend the salary of Miss Butcher, needlewoman, be advanced from £22 to £24 per annum and that of Alice Lee, cook, from £16 to £18 per annum. The advance from 1 January 1897.

7 July 1897. The laundress Mrs Holliday tendered her resignation. The governess, Miss A. E. Baker also resigned. The reason of their resignations is not given.

4 August 1897. Miss Winifred Atkins of Coventry is appointed schoolmistress for £35 per annum including board, lodging and washing, with three months' notice on every side. Miss Fisher of Huddersfield didn't get the job.

18 August 1897. The resignation of the cook. The Ladies Committee to fill the vacancy.

7 December 1898. A letter was received from the schoolmistress, Miss Atkins, resigning her situation.

1 February 1899. Miss A. Bannister is appointed schoolmistress for £35 per annum, including board, lodging and washing.

6 September 1899. Fourteen days leave of absence be granted to the schoolmaster and schoolmistress.

20 September 1899. It is reported that Miss Lukey is undertaking the duties of schoolmistress.

4 October 1899. Recommendation as to the employment of a laundrymaid and housemaid was approved and the appointment was left in the hands of the Ladies Committee.

1 November 1899. The wages of the cook were raised from £20 to £24 per annum.

4 April 1900. The schoolmistress made application for a rise. It was suggested to give her an advance of £5 after six months. Gratuities of £5 to the master and £2 to the needlewoman were granted in recognition of their special work during recent alterations and the removal of the children to Malvern.

18 April 1900. 'The needlewoman, Miss Butcher be granted 14 days leave of absence subject to satisfactory arrangements being made for the discharge of her duties.'

2 May 1900. Miss Andrews of Malvern Link to superintend the laundry and other domestic work at a salary of £24 per annum. The schoolmistress's salary to be increased to £40 after 18 months completed, provided that her duties were successfully carried out.

17 October 1900. 'Permission be given for the master's sister to spend a few days at the orphanage.' It was reported that the cook, Minnie Eggington, had been discharged for immorality!

5 December 1900. 'That Mrs Barker's appointment as cook in place of Miss Eggington at a commencing salary of £20 per annum is approved.'

18 December 1901. 'On the death of Frank Everill, Mr G. W. Bull be appointed secretary at a salary of £60 per annum.'

6 August 1902. Miss Bannister, schoolmistress, announced her resignation.

17 September 1902. 'Resolved that Miss Margaret Smith-Goode be appointed schoolmistress at a salary of £35 per annum to commence on 29 October.'

1 October 1902. 'The wages of the cook, Jane Wood, be increased by £2 per annum. Such increase to take effect from 20 May 1902.'

3 December 1902. 'That a new carpet be provided for the governess's sitting room and that the Ladies Committee be asked to kindly arrange the matter.'

7 January 1903. The schoolmaster, Mr Lord, asks for a testimonial.

21 January 1903. Mr Lord resigns as schoolmaster. His successor to be advertised at a salary of £45 per annum.

18 February 1903. It is resolved that Mr Claude Vaughan of Southsea be appointed schoolmaster. Salary £45 per annum. Mr G. G. Davidson of Sunderland was unsuccessful.

1 April 1903. Secretary instructed to advertise for a successor to the cook, Jane Wood, who is leaving. The appointment to be left to the Ladies Committee.

4 November 1903. The complaint was made that the schoolmistress, Miss Smith-Goode, was out frequently until late at night. After consideration the committee decided that the matter should be left to the chairman to communicate with Miss Smith-Goode and take such action as he might deem desirable!

18 November 1903. The chairman wrote to the schoolmistress, Miss Smith-Goode, as follows: 'Acting on the powers given me at the last meeting I have informed the schoolmistress that she must not be absent from the orphanage after 7 o'clock in the evening.'

2 December 1903. The chairman reported that he had an interview with Miss Smith-Goode, the schoolmistress and that she desired to resign her position. It was decided to accept the resignation of Miss Smith-Goode and it was accepted that the chairman and the Rev. T. L. Wheeler be authorised to advertise for a successor and make a selection from the applications received. Salary to commence at £35 per annum.

16 December 1903. 'That the master be authorised to purchase some store pigs from Rev. T. L. Wheeler on the valuation of Mr Meredith. That the master be authorised to purchase two tons of potatoes from Mr Green at £4 per ton.'

20 January 1904. 'That the action of Mrs Carr in accepting the situation as kitchenmaid for Edith Weaver is hereby confirmed. That the master be granted two days' leave of absence to take Edith Weaver to her situation at Dartford.'

3 February 1904. That Miss Christine Whitgrove is hereby appointed schoolmistress at a commencing salary of £35 per annum.

2 March 1904. A letter from the schoolmaster was read stating that he had been offered an appointment elsewhere at a much higher salary and asking permission to leave before the end of March. The schoolmaster, Mr Vaughan, was interviewed and offered an increase of salary of £10 per annum making it £55 per annum, conditionally on an undertaking being given to remain at the orphanage at that salary for one year. This the schoolmaster said he was unable to accept. The chairman was asked to endeavour to find someone to take the schoolmaster's place temporarily and if able to do so to permit the present schoolmaster to leave as desired.

It was decided that a schoolmaster be advertised for with a commencing salary of £50 per annum. It was proposed by the Rev. T. L. Wheeler and seconded by Mr Rogers, 'That the services of the schoolmaster be subject to one month's notice either side, such notice to run from the first of the month.' Mr F. J. A. Wood proposed an amendment that the notice be two months. This was seconded by the chairman but received no further support and the original resolution was therefore carried.

6 April 1904. The chairman reported that after the last meeting the schoolmaster, Mr Vaughan, explained that his resignation had been given under misapprehension and he, the chairman, gave permission for him to withdraw it. A letter from Mr Vaughan was read stating that he should be glad to be allowed to withdraw his resignation and remain on the terms offered him at the last meeting of the committee. This was agreed.

20 April 1904. 'That the schoolmistress be permitted to be out not later than 10 o'clock at night.'

6 July 1904. The secretary's salary to be increased to £75 per annum on the understanding that this would be the maximum. This rise was to take effect from 1 July.

1 February 1905. The salary of Miss Butcher, the needlewoman, to be increased from £24 to £28 per annum.

5 April 1905. A letter from the schoolmaster, Mr Vaughan, was read asking for an increase of salary. It was resolved that his salary be increased by £5 per annum from £55 to £60 per annum.

19 April 1905. 'That Mr C. Wootton be offered the appointment of teacher of carpentry in place of Mr J. Quick deceased, on terms of 5/-

per lesson of three hours, on condition that he can carry out the requirements of the master.'

19 July 1905. The schoolmistress, Miss Whitgrove, was granted three weeks' leave of absence.

6 December 1905. A letter of resignation from Mr Vaughan was received, resigning his position of schoolmaster on account of ill health. Thanks of the committee were to be expressed to Mr Vaughan. It was resolved to advertise for a successor at £50 per annum.

3 January 1906. Two candidates appeared before the committee for the appointment of schoolmaster: Mr H. O. Knight of the Blue Coat School, Reading and Mr E. J. Sibthorpe of the Infant Orphan Asylum, Wanstead. It was resolved unanimously that Mr H. O. Knight be appointed schoolmaster at a commencing salary of £50 per annum and to commence his post on 15 January 1906.

7 March 1906. That a new carpet be purchased for the master's sitting room.

16 May 1906. That permission be given to the matron for a lady friend to stay with her for a few days.

5 September 1906. An application was received from the schoolmistress, Miss Christine Whitgrove, for an increase in salary. It was resolved to be increased as from 1 October, at £5 per annum, from £35 to £40 per annum.

5 December 1906. Mr H. O. Knight appeared before the committee and stated that he had arranged to be married early in the new year. He suggested that this would not interfere with his duties at the orphanage!

12 December 1906. 'That the schoolmaster, Mr H. O. Knight having stated his intention to be married he be requested to tender his resignation to expire in three months from 1 January 1907.'

19 December 1906. A letter resigning his position after three months from 1 January 1907 was received from Mr Knight stating he had arranged to be married at the end of January. Mr Knight suggested that he should be allowed to retain his position until 30 April. The secretary was to inform Mr Knight that the committee could not agree to his suggestion.

2 January 1907. 'That the schoolmaster be advertised at a commencing salary of £50 per annum. Preference given to the man able to teach singing and conduct drilling exercises.'

6 February 1907. The following candidates for the position of schoolmaster were interviewed: Mr D. J. Morrison, Mr H. J. Parry and Mr F. J. Stephenson. It was resolved that Mr D. J. Morrison be appointed schoolmaster on £50 per annum subject to three months notice on either side.

3 April 1907. The sewing maid, Miss Butcher, was granted fourteen days leave of absence.

5 June 1907. The master, Mr Richens, stated the intention of matron and himself to place their resignation in the hands of the committee. Their reason for doing so was that the matron's health was not good and she did not now feel equal to the work of the institution. He mentioned that the number of children in the orphanage had increased from 47 to 90 during their twenty-five years service, while no addition had been made to the staff. Mrs Richens felt the strain and considered the time had arrived when she should give way to someone younger.

The committee expressed their appreciation to Mr and Mrs Richens and expressed great regret that they should find it necessary to retire. The committee suggested that if a long holiday would be likely to restore the matron's health, they would be willing to grant this and would sanction some further assistance if it would enable the master and matron to continue their services.

17 July 1907. Mr and Mrs Richens, the master and matron, were to go on a fortnight's holiday before their proposed retirement at the end of August.

31 August 1907. Mr and Mrs Richens, the master and matron retire.

The stage was set for the appointment of David and Agnes Whitehead, both of Scottish descent, as master and matron. They were to hold this position from September 1907 until the mid 1930s and many of those who give their personal testimonies were under their care.

The following pages contain testimonies of the boys and girls who lived at the Royal Albert Orphanage. The dates after their names are the years they were there.

Royal Albert Orphanage, Worcester (1908). Mr Whitehead (headmaster) is in the front row

2

THE 1910s

This decade saw the dawn of a new Georgian age with the accession of George V. The Edwardian era came to an end with the death of Edward VII on 6 May 1910, but by the end of the decade the history of the world had been rewritten. The King's cousin the Tsar and his family had been assassinated and Russia had become a Communist state. The King's other cousin, the Kaiser, had been driven into exile after the defeat of Germany. Many of the old Imperial heads throughout Europe had fallen but Britain's remained.

Thirteen old boys of the Royal Albert Orphanage paid the price in the Great War.

	Killed	*Aged*
**Arthur Barnett*	*1917*	*26*
John Frederick Brookings	*1918*	*20*
Sidney Brooks	*1915*	*21*
**Benjamin Bunn*	*1917*	*25*
**Harry Waterman Dowling*	*1916*	*24*
Tom Dowling	*1917*	*21*
**Wilfred John Finney*	*1917*	*21*
Joseph Gwilliam	*1917*	*30*
James Hoskins	*1917*	*20*
Harry Mason	*1915*	*22*
John Henry Matthews	*1915*	*23*
George Henry Prescott	*1916*	*25*
James Hawker Winwood	*1917*	*21*

**Who had earlier emigrated to Canada.*

John Devereuse died under training in 1916. He was 23.

Archibald Richard Corgett won the Military Medal in 1917. He was 23.

THOMAS REGINALD CRACROFT (1910–14)

I entered the Royal Albert Orphanage before I was seven years of age, the first child to be admitted under seven. The reason why I was given permission to go into the orphanage was because my father had worked at the Lea and Perrin's sauce factory in Worcester and Mr Perrin who was on the board of governors had a great say in the running of the Royal Albert Orphanage.

I can't remember my first day at the Royal, but my first impression was that it was grand to be in there. The work duties were carried out by the girls and boys, each one being allotted a certain job to be done each day. Some of the girls were in the kitchen, others did the dusting and polishing and the boys did gardening and shared in the dusting and polishing. Each one knew what he had to do each day.

The staff consisted of Mr Whitehead (headmaster), Mrs Whitehead (matron), Mr Knight (schoolmaster), Mr Archer (head gardener) and Mrs Archer (head in the cookhouse).

The school was in the Royal and Mr Knight took all the classes. It was very good.

When you reached the age of sixteen you had the choice of having a job found for you, or going to Canada where a job was waiting for you. The boys were up to sixteen years of age before they left the orphanage and some of them were quite young men. I was put under one of the boys, Bill Turner. He was quite a big fellow. He used to make me go to the lavatory every night before I went to bed. 'Off you go.' 'Oh! It's pitch dark out there. No, I don't want to go. I'm frightened, Bill.' 'OFF!' and off I went, across part of the playing field from the gymnasium to the lavatory. Every night I had to go. Oh dear!

Discipline was the major feature of life in the orphanage. Every month you were ordered into the school classroom by the headmaster, Mr David Whitehead. When I went in there I used to think, Oh my God! Have I done anything wrong? He would then read out from the punishment book the things that the boys had done. 'Laddie, did you go into the stores and steal some carrots last week?' 'Yes, sir.' 'Fine!' And if that was it the boy would be punished. Out he had to go in front of everybody.

David Whitehead was over six feet tall and the cane went right over the top of his head. Six whacks on the lads' hands with a thick stick which left three weals on his left and three weals on his right. God! It used to make me shudder! The lad couldn't hold his knife and fork to eat or his pen to write for days.

For serious offences it didn't matter how big you were or how small you were. 'Take your trousers down,' and the master would get one of the big boys to stand bent and the victim would have to lie over his back and hold out his hands over their shoulders – the victim was practically tied to the other boy. Dear oh dear! No use screaming blue murder: you had it. He would have six heavy blows across his bare backside and he couldn't sit down for a month. Boys rarely came back a second time if they were punished. The worst punishment was to be denied seeing any festivities for that month.

I escaped all such punishments both from Mr Whitehead and from the school teacher Mr Knight, but I remember how the boys and girls went white with fear whenever they were called into the headmaster's office. When you had this punishment you were allowed no visitors. You were put in your dormitory when the visitors came. 'Very sorry, he's poorly!' The visitors were not allowed to see their children who had been punished. Perhaps they had got weals on their hands or their backside. Visitors were not allowed up the stairs. The visiting was once a month.

It's a funny thing, I can honestly say I didn't miss my mother. I wasn't homesick because I used to get on so well there.

Climbing the roof was strictly forbidden. They did do that whilst I was there but by Jove they were running a risk climbing up and down drainpipes and guttering if they were caught. No, no! I didn't go on the roof, it was more than my life was worth.

The first time I jumped into the three-foot shallow end of the orphanage pool the waters came up to my forehead! One of the bigger boys jumped in and lifted me up to the pipes around the pool. But I learnt to swim the first year I was there and the boss, David Whitehead, really took to me. There's no doubt I was a favourite.

I was never thrown in the deep end of the swimming pool, whereas if a boy didn't learn to swim in the first year that was his punishment, thrown in the deep end! If he didn't learn the next year the boss would call him up to the deep end. Of course he had to go. He knew what he was going to go through. The boss would have about five, perhaps six, of the big boys treading water. Then he would be thrown in the deep end. The other non-swimmers would be screaming blue murder because they'd seen him go under. When they came out there was no playing about in the swimming pool after that, they would learn to swim!

We had pantomimes and dances at Christmastime. I always had Phyllis Newman as my dancing partner and we danced up on the stage. Phyllis Newman was a little girl just the same size as me. That is why they put us together. Boys and girls didn't mix except at Christmastime. You never did see a girl, barring when you were in the dining hall for meals. The girls used to march in and go up one side and we used to march in and go down the other side. The girls sat on one half of the dining hall and the boys on the other.

The orphanage was such a lovely building in those days. The steps were as white as driven snow. One of the boys whitened them every morning whether they wanted doing or not! About three boys would have to clean the drains every morning and it didn't matter whether it was raining or not. They had to be done.

The matron and the boss, of course, David Whitehead felt a great deal for me because I was so small and every morning they allowed me to pick six boys who I liked – seven or eight years of age. Of course they were looking forward for me to pick them. I would get them in a line. Then I marched by the side of them as though I was an officer. I took them from the boys' side, right the way round to the girls' side into the cookhouse and we'd have a piece of bread and dripping at about half-past ten or eleven o'clock in the morning. Nobody else had any.

I can remember the matron standing in front of my mother when she got better and came to visit me. 'Your Tom's one of the favourites, you know, Mrs Cracroft. He picks up six boys and marches them round to the cookhouse and he has a piece of bread and butter.' And I says, 'Not butter, matron, bread and dripping.' Well, I suppose I was so small and they thought I wanted feeding up. But I was just as small, very nearly, when I left the orphanage. I didn't start to grow until I was seventeen or eighteen.

The gardens at the front were kept spick and span. Beyond the orphanage building were the playing fields, two meadows and the cricket pitch which were kept beautiful. The boss, David Whitehead, was a very keen cricketer. In fact I believe he played for Hampshire in his younger days. He was very keen to see we had a first-class team and we played all the best teams around Worcester. When the boys were playing a match on Saturday he used to have them up there on a Friday night throwing a ball to them and by Jove he could throw, and they had to catch. I used to umpire at home matches.

There used to be cows up there in the cowshed. A man called Archer was overseer of the gardens. He would have a dozen boys under him all day when they'd left school at fourteen. Archer was the husband of the cook.

The floor had to be scrubbed every day. You'd do a patch about 10 feet by 10 feet and the boy next to you would do another patch of similar size. Everything was cleaned every day. Nothing was missed. The place was kept immaculate. We always had to make our own bed, right and proper so as it looked neat when the boss came to walk round the dormitory to inspect. By Jove!

It's a funny thing, in the dormitory you would have a nice joke and talk. But you weren't long before you were off to sleep because we had been playing around for about two hours. We would have a bit of a pillow fight and all that sort of game. We went to bed at 8 o'clock. We certainly weren't allowed to go into the girls' dormitory. They were kept in one half of the building and we were in the other. We wore white nightshirts in bed and we had a bath every Friday night. There was a strong smell of carbolic soap. We were usually two in a bath. It was Bill Turner's evening duty to see us all bathed and as I was under him he'd come and see as I was bathed and bath me. Bill was getting on, he was fifteen. Quite a big fellow.

After living in a tiny house in Severn Street, the huge Henwick Road Orphanage seemed like a mansion to me, a beautiful big place to live in.

There were bullies in the orphanage, but of course they didn't bully me because Bill Turner was about the biggest one up there and he would have put them in their place. I was so small that they put Bill to look after me. When we went to church at St John's, I sat next to him.

Boxing gloves were available in the gym when you wanted a session with somebody. Top championship tennis was played at Malvern in the summer. The night before the championships it was decided by the master who would travel the next day from Henwick Station[1] to Malvern to be ball-boys at these championships. You'd be in the classroom and the master would call the numbers out, not by your name but by your number. My number was 5. I was a real favourite there and when the master called the numbers out my number was always among them.

I've been a ball-boy to the lady champion and the gent champion. I can remember the lady champion as plain as punch, Mrs Larcombe, and that's going back to 1911 or 1912. But I was the only boy up at the orphanage that went every day. There was one player there, a Mr

[1] Henwick Station was demolished after the Beeching purge of the 1960s.

Thomas, who used to give the ballboys a half-a-crown. So I had *2s. 6d.* nearly every day I went to Malvern. Mr Thomas, apart from the singles, would be partnered in the men's doubles and mixed doubles. There were four of us on court for him. Before we came away I would give my money to the boss as he knew I was saving mine. Half-a-crown was really a fortune to a boy in those days. What a great day out!

When the orphanage was giving anything away after a 'do' they would call your number up for a bit of supper. The master would have a tray of sandwiches and cakes. My number 5 was always called. I was such a favourite that I was let off all work in the orphanage. The reason was I was so small. The master would call 'Cracroft' and I would have to walk round to see if all the boys and girls had cleaned the drains in their morning's work. Then I would go and check the flower beds to see if the flowers were clear of weeds. I never had a job to do all the time I was there! I never did any scrubbing but the master would get me to check other boys' and girls' work.

I seemed to be a favourite from the start with the staff and other children. In the very first year I arrived just before Christmas, I hung up my stocking on Christmas Eve much to the amusement of the other boys in the dormitory. 'You'll get nothing in there, you have no chance of getting any gifts in a stocking in here. The orphanage presents are handed out the following morning.' But to everyone's surprise, we woke to find my stocking packed full of goodies! Apples, oranges and sweets and that really upset quite a few in the dormitory.

There would be about ten or twelve girls in the cookhouse peeling the potatoes and preparing the cabbage. Old Mrs Archer, the cook, was there to supervise in the cooking. The food was a bit rough and the pieces of bread would be that thick with a dollop of butter or margarine. You always had a real nice dinner. It would be cooked with potatoes and greens and tinned meat. We had a decent tea but I can assure you we were always ready for it. We never had too much! We were not exactly hungry but we were always ready for our meals. Breakfast was always porridge. We had three meals every day which were well prepared for you. The orphanage food was good, but not ample and all the youngsters were dressed well.

Mr Whitehead, the boss, would be walking round every night to see if the boys were in bed and asleep. He would be smoking a cigar, blow some smoke into my face, wake me up and give me a bit of cake. 'Goodnight,' he said. Nobody else had any!

A kit inspection was held every Sunday morning on the playground. We would be wearing our Sunday clothes: suits with a Norfolk jacket of rough sort of material that was dark grey. Young boys would wear short trousers. Those that had left school, they'd be in long trousers. You'd have to lift up your leg to the master to let him have a look at the bottom of your boots as he walked along the line behind you. In front of you would be laid out your working clothes, your working boots, your school clothes and your school boots. If you wanted a new pair of boots you'd have to go round to the stores and get a pair. All the boots were black. If it was raining the kit inspection would not take place that week.

After kit inspection we would march to St John's parish church and I can assure you we all had to be very smart for church. On Sunday afternoons we would go for a walk, under supervision, round St John's when the weather permitted.

Boys and girls had the option of emigrating to Canada or Australia. Most went to Canada. When they were departing for Canada we'd go to Henwick Station to wave them goodbye.

It didn't matter how high the horse was in the gymnasium, you had to jump it. The boss was the other side of the horse to catch you. There was a springboard to jump off. Whether you only hit it halfway up you had to go over it. We had to go up the ladder whether we liked it or not. It was compulsory. I had to be lifted up to go along it I was so small!

It was very cold at the orphanage: I would go and sit on the hot pipes which went round the rooms.

I swam for the orphanage in the swimming barge that was in the River Severn. I won a prize against the other schools in Worcester for being the neatest breast stroke swimmer. The swimming barge was the same side as the Worcester Royal Infirmary and the Worcester Racecourse. The water from the River Severn flowed through the barge. In those days there were two big steamers on the River Severn, the *Avonmore* and the *Old Castle*. Orphanage boys and girls were invited to go on them and sail up and down the river.

I never saw the sea until ten years or so after I left the orphanage. We didn't travel much in those days.

When the orphanage was playing Malvern College at cricket it wasn't every one of the boys went, but Tom Cracroft went! It didn't matter what was on you, could guarantee No. 5 was called out to go. At Malvern College, which was a public school they used to give us cakes and a cup of tea in the interval. The famous Foster brothers, I think there were five or seven of them, played cricket at one time for Malvern College. When they played for Worcestershire it was know as 'Fostershire'. I saw the Foster brothers play many times.

It must have been 1911 or 1912 that I watched Jack Hobbs play at the Worcester Cricket Ground. He was a professional and played for Surrey. The orphanage received some complimentary tickets from the WCC to watch him play. The amateurs used to come down from the pavilion steps but the professionals came out from a small building on the side of the pavilion. They were segregated in those days.

I saw Lord Coventry get a nine at the Worcester Cricket Ground. He had a job to run for the fifth and the fellow had a shy at the wicket and missed and it went to the boundary. They ran five and had four given them.

We had a cricketer from the orphanage who later played cricket for Worcestershire. He learnt his cricket at the orphanage and was older than me by three or four years. Archie Corbett played for the orphanage cricket team whilst I was there. He was a fine cricketer. Another good cricketer was Cecil Tomkins but he didn't go on to play for Worcestershire.

I can honestly say that my days that I had at the Royal Albert Orphanage were a very happy time because I was looked after a little bit above the others. Well, I'm quite positive of that. My mother remarried and I was allowed to go home again in 1913.

CECIL JAMES TOMKINS (1911–20)

Cecil Tomkins was perhaps the most well-known of the old boys and girls. People I spoke to said, 'Have you seen Cecil Tomkins? Go and see him. In his youth he was a brilliant cricketer.' Cecil was even mentioned in John Brown's Diary (3 June 1923). When I did meet Cecil I was welcomed by him and his wife but it was very difficult. His wife was handicapped and in a wheelchair, a former hospital sister and quite a formidable lady! Cecil was nearly stone deaf.

We lived at Bransford Road. I had lost my father and May, my sister, and I were put into the orphanage. I was taken the next year to the RAO because they realised my mother was unable to go on any more. She had given birth to a baby boy six months before Father died. His name was Stan. In total Mother had eleven children.

My mother took me to the orphanage and when I realised that she was leaving me there, I'm afraid I was in tears. Well, she was in tears herself and she said, 'I'll be seeing you for sure. Visiting you,' because Wednesday was visiting day for the institution and that helped. There were six boys and three girls admitted that day, making a total of 62 boys and 34 girls in the orphanage. It was Mrs Stallard who introduced me to the orphanage because my father had been gardener at her big house in Bromyard Road.

Scrubbing floors was part of the daily routine which began when 96 children were woken by the handbell. The boys and girls were given work duties throughout the day. The whole institution was kept spotless. The floors were beautifully clean.

As things went on we realised that life was going to change a lot for us, for the six of us who were introduced into the orphanage that day, 19 April 1911. I was 7 years and 4 months. Gradually as things went on you realised that life was not as bad as it seemed. We had two big fields for football and cricket. Mr Whitehead, thank goodness, taught us how to play cricket and things got better and better.

We soon realised that we had one or two bullies. As youngsters we had rather a rough time. The bigger boys encouraged the youngsters to fight each other. Mind you there were sixty-two of us at the time and things were a bit tough. The bullies were never found out, that's why they were not punished and therefore the teachers didn't do anything about it.

Boxing was encouraged as I grew up. Bouts were held in one of the rooms of the orphanage. Boxing taught us how to look after ourselves

Cecil Tomkins in 1915 (middle row left). Archie Corbett later played cricket for Worcestershire (standing front right)

and was recommended by the Scoutmaster, Mr Price. It was he who introduced Scouting into the orphanage. It did a very good job. One lad became quite pally with me and we gradually were able to stand up for ourselves. The girls, they also had a tough time there.

The bell was run twice for each meal, breakfast, dinner and tea. We then marched into the dining hall. Grace was sung before and after meals, 'For what we are about to receive may the Lord make us truly thankful.'

The food was very plain. We didn't get a pudding until quite a time after I was there! When they started issuing the pudding things improved a lot. Tuesday was the best because we could see the kitchen people bring in the roll of plum-duff, just the plain treacle duff. That was good. Yes! That was good. But there were occasions when some of the bigger lads got on to those below them and were inclined to rob them of some of their grub. That is just one of the unfortunate things that happened.

After tea we had what was like a church service, well, as good as! It comprised a hymn, a prayer, a chapter from the Old Testament, another hymn, a chapter from the New Testament and the final hymn. That was every day after tea-time. Mr Price would lead us in the singing. He was a very good musician and taught us how to sing first and seconds. One of the lady teachers was the pianist.

I was taken out of school, aged fourteen, and put to help with four other boys with the digging of the vast garden around the building. I was put under the cowman, a man called Archer. I worked six hours per day. We had three cows which provided the necessary milk for the orphanage, and two large fields for grazing. One day I was helping the cowman, Mr Archer; we were pulling up a patch of carrots and he asked me if I wanted one to eat. We liked the carrots as much as the apples, they were very nice. The orphanage had a massive ground and orchard, all laid out, beautiful.

It just so happened the master, Whitehead, came along. He found me eating one of the carrots, took it off me and gave me a clout across here. He told me that would be my tea and when we had our meal that evening there were the remains of the carrot sitting on my plate. Whitehead took the plain thick piece of bread and butter off my other plate. It upset me somewhat, but one of the lads further down the table prompted me to eat the carrot, as they thought that defying the headmaster would result in a serious hiding for me. Nevertheless, it surprised Whitehead that I ate the carrot just before the start of the hymns. Two of my friends couldn't bear to see me go hungry and slipped half of their meal into my pockets!

Swimming was part of orphanage life. We had a very good swimming pool but things were a bit rough. Some of the older lads who had got on well with their swimming weren't particular about ducking the youngsters. Still, that was just one of those things that you had to get used to. When I was older I was able to teach boys swimming. How to learn life-saving methods was all part of our Boy Scout training.

At fifteen, I was given the job to attend the boiler which heated the whole orphanage building, using coke. The fire was never allowed to go out. It was a responsible job doing the heating, but I didn't mind at all because it got me off the scrubbing and I could go to Henwick Station when I wanted and there was a sweet shop a little further down. Friends would give me their pocket money and I'd get them sweets and charge a quarter for them! The fumes when stoking up the fires and clearing the boiler out didn't do me any good. It gave me a headache. Doing this job caused me to have an epileptic attack, which was to occur again in the future. Cold sweats came over me while sitting at the meal table. It was during this period of my life that I had my first wet dream. I was sixteen years of age.

Cricket was my first love. Occasionally we were taken to Malvern to play some of the lads of our own age. Malvern College was a public school. At the orphanage we had two vast fields, one for football and one for cricket. I would like to say a big thank you to many of the factory workers who came to give us a game of football or cricket on Saturday afternoons or weekday evenings in the summer.

There were twelve steps into the main entrance of the orphanage. They were kept beautiful and white, scrubbed with whitening on Saturday mornings. The girls helped with this job as well.

Before church on a Sunday morning we had what can be best be described as a military parade. We were inspected for our cleanliness and our clothes. If anyone hadn't cleaned his boots properly it would be just too bad for him. It was not only the one that had dirty boots who would be in trouble, it would also be the dormitory boy or senior boy of that particular dormitory. Discipline was always strict but good at the Royal Albert Orphanage and if the inmates broke the rules they were taught a lesson. If we were caught stealing we had to touch our toes and have three strokes of the cane.

After Sunday's kit inspection we were brought to attention, and when

I was fourteen, I was one of the senior boys who marched the younger ones to church.

We went regularly to St John's church at 11 o'clock. We marched four abreast. Six of the senior boys were invited to sing in the choir at St John's and when the parish was changed over we moved to St Clement's. Friday evening was choir practice. I really enjoyed singing in the choir. It was one of the best things that was introduced in my time.

There were four dormitories for the boys. We were not allowed to talk in the dormitories but we did. One boy in our dormitory was clever. He went into the senior dormitory where one of the boys was reading from *Comic Cuts*. He then returned to our dormitory having memorised it and recited it to us. In the mornings we made our own beds except Dorm 1 where the youngsters had their bed made for them till they knew how to do it for themselves. All four boys' dormitories were scrubbed once a month by the boys before going to school. Because the floors were scrubbed smooth none of the boys had trouble with their feet.

Thursday afternoon was the regular walk and the boys and girls were able to spend their few pennies on sweets at a local sweet shop. There used to be a very good shop down Henwick Road but that's all built over now. Whoever bought the sweets had a quarter. My mother gave me 3*d.* a month for sweets but May my sister got 6*d.* 'Royal Duchess' were square toffees, there were five for ½*d.* Sticks of liquorice were ½*d.* apiece. 'Jumbles', as we called gobstoppers, were four for a penny. We had ½*d.* worth and they lasted all day long.

Fetching the Orphanage Committee Books was a job I had at fourteen. The books were laid out on a table outside the headmaster's office. Then I took them in a green bag down to Worcester at the office of a Mr Bowen, opposite the Star Hotel, near Foregate Street. Their committee meeting was the third Wednesday of the month. I obtained a few pence for doing this.

The orphanage was very much like a hotel. Every Friday night it was the job of one of the senior boys to see to the bathing of the whole lot of us, with three younger boys at the most in one bath. There were quite sixteen boys in each dormitory. Toenails were cut once a month. The headmaster, Whitehead the Scotsman, weighed and measured us every six months.

We wore short trousers till thirteen, then long trousers. They were very good material which came from Russell and Dorrell in Worcester.

A resident teacher introduced us to the game of chess. Mr Collins and Mr Price often played the game with us.

We all had our own garden, a piece of land around the playground rails where we grew flowers, sweet peas and godetia. The matron was often helping herself.

Holidays were twice a year in April and October. I was having three days. I left the orphanage on Saturday morning and I was back on Monday night.

When boys reached the age of fourteen the institution informed the parents to encourage the individual about going to Canada. By the time they were sixteen if they wanted to go they had the opportunity. It wasn't at the expense of the institution here. The children were paid for by the institution in Montreal.

Soon after I went to the orphanage, Mr Knight, the senior teacher, was invited to accept a post in Canada where he was in charge of boys from the RAO. Some parents wished their sons should be sent to Mr Knight's home in Canada and he accepted boys from other homes and orphanages. Mr Knight was able to take his wife and son. He found work and homes for those in his care. Mr Whitehead often read letters from those he had sent to Mr Knight and also reports from those they were working for.

Boys when they left school at fourteen worked on the gardens and farm. Girls helped in the kitchen and laundry from fourteen to sixteen. The girls when they left the orphanage were usually put into service.

There's no doubt about it, I was not happy at the orphanage. It's true I would have rather been at home with my mother, but it was not so much being at home with her, it was the heartbreak of being without her. I MISSED MY MOTHER!

At this point Cecil broke down in tears. Mrs Tomkins said, 'I think he's had enough. Don't take him back any more!' We had refreshments and spent a pleasant evening. When I left they both said, 'Come and see us again.' I said goodbye to this good man and his wife. Sadly I never went back.

WILLIAM TAYLOR (1914–22)

My mother took my brother and me to the orphanage because my father had been killed not long before. I remember they shut the gates at the level crossing by Henwick Station to let a goods train go through.

As I went into the orphanage I cried my eyes out and my mother cried. Bertie my brother cried and I was broken-hearted. I remember it was just before noon we went there. The orphanage building frightened me to

Royal Albert Orphanage, Worcester (1919) staff
Charlotte Wright (laundress), Mrs Archer (cook), Mr Lockey (top class teacher), Miss Atkins (needlework teacher), Helen Tovey (parlour maid), Mrs Whitehead (matron), Mr Whitehead (headmaster), Miss Bird (infant class teacher), Miss Williamson (middle class teacher)

death. To tell you the truth it looked like the mouths of hell had opened as I went up the steps into the entrance hall! A vile place! And I was only a little tot! I was too little and small to think I was leaving my mother.

We lived down Lower Chestnut Street. There were seven children. My elder brother Bert and I went that day into the orphanage, 22 April 1914. I was eight years old. Bert was a proper good footballer and I was very good at cricket. He was a ruffian type but a damned good fellow, Albert. And he ran away and he took his rabbit with him but they caught him just down the road. He had a pet rabbit. I remember that well.

They used to take us some lovely walks. We went with the boss, a chap named Lockey. He was in charge of the school and also of the Scouts. I didn't like Lockey. When we had our meals Lockey would be sat up on the rostrum with his arms on the table, biting his nails and his beady eyes looking round the room at us all. If he saw anyone with their backs not smart, and they were slouching having their meal he would get up, walk down these two steps and come and give them quite a clout across the back of their neck. He walloped me some bloody times. He really had got no nails. He'd bitten them all away! I do believe he came out from the forces, this Lockey. He was an army captain, at least that's what we were told. He was everything to us kids but he was a hell of a bully. The number of times he hit us.

Now one or two of us, we'd be bowling at him for a devil of a long time, but he was batting, he wouldn't let us bat. He'd got to do all the batting and we other kids that played in the team, we had to keep bowling at him. He wouldn't let us bat! Some of us kids were good at sport but this chap always seemed to have it over us. He was a swine of a fella!

Two or three boys went to Canada and they arrived at a sort of home where they put them to learn and to find a job. Most of them went to work on farms.

I liked Miss Bird, she was one of the teachers. She was very nice. David Whitehead, the headmaster, he was a gentleman.

The main entrance steps, I used to scrub them for weeks. We had a rag in a tin with whitening stuff and squeezed it out. They always looked so nice when they were finished.

Wednesday was the big board meeting. The officials would go into the boardroom of the orphanage. They would all climb up the main steps and that is why they had to be whitened and made spick and span for them.

Cecil Tomkins was a damned good cricketer, excellent, but I don't think he liked football. I loved cricket and I loved football. I liked the lot.

That Lockey I loathed – he'd come round of a Wednesday, visiting day, that bugger Lockey and in front of my mother he'd say, 'Hello, Willie,' tussle my hair a little bit and mouth, 'He's a lad.' You know what I was thinking and I was only a little 'un! And I wasn't the only one. He's dead now! I hope! Oh, he was a bastard, that Lockey! God, I don't know why God put him on the earth! Honest! He was the worst thing ever! If ever I was out after I'd left the orphanage and I spotted him, I ran like hell, right out of his way, I didn't want to see him. He said to somebody one day, 'Every time I see that Taylor, he runs away!' Well, I did. I never wanted anything to do with him after I'd left.

There were some ruffians in the orphanage, they'd go through your bloody pockets while you weren't looking! The thieving swine!

Oh, we used to squint through the bedroom keyhole to watch Lockey going to bed. But he caught one of the kids who squealed about us other buggers watching him go to bed. Lockey always had his squealers. He was a lousy sod! We got well punished for this. Lockey was in charge of our dormitory; his room was opposite a few yards away. We didn't do much talking as Lockey was always creeping about. I was in the big dormitory but when I first went in I was in the little one. We all wore white nightshirts in bed.

I don't think I ever left food. Mind you if I had done I would have had a smack across the ear-hole. So you had your choice! Haricot beans we had on a Tuesday and lentils on a Wednesday. I know haricot beans was my favourite.

I wouldn't trust anybody! Probably the only one was Bobby Ross and he went to Canada.

Lockey hated about seven or eight of us. He would catch hold of our ears and throw us to the ground with the cry of 'CRRRRRR!' and I thought, you swine, I'll put a brick through your head, but of course you couldn't go that far!

It was Golden Balls who climbed to the top of the orphanage building. His real name was Brian Ball but because of his bright flaxen hair he was called by friend and foe alike, Golden Balls. He was a colossus and some three years older than me. The orphanage was run by him and he usually had four or five of his henchman following him. It was a very fortunate thing not to get on the wrong side of Golden Balls. He could be a right bastard!

Golden Balls climbed the building with the help of his henchman and went right to the top, to the highest spar. They climbed it with ropes when the staff weren't about otherwise they would have been in trouble with the headmaster Whitehead, and of course Lockey. There would always be some bugger who would squeal on them but I think they were too afraid of Golden Balls to do this. That was the only time as far as I know that the orphanage building was climbed.

We did our share of the gardening. Six of us would work on a patch six abreast. There was a pear tree we called 'the bendy tree'. We would raid the orchard for fruit. We had some lovely fruit there. We also milked the cows in the cowshed and looked after the pigs in the pigsty.

I didn't mind at all going to church to St John's. I would look at the girls and say to the boy next to me, 'I fancy her!' The girls sat on the other side of the church.

Packing up to go on our holidays we went mad with excitement. We always had someone to help us with our cases. Then of course [with a drop in his voice] we'd got to come back!

I would rather jump in the river than go through my orphanage days again. I shouldn't like other kids to have to put up with what I had to put up with.

I had been at the orphanage eight years and four months when I left. Well, I was as happy as a pig with two tails when I went down that bloody drive. Lockey, the swine, said, 'I'm glad you're going. I hope I never sees you again!' 'Yes!' I says, 'I don't want to see your bloody face again either. I'm getting bigger!' I bet I hadn't grown an inch in eight years!

Miss Lawton, the schoolteacher, she was ever so nice. She came from Ledbury. Lockey married her or she married him!

ALBERT EDWARD GOULD (1914–22)

I thank you for the opportunity to contribute a few facts regarding my eight and a quarter years spent at the Royal Albert Orphanage, Henwick Road, Worcester and if I answer the guidelines given it will help me to give you the story as far as I can remember.

I entered the RAO in early April 1914 just seven years and ten months of age, being taken there by my mother. Not having travelled away from home before it was something of an adventure until my mother departed, leaving me to cry.

I had curly hair, so curly the matron (Mrs Whitehead) called me Bubbles, but they were soon cut off by a barber in St John's. I remember getting excited on seeing my first tram and was told to sit down and be quiet.

The orphanage buildings were large, unlike any I had seen before, making me somewhat terrified especially when I realised I was cut off from the outside world.

Work duties were reviewed each year and as you got older the workload increased. I remember cleaning Mr Lockey's boots; they were the army type and had to be polished as if he was still in the army. The large front hall and the many corridors had to be cleaned each day to the satisfaction of the matron. The dormitories were scrubbed once a week, the matron sitting on one of the beds directing operations. Wash, scrub, remove soap and finally dry; this was done by a number working in a line, beds having to be moved as the work proceeded.

One of my duties was cleaning large steps leading up to the main entrance. You worked with a chalky substance and you had to make lines along each step by drawing the floor cloth along the steps, and if someone, a visitor, made a footprint whilst you were still there, the mark had to be removed.

Mr and Mrs Whitehead were master and matron; there was Miss Bird (called Dicky); Mr Collins was the schoolmaster (called Pat after the Fair Proprietor I assume). He was only there for a short time; we believe he was called to the forces. He introduced the game of chess, often interrupted by the sirens sounding off when to bed we went. Miss Atkins was the sewing mistress, Mr Lodge the gardener, Mr Coombs the cowman. Three cows were kept: Beauty, Christobel and Topsy. Teachers who came later were Miss Williamson, Miss Lawton, Mr West and Mr Lockey. (Lockey was not a favourite.)

Talking was not allowed in the dormitories, but if we thought the coast was clear, those able to do so would tell stories. On one occasion someone asked, 'What would it be if a bomb dropped in a field where a bull was?' Someone a little louder than usual said, 'Abominable.' The door opened and Lockey said, 'It is abominable,' and the slipper was administered to two or three bottoms and it did hurt.

Going to bed early was very tedious especially in the light nights and one would try and read a comic or easily folded literature before going to sleep. The boys had a play shed to use in the summer and the schoolroom in the winter. Several good chess players emerged as one strove to play the best player, thus ensuring good games.

The dining hall at first seemed large but, as you got accustomed to it, it did not appear so awe inspiring. The kitchen was taboo for the boys, the girls helping with the cooking.

Swimming was a nightmare to the newcomers and the younger ones because the older lads played tricks, but almost everyone learnt to swim by the end of the season. Again the swimming pool looked large until you really got used to it and was able to swim.

Discipline was as strict as any army barracks, partly no doubt to command respect. We marched to church each Sunday morning and had to keep ranks and in step, otherwise you found the lads marching a few rounds of the playground on return from church! Inspection was made before marching and boots had to be clean and collars tidy; your ears had to be clean and everything had to be smart. The girls walked down to church in ranks, but not marching.

The cane was used regularly and it was quite common to receive six strokes either on the hands or the bottom. Out of bounds, talking in the dormitories, caught in the act of bullying (which was prevalent), and misbehaviour was generally liable for punishment.

The officers' (staff) dinner time was always the occasion for trying out any prank that came to mind. One lunchtime a couple of boys decided to climb up the orphanage building and managed to reach the pinnacle, led by the biggest boy in the orphanage who was known as Golden Balls. As they endeavoured to climb down, they slid down the roof and were saved by the dormer window surface and as they were watched by all of the children standing in the playground there was great relief to see them get down safely!

Sport was Mr Whitehead's one ambition for the boys, football in the autumn and winter and cricket in the summer. The orphanage played against the schools in Worcester and if they lost a match there was the usual lecture and reference made to former years when he said he was proud of the lads he had then. There was a cricket eleven called the 'nondescripts' which we used to watch. During weekdays the lads were encouraged to play and if you were caught larking about you would sometimes have to roll the lawn in front of the orphanage. That way the master would get a job done that he did not like to ask anyone to do. Swimming was another sport in which the orphanage did well against other teams.

At the age of fourteen one became a gardening boy and schooling was finished. Personally I did well and stayed in school until I left because I was short of stature and also a good scholar (pardon the reference to myself!). I do feel that staying in the orphanage school until the age of sixteen, I had a good sound instruction in the three 'Rs' which stood me in good stead to obtain an office job. All aspects of gardening were taught and the orphanage relied on our work to provide the vegetables and fruit. There was a huge garden and it was dug in the old fashioned way. There was plenty of manure from the pigs, cows and poultry. During the summer holidays the under-fourteens would be used for picking and stripping peas and pulling up the haulms. There was a large rhubarb patch. The first of the rhubarb, apples and plums, gooseberries and currants red and black were sent to market to help the funds of the orphanage. We had fruit at mealtimes in the autumn and winter.

ROYAL ALBERT ORPHANAGE.

DINNER. 12.30.

Sunday.
Roast Beef, Potatoes, Vegetables, Rice Pudding made with milk.

Monday.
Alternate weeks. Boiled Bacon & Harricot Beans, or Irish Stew and Bread.

Tuesday.
Pea or Lentil Soup 1 pint to 1½ pints according to age. Bread. Suet Pudding made with Fruit in season or Jam or Treacle.

Wednesday.
Roast or Boiled Mutton, Potatoes & Vegetables.

Thursday.
Cottage Pie, Bread Pudding made with milk.

Friday.
Fish & Potatoes. Milk Puddings (Sago, Hominy or Rice).

Saturday.
Thick Soup made of Shin of Beef and Vegetables. Bread and Cheese.

N.B. This Dietary to be varied according to produce of Farm and Garden. Pork, Eggs and Fruit.

BREAKFAST. 7.30.

Three times a week.
Porridge with Treacle or Sugar.
Bread & Butter & Cocoa with Milk & Sugar (little ones milk to drink).
or
Bread & Milk (1 pint) instead of porridge.

Three times a week.
Bread & dripping or butter.
Cocoa with Milk & Sugar.

Sunday.
Bread & Butter & Coffee.

LUNCH 11 o'clock.

A 2 oz. Biscuit or piece of Bread. Young children also cup of milk. Elder girls and boys who work, Bread and Cheese.

TEA. 5.45 to 6.15.

Three times a week. Bread & Butter. Tea with Milk and Sugar.
Three times a week. Bread & Jam. ditto
Once a week. Bread & Treacle. ditto.
Cake once a week or oftener.

APPROVED. Geo. W. Crowe, E. Lancelot Bunting } Medical Officers.

Worcester.

March 31. 1913.

School started at nine o'clock after all the jobs had been done. Personally I found it enjoyable, except that I did not get on well with Lockey who would often chide me for my free drawing saying if I did not like a subject I did not try, but I always tried my hardest.

We often went on walks as far as Hallow but at holiday times we would go longer distances.

Food was substantial in that it kept us fit, but everyone felt they could have eaten more. The menus for the week were as follows:

Breakfast:	bread and margarine, porridge once or twice a week.
Tea:	bread and margarine, jam occasionally, cake once a week.
Sunday lunch:	beef, potatoes, cabbage and rice pudding.
Monday lunch:	hash made from the Sunday beef.
Tuesday lunch:	pea soup and suet pudding.
Wednesday lunch:	mutton, potatoes and cabbage.
Thursday lunch:	shepherd's pie made from Wednesday's mutton, followed by bread pudding.
Friday lunch:	sausage, potatoes and cabbage.
Saturday lunch:	vegetable soup which we called carrot water and was the worst of the week.

We were graded by height by Lockey for position up the tables. Many like me suffered because some older boys were lower down the tables than some younger boys who were taller!

We had an annual trip in the summer by the steamer *Belle* to Tewkesbury one year and Holt Fleet the next.

The lads acted as ball-boys at the Malvern Priory Lawn Tennis Tournament. We usually trekked there pushing a loaded handcart. The tournament lasted a fortnight. We really enjoyed camping out, such a change from the daily routine at the orphanage. Sir George Thomas (a British chess champion), Sir Leo Lyle and Miss Tumbly Ellis were people who played there.

Our uniform was of a charcoal colour, the younger boys wearing short trousers and the over fourteens long trousers. It was made of material called 'never-tear' and was obtained from the firm Russell and Dorrells near Worcester Cathedral. Our boots had always to be clean. You only had a new suit or perhaps one handed down if your present suit was beyond repair. Caps with a RAO badge always had to be worn when outside the orphanage. Regarding our school outfit I am not aware how others were fitted out upon leaving, but in my case I had the misfortune to be fitted out hurriedly!

I had been on holiday for a week and was informed that if I could find a job I could leave. Several factories were visited and on the Thursday I had an interview with a large spring making firm. I was small for my age and probably did not appear a suitable candidate for the vacancy in their Costs Department, but after having an hour's examination in arithmetic I was offered the position of a junior with the firm. I was greatly relieved and foolishly said I could start on the following Monday! (24 July 1922). I was accompanied by my two elder sisters on my return to the orphanage on Saturday (22 July). After explaining that I had secured a job and having said I was engaged to start on the following Monday there seemed to be some annoyance by the headmaster Mr Whitehead for acting so quickly and saying I wished to return home to Redditch with my sisters.

The master took me into Worcester and fitted me out. Being short and not wanting short trousers I was fitted out with knickerbockers! I cannot remember what else I was given but I feel that if I had not acted so hurriedly I must have done better.

MARJORIE ADA DARBY (1916–22)

The following story is a combination of two interviews, one by Karen Demonte and one later by myself when I visited Marjorie in her Birmingham high rise flat on the 13th floor.

I was taken to the orphanage on 18 October 1916 by my older sister. I didn't notice the building, I was too full of grief over my mother who was very ill. Oh, I did a lot of weeping that day. I remember standing waiting on the steps of the main entrance, waiting for them to answer the doorbell. The matron greeted us. She was a very big woman but very pleasant. We were shown into the boardroom, the room immediately to our right, where we sat and talked. I don't remember what was said, most of it was above my head, and remember only that it was very cold, it was chilly and I remember the smell of the soap. Oh, I can remember the smell of the soap, that bad. It was carbolic! My sister and the matron talked on and on about my future as though I wasn't even there!

My brother came into the orphanage six months after me. He came in the spring. I'm an hour older than Bert. My brother was the weaker one, and was having to be carried about on a cushion when I could walk. Bert had a bad time with his hands in the orphanage. He used to get chilblains. His fingers were like fat sausages with the chilblains because the boys and girls had to scrub the bedroom floors. Like the rest, I did my share. I was ten years old when I went into the orphanage.

We rose at six o'clock to prepare breakfast Girls and boys had meals in the same dining hall but we were not allowed to talk. Grace was said before meals. 'For what we are about to receive may the Lord make us truly thankful.' One lady who visited the orphanage said, 'Yes, but are they singing it in Latin?'

One verse I remember from the orphanage:

It's a beautiful place to look at
But come inside and see
You'll see the kids do slaving
With half a length[2] for tea
When *she*'s dressed in navy blue
Tucking in to rhubarb stew.

We, the girls, had the cane for talking in the dormitory and I had it once for fighting a red-haired boy.

At first we didn't do any work but gradually we were given different jobs to do as we got older. At fourteen when I left school, I had to do domestic work full time for two years until I left the orphanage at sixteen.

Children were not allowed in the boardroom. Here the staff had their meals and the orphanage committee met once a month.

Oh, the building was very nice and very clean and well-run by the matron, Mrs Whitehead, who was a Scotch lady. The orphanage sign bearing the words 'Royal Albert Orphanage' in huge letters was enormous. 'Royal Army Oranges', the children used to call us when we were out for a walk. These children we called 'outsiders' – outside of the orphanage! We had straw hats, strawbrimmers we called them. Round the hats was a royal blue band on which was printed RAO. Fancy the children calling us 'Royal Army Oranges', it was a funny title. Well, that was children for you!

We went to St John's Church on a Sunday and I remember we listened to a sermon by the man who gave out cigarettes to the soldiers in the First World War. His name was Woodbine Willie (Rev. Geoffrey Anketell Studdert-Kennedy). Well, he was only a small man and he had got such a big wife. Oh, she was bossy! I don't know how he put up with her, I'm sure. She bossed him about like nobody's business. But he was

[2] Half a length of a 4 lb. loaf.

a very nice clergyman. We went to this special service at the end of the war, 1918 that would be. He was very good to listen to. His wife was introduced to us amongst the crowd. He was very famous. What hit me was she was so big and he was so small. He was only a little man or at least in my memory of him, he was.

Woodbine Willie died in 1929 aged forty-six. It was rumoured that he would be buried in Westminster Abbey but this was rejected by the Dean as he was a socialist! At his funeral which was held in Worcester Cathedral, thousands of ex-servicemen lined the route and threw packets of Woodbines onto the coffin as the cortege passed, out of respect to this good man.

The teachers were on duty at different times. We often had Miss Lawton who taught the girls. She married Mr Lockey in the end!

Your first job was taps, mats and boots; you were the taps, mats and boots girl. You had to polish the taps, brush mats and clean the boots. Yes, all the boots!

There was a time when I set the wash-house on fire. It was the girl before me who was really to blame as she was supposed to have filled the boiler and laid the fire underneath. So all the girl on a Monday morning had to do was put a match to the fire. I did so without looking in the boiler to see if it was full of water and it hadn't been filled. Oh, it was a mess! The drier had been burnt out so there was nowhere to dry the washing. I don't know who they blamed, really, but I wasn't punished.

Monday was washday. About three washerwomen came in to do the washing and the older girls helped them when they left school, for the last two years of their time at the orphanage. When I left school I helped them with the washing and then on Tuesdays and Wednesdays you were in the laundry room doing the ironing and my legs used to ache with the standing up. They were the old flat irons then, not like the amenities we've got today. We changed our duties on a Sunday. It was cold, very cold. One Monday I put a match to the fire under the boiler, then went to breakfast. The boiler room was full of smoke! No washing that day!

There was always plenty of washing-up. We had to kneel on the scullery floor to do the vegetables. Oh, it was cold! You all knelt round a tin bath full of vegetables and proceeded to peel them. At the same time other girls were also peeling vegetables in the sink.

I carried things that were too heavy. If any crash came they always yelled out, 'Is it Marjorie Darby?' Yes, it was Marjorie Darby, she had fallen with a pile of plates. It seemed I was always falling over!

The boys did the farming and cut the lawn. We helped to pick the apples when they were ripe. We had a beautiful orchard at the back, Worcesters and all the different varieties of apples.

The orphanage kept cows. We did the milking in the morning and skimmed the milk. It was my job for a while when I was kitchen girl. The kitchens were kept very, very clean by the staff and children. The cook, Mrs Archer, lived in a cottage on her own, out at the back. Miss Tovey, the parlourmaid, spent a great deal of time helping the cook.

As I've mentioned earlier, when you left school you went into the laundry. You had a week doing 'laundry work', a week doing 'kitchen work' and worst of all, a week doing 'pile of work', as they called it! 'Pile of work' was looking after the staff with their meals. It was housemaids' work. We waited at table and served their food in the boardroom. This was hard work carrying the food from the kitchens at the back of the orphanage along the tiled passages to the front.

They called Mrs Archer 'the old lady' but she was quite nice and I enjoyed the kitchen work with her. She was a good cook. Everything was done on a big scale. It was a massive place to look after.

Everything was kept clean. The kitchen used to look really cheerful. The table was scrubbed and scrubbed. The worst job was the kitchen range, that was shocking to clean. The heat from the fire, it really was H-O-T! They had steel fronts which we had to clean.

There were the girls who got up at 6 o'clock in the morning, a job we all did when we got older. 'The early girls' had to see the tables, slice the bread and prepare the breakfast. We had our breakfast at 7.30 in the morning, weekdays and Sundays, but we didn't have much! It was a cup of weak cocoa and one slice of bread. Cocoa one week and tea the next.

Dinner was at half-past twelve. We had roast beef on Sunday. On Monday it was hash from the Sunday joint. Tuesday it was soup and plum-duff but we could never sing properly after we'd eaten it, that's why we called it 'silent Tuesday'!

We had an egg once a year! If we had rhubarb, we had dry bread with it. You didn't have any margarine on your bread, they just gave you a piece of dry bread. It was only occasionally we had this, when the rhubarb was in season. I think we had it for tea. A plate of rhubarb and dry bread. The bread was off the big 4 lb. long loaves.

The girls sometimes took a piece of bread and put it in their knickers, and the bread didn't fall out as the knickers had elastic tops and bottoms then. But it wasn't really much fun because the only place you could eat it was in the lavatory! Oh no, we weren't allowed to eat food upstairs in the dormitory.

We were caned for reading in bed. Oh yes, I was amongst the ones that were caned. Miss Williamson, the middle-class teacher, carried out the punishment. We had six of the best across our hands, three on each hand. She certainly could lay it on. Miss Williamson was a beautiful looking woman, the double of Greta Garbo, but she wasn't very beautiful when it came to punishment. We were caned for talking in the dormitory after lights were out and caned for getting up to the windows. What we expected to see out of the windows, I'm not sure. Oh, probably boys! But the boys were on the other side of the building. We didn't see a great deal of them, only if we had a dance at dancetime and Christmas.

Miss Williamson may have been free with the cane but she could read a good story. She read us some nice books on different afternoons at lesson time.

The orphanage was a very cold place. In 1916 the windows were frozen over. There was no heating upstairs in the dormitories and we suffered badly from chilblains. We pretended our hands were fat sausages, caused by scrubbing dormitory floors. We were not allowed to wear shoes upstairs. In the playroom the girls sat with their hands on the hot pipes, stooping down with their faces to the wall.

I was kept in bed in 1917, when the River Severn was frozen over. The children from the orphanage went on the ice, they skated or walked across the river. I was in bed with chilblains, so couldn't go. I know it hasn't been frozen since. 1917 must have been so cold.

Oh, it was cold at times! They had central heating in the girls' playroom and we would kneel down and put our hands on the pipes. This was of course the worst thing you could do really because it gave you chilblains. We had an apron on in the orphanage, which had a bib so we were able to put our hands in our bib to try and keep ourselves warm. The playroom had a seat all round the walls and the lockers were at one end where you kept your brush and comb and your own personal things. It was quite a big room, though not as large as the dining hall. There was a dressing room attached to the playroom where all the girls' coats were kept.

You were bathed on a Friday night once a week and you had your hair washed at the same time. They bathed you two at a time when you were smaller of course. You bathed yourself as you got older.

Then on a Saturday morning when you were fourteen years old you had to queue up and go into the sewing room which was next to the schoolroom. They were quite big rooms. I had trouble with the sewing mistress. We were not allowed out of the sewing room. I pulled all the leaves off a plant. We had to help make the girls' dresses all by hand: seams and all that darning.

We had one girl die, but I don't know what was wrong with her. She was too young to die, wasn't she? Because she couldn't have been sixteen; if she'd been sixteen she would have gone from there. I should think she was fourteen or fifteen. She had a big sore on her face. I don't know whether it was an abscess or what. June Garland was her name. June lay in the sick room and we were allowed to see her when she died. All I remember was her lying down on a pile of capes. The girls wore capes when they first went into the orphanage years before I went there and these were kept in a pile in the dressing room. So when June was feeling bad she would lie down on them. Then she was taken to the sick room when she was very ill and the doctor came to see her. We never wore these capes; they were out of fashion when we went there. We wore coats but I suppose they kept these capes in case they were needed to make something with in the sewing room. The capes were kept in the dressing room next to the playroom at the top of the high cupboards. I think June was so cold, she'd take these capes down from the cupboards, put them on the floor and lie on them. They were furry, brown fur. She lay herself down in the sewing room for a bit of peace and quiet. When June was dead we all trooped up to the sick room to see her lying there, all laid out. The boys didn't see her, or the younger girls. Only the older girls. I saw her.

There was another girl, Louise Giles. They looked after her. She was ill a lot with asthma of some kind. She used to have to use powder on a tray and inhale it. Her illness I believe was called emphysema. Louise spent days in bed.

One of our more exciting duties was fire drill practice which was a regular orphanage ritual. We girls had to escape from the dormitory via the bathroom window by going down through a shoot into the playground. The shoot was like a long bag that stretched from the bathroom window down to the playground. I can't remember who it was, but somebody must have shot me through!

When we went to the orphanage swimming baths the water was icy cold. We had no warmers in those days. You either stood around in the cold or you got in! Some of them jumped in but I was always afraid to. We didn't have a teacher to teach us but I taught myself by going round the whole of the bath by holding onto the pipe with one arm and swimming with two legs and one arm till I had the confidence to let go the other hand. Then I did across the breadth of the bath and eventually I learnt to swim. I assume my brother got on all right and learnt to swim as he was a Sea Scout in Windermere. One girl who didn't want the trouble of getting in the swimming pool was Nellie Camm. She'd always got a cheeky answer for the teachers and she always got into trouble. Nellie never did what she was supposed to do. She was a bit of a bully and I used to keep out of her way. She had got a lot about her. The teacher had to run her all round the bath to even get hold of her. She used to lead them a dance!

We played basketball and stoolball. Stoolball is like cricket and was a popular girls' game. The wicket is a board a foot square on a pole 4 feet 8 inches high; the bat has a round striking surface and the ball is rubber. Wickets are 16 yards apart and eight balls constitute an over.

The day of my mother's funeral on 14 May 1917 (three weeks after my twin brother came to the orphanage) they dressed me up in someone else's bloomers, a pair of thick knickers. We were fetched from the Boat Inn at Worcester. It was an open cart. We had to wait hours for them to come. The dress I wore fastened down the front; it was navy blue serge with white braid on the collar and cuffs. It looked very nice. This is what we wore on Sundays. My brother wore his Norfolk suit and black lace-up boots. We had our photograph taken that day in West Bromwich. We looked quite neat.

When I came home once for a holiday – you had one week a year – Madge, my half-sister, had made me a beautiful lace collar. She was a good seamstress. After the holiday much to my surprise the matron took a fancy to the collar and because she liked it the girls were allowed to wear lace collars after that.

We had very little to do with the boys. My brother Bert's nickname was 'Dab for Darby'.

My number was 72, though they didn't call you by it. They called you by your name. The number was used for checking the clothes on a Friday night or Saturday because they all had to be put together for washing and ironing. A lot to do!

I really did admire the matron's niece, she was lovely. I'm trying to remember her name but I can't.

Well, I think the staff did their best for you with what they'd got.

We all went Christmas shopping at Christmas. You bought what you fancied with your own money, of course.

When we left we were given a tin trunk. Well, the girls did, I don't know about the boys. It was too big for us to carry and two boys had to take it to Henwick Station. Oh, yes, the tin trunk became your own. I don't know what I did with it – I couldn't say.

You see because you went into service you were bought your clothes. I mean you were paid how much? About 3*s*. 6*d*. was it? So much and your clothes, uniform and that. I went to two sisters who lived at Bromsgrove. I know how their memories used to go, they couldn't remember where they had put anything or what. That's like me now. I put things down and I don't know where I've put them!

I was always the shy kind, so I didn't make friends frightfully easy. Edwina Phillips was quite a nice girl. There were the Newman girls, Phyllis, Doris and Nellie.

I went with Nellie, Phyllis and Doris Newman one weekend to stay with the Canon of Worcester Cathedral. We slept in linen sheets. We had a writing table in the bedroom. There was a parlourmaid and a kitchenmaid. The smell of the breakfast was lovely. The garden looked down on the river. The girls were something to do with the Cathedral and Nellie was invited for the weekend, so I went. She chose someone and she chose me. We went for the whole weekend and we smelt bacon, oh, it was beautiful, the smell of bacon! I think the man who looked after us was the Canon and these three girls eventually went to Australia from the orphanage. This weekend with Nellie Newman was sheer luxury, sleeping in linen sheets and having writing paper on the table and oh, we had a wonderful time! Cooking for breakfast, we hadn't smelt any before this, we didn't have bacon at the orphanage, we never had a cooked breakfast. They had housemaids and servants. I didn't do anything. It was all done for me! Nellie was something to do with the Canon in some way. I don't know whether they were godchildren of his. Everything was nice of course and they had a beautiful garden in the cathedral grounds. They'd got a parlourmaid, cook and housekeeper to look after us.

The girls had a sick room. Menstruation was kept a secret. Matron did not help; we kept it to ourselves. Nobody told me a thing and we did not have napkins. It was a bit of a mess. Yes, it was a bit of a nuisance when you came to your periods. But I was late starting, so I didn't have that trouble. The girls had to keep the towels they used in a bag in the wardrobe. Everything was kept a secret then. So the girls suddenly had a period without knowing what it was and they had to do the best they could. You were given a piece of tape to tie your towel on. They were made for you. They didn't buy them, they were made in the sewing room. But you were never supposed to say anything to anyone about it and I don't think you would anyway. I wouldn't know if the staff let the girls know, because as I say it was nearly time for me to leave the orphanage when I came on, I believe. I don't know whether any of the girls were caught out by periods as you didn't talk about these things. All girls start at different times. Some start at ten, like my sister. I must have been nearer sixteen when I started.

They didn't do much for the eyes. I didn't think they did. No, I don't remember seeing an eye man. But I know we used to go to the dentist. One girl who was much younger than me wore very thick lenses so they may have done something for her. But I don't remember going. I didn't have very good eyesight but I don't think they ever did anything for me as regards the eyes.

'Oh!' the teacher told me, 'are you looking at me or are you looking over there!' And I used to say, 'No, I'm looking at you.' Of course they wouldn't do me later on because they thought I might have double vision. I've got what do you call it, a squint. (I've got a lazy eye. I can only use one eye at a time.) The teacher must have thought I had a squint.

Two girls ran away one night. They only got as far as Droitwich. Effie Smith and Violet Walton were the culprits and of course they had to go upon the platform in the dining hall when they came back and Violet Walton fainted, I believe from the shock of having to stand up in front of all the children for running away. I don't remember what punishment they had, or who found them in Droitwich. Not very far, only five or six miles away. Effie Smith married quite early when she left the orphanage. She brought her little girl Gloria to see us.

Miss Bird was our favourite teacher. Her brother used to keep bees if I remember rightly. She was only in her forties, Miss Bird, when she died of cancer. She didn't die in the orphanage but that was after I'd left.

The orphanage was a marvellous looking building, wasn't it?

Matron's birthday was on 26 October, I remember that, which we celebrated with a dance in the dining hall.

I had croup once and the matron sat on my bed all night and they used to soak my feet in mustard water and then you had to drink Vaseline and black treacle to help your throat. Well, you had it as a sort of medicine.

The Scotch couple, the headmaster and his matron wife, were as kind as they knew how.

Twins Marjorie and Bert Darby in 1916, the year they went into the orphanage

Most girls went into service when they left the orphanage. When I came to leave I found the clothes didn't fit me. The clothes were made the year before and when I came to put mine on I found I'd outgrown them. So I had to borrow a pair of scissors and nip the knicker leg. Navy blue knickers we wore then. They weren't too bad really!

BERT WILLIAM DARBY (1917–23)

Wednesday 18 April 1917 I came to the Royal Albert Orphanage. I was scared stiff! I was ten, nearly eleven. Children eleven and over were not allowed to enter.

I had lived with my mother and father in Birmingham. My father died in June 1916 and Marjorie my twin sister went into the orphanage in October 1916. I couldn't say why we didn't go in together; it may have been because there was a place for a girl but not for a boy, though at that time my mother was still able to support one of us. If my memory is correct I believe our sponsors to the orphanage were the firm of Chason Hunt of Alwyn, glass manufacturers.

From living with my mother in the Birmingham area, I had travelled down with my older sister, who was twelve years older than me, by train from Langley Green to Worcester in a snow shower.

I walked with my sister from Foregate Street Station rather than take the tram as we didn't have much luggage. We walked across the Severn Bridge and looked up at the magnificent cathedral. It was while on the bridge that my sister pointed out to me the orphanage and I remember looking into the distance with a sense of foreboding at this vision of turrets and towers. As we approached the house along Henwick Road I wondered what the hell I was going into. We turned into the grounds through the huge iron gates passing an enormous wooden board on which were printed in very large letters 'The Royal Albert Orphanage'. We must have got there just before lunch, about 12 noon.

What hit me as we climbed the steps into the main hall was a strong smell of disinfectant. I forget the name of the brand; I don't think it was carbolic, I think it was Sanitas.

Nobody greeted us. My sister had to go in to report to the headmaster's office. I can't remember going there that day though I did many times later. I believe she walked round the house with us, then she left before dinner time and I felt very alone. I believe my sister had come that morning with two missions – to bring me and to take my twin sister home to see her mother for the last time. However, the matron wouldn't allow her to go as it wasn't holiday time. My mother died three weeks later on 9 May and Marjorie never forgave the orphanage for not allowing her to see her mother before she died.

When I went into that huge great dining hall on that first day, it scared me stiff. One hundred children and not a word spoken. In other places they might have appointed another boy to look after you on your first day, but here, God no! It was terrifying. To a small boy like me it was the thought that I might get lost that was part of my fright. The fright of being left on my own, but also the sheer size of the place. So I ended up in this dining hall; no one escorted me to a seat or found me a chair. Actually we sat on forms. Somebody said where you had got to go and you went.

Going into the dormitory on that first night shook me a bit. They locked the dormitory doors at night so we couldn't get out. We had to use the chamber pots under the beds if we wanted to go to the toilet. There wasn't one for each bed; three or four boys had to share the same chamber pot. There were four dormitories and the doors were unlocked in the morning when they called us. I wondered whether they locked the doors to stop boys running away. We never knew why.

All I can remember on my first day at the orphanage was that I was frightened, I was very frightened. I remember one of the older boys (it wasn't one of the bullies) who said, 'Have you ever seen a monkey?' I said, 'No!' Then he got a mirror and put it up to my face and said, 'There's a monkey.' Not the kindest thing to be told on your first day!

I was very unhappy there. I was a boy who was free and a bit wild and you were shut away completely and then you weren't allowed outside this playground with iron railings round. Out of bounds meant six of the best. When we were doing our school work we weren't allowed back into the dormitories once we were up and downstairs; the dormitories were out of bounds until you went to bed unless you were sent up there for any special reason. I remember boys climbing out of the dormitory windows at night and down the drainpipes to steal some fruit out of the orchard which was out of bounds. Then climbing back up the drainpipes into the dormitory.

The chap who said, 'Four walls do not a prison make, nor iron bars a cage,' had never been in the Royal Albert Orphanage – not after having freedom! The notice should have read, 'Abandon hope all ye who enter here!'

We all wore caps which had a badge with RAO on it. The cap was blue with a white shield and the letters RAO stood for Royal Albert Orphanage.

No one was ever expelled to my knowledge. If you were expelled then everyone would have been misbehaving, wanting to be expelled!

One of the masters was a sadist. He taught by fear and we were terrified. The headmaster Mr Whitehead died in 1953, his wife the matron died in 1949. One of the favourite sayings of Mr Whitehead was this: 'There's a fool in every family, and I think all the mothers have sent all the fools to me!' This saying wasn't inclined to do one's confidence much good.

What I didn't like was the tremendous amount of bullying that went on. Life was a living hell. There were five of them who bullied me. What they did for years was to make my existence a misery. I remember their names and their faces haunt me still. They were already at the orphanage when I got there. They all stuck together and there was nothing I could do. My desire when I left the orphanage was to try and track them down and tell them what I thought of them.

The ringleader of these bullies was the worst His name was Golden Balls. He made my life a living hell. Every time he could persecute me in any way he did so, by force and mentally. He made my life unbearable. Of course he was bigger and probably three or four years older than me and much stronger, but even so I did try and have a go at him but he overpowered me easily enough. And there's one thing I didn't do: I couldn't go and tell the schoolmaster but I think they all must have known it went on.

My life was better once the bullies had left. I made a vow that when I left the orphanage I would seek out and find Golden Balls and give him a piece of my mind. Years later I very nearly tracked him down but it took me a quarter of a century! I found out he was Inspector of the Midland Red Bus Company and their headquarters was in Bearwood, Birmingham. This was in 1949, but when I got there Golden Balls had left the company two days before. He went to another company – the Walsall Bus Corporation. I was very annoyed but finally gave up as I lived a good distance from Birmingham at the time.

Though we had a Christian upbringing I didn't like having to say grace before and after every meal, or singing two or three hymns and having the Bible read to us at tea-time.

Meals never varied all the time I was there. Breakfast was bread and margarine and lukewarm cocoa at 8 o'clock. We got up at 7 o'clock, then before breakfast it was scrubbing, dusting and polishing. All the floors were whitewood and scrubbed. We scrubbed the dining hall once a week on Fridays. The laundry, dormitories and wash-house all had to be scrubbed. As you grew older (aged fourteen) you worked all the time – no lessons. We were detailed to do jobs and stuck to it every day. My knees were sore. We only had a wooden kneeler. 'Bloody scrubbing!'

On Mondays we had to go in the wash-house. The wash-house and laundry were run by female workers. We had to do all the stockings and handkerchiefs and turn this bloody great mangle for a good year or two. There was gardening from 9 a.m. to 12 noon and then again in the afternoons. We had loads of rhubarb. We used to get it at tea-time.

The biggest dormitory had twenty beds, the others had twelve. The dormitories were as cold as ice in winter, we couldn't have the windows shut. All we did in winter was shiver. We had to be in bed by 8 o'clock in the summer, 7 o'clock in the winter. We were not allowed to talk. I saw my twin sister at meal-times but I was not allowed to talk to her except at Christmas! We finished school every day about 4 o'clock then worked in the gardens.

Two girls ran away from the orphanage but I don't remember any cases of boys running away. There might have been but I don't think so. Not in my time.

We had electric light. The orphanage was heated by coke. There was no heating upstairs in the dormitories, only in the classrooms and dining hall. We had to use the classrooms for recreation. The gymnasium was heated.

When we were washing, we were inspected like prize cattle. They boxed our ears 'until we could hear the angels sing'!

Everybody made their own bed. It was not warm enough in the winter. There were only bare boards – no carpets. The walls were a greeny colour and the windows and doors, dark brown. We had a bath once a week, two in at a time. Everything was done in silence.

When sick we went to the infirmary or hospital in the orphanage. The orphanage was built in 1868 by voluntary contributions, endowments and bequests. I believe it is now a listed building. The Committee met the first Wednesday of every month. There was an annual prizegiving for school work and behaviour – not sport. This was always held at the end of March.

It was basically an elementary education in the orphanage school which was from 9.30 a.m. to 12 noon and 2 p.m. to 4 or 4.30 p.m.

Two passages of poetry I can still remember having learnt at the orphanage school are from 'Horatius' from Macaulay's *Lays of Ancient Rome.*

Shame on the false Etruscan
Who lingers in his home
When Lars Porsena of Clusium
Is on his march from Rome.

Then out spake brave Horatius,
The Captain of the Gate:
'To every man upon this Earth
Death cometh soon or late.
And how can man die better
Than facing fearful odds,
For the ashes of his fathers,
And the temples of his Gods?'

They don't learn poetry at school now, not like we used to. We learnt poems by Shelley, Keats, Byron, Southey, Wordsworth, Tennyson and Browning.

We had to learn parts of the Bible by heart and the Collect for Sunday. One poem I remember we learnt but I can't remember much of it now was 'The Prisoner of Chillon', by Byron. I would like to read that again, it was very good. We did try a bit of Shakespeare. I fell foul of the schoolmaster because I wouldn't go in the play, *A Midsummer Night's Dream*. They wanted me to play one of the fools I think!

The dinners never varied:

Sunday:	roast beef	milk pudding
Monday:	hash	no pudding!!!
Tuesday:	lentil soup	duff (suet pudding and treacle)
Wednesday:	roast beef	milk pudding
Thursday:	shepherd's pie	bread pudding
Friday:	sausage	boiled rice and treacle
Saturday:	vegetable soup	bread and cheese

To my knowledge we never had fish!

The food was prepared by the girls. The dining hall was filled with long tables and forms to accommodate sixty boys and forty girls. We marched in and stood by the tables. Grace was said. We sat and gobbled what there was. Grace again, followed by a prayer, then lessons from the Bible. At breakfast and tea-time bread and marg. was dished out on plates, waiting! Some boys were detailed to serve the food, 'Like one of Dickens' workhouses,' my friend Charlie Mitchell used to say.

There was no library but there were books on shelves. Visiting day was once a month. Those with a father or mother had visitors.

We had a piece of ground near the railway. When a train came along we left our gardening and digging and looked over the hedge to see the trains of the Great Western Railway go by. I can still remember the names of the engines: *Queensland*, *Brisbane*, *City of Bath*, *GWR*, *San Francisco* and *Alexander Hubbard*. I loved steam trains. I always wanted to be an engine driver. We knew the times of all the trains.

Our biggest room was the dining hall – that's where we had prayers. One August, some people came to look round. One said, 'What a nice lot of well-behaved boys.' As soon as they had gone we set to and knocked each other about. We each got six or twelve of the best and I was in solitary confinement for a week. The boy I fought was called

'Hippo' and his brother was 'Rhino'. All the boys were yelling their heads off, that's what brought the master on the scene.

We were taught to swim in the outdoor pool, or rather we taught ourselves more than anything. At the carpenter's shop they taught us a bit about carpentry. One special day they hired a tram for us at the orphanage. We watched the troops marching at the Armistice Celebrations which were held some six months after the Armistice.

You could always visit the orphanage after you had left and spend the night there – I went several times. They were always pleased to see you.

Punishment was half a dozen of the best with the cane. Today's muggers and vandalism would never have been allowed.

The first time we went to Scout camp I remember waking up and hearing a nightjar and a corncrake. It was two on to cook grub, and two to keep the fire going. It was always our job to put up our own tents. Our Scoutmaster, Mr Lockey, was very good. He was very fair.

For a fortnight we were ball-boys at the Malvern Tennis Tournament with two on each court as ball-boys, but only the senior boys went. There were a dozen courts. We didn't get paid. At the end of the session the club gave us an evening supper with waitresses serving us – all sorts of food we hadn't met. Sometimes the players gave us a tip but we weren't allowed to keep it. We had to hand it in. Some tried to keep it and were sent back to the orphanage in disgrace. We wore plimsolls supplied by the orphanage and shorts and cricket shirts.

We used to go to county cricket matches. I first saw the Australians in 1919 one glorious afternoon.

At Christmas we had a tree with a present for each child. We went up and they handed the presents to us. It was usually a book, a toy, a puzzle or a small game. The women schoolteachers decorated the tree. We had dancing at the party. We danced the lancers and the barn dance to the music of the piano, with the girls.

We had loads of apples and plums. We liked picking the fruit which was all sent by rail to market in Manchester. They loaded it into sieves onto the railway horse and cart. There was quite an acreage of gardens and playing fields. The orphanage kept a couple of cows, a cowman, two gardeners and us boys. We kept ourselves in vegetables. Though we had many fowls we only had eggs once a year at Easter. We had a piece of cake at Easter and Christmas – no other times. For years our supper was one piece of bread and dripping. I could have done with six pieces.

Church was twice on Sundays to St John's, but not to the 'Glover's

Needle' as St Andrew's was known. There were no visiting or outside speakers, only the vicar who gave confirmation classes – 'a damned nuisance'. We always wore our Sunday best clothes when going to church but when coming back from church in the afternoon, we had to change back into other clothes. All clothes were provided by charity including the Norfolk suit.

In 1924 the Scouts went to the Wembley Exhibition and gave displays. I think they also went to camp in France. Once a year in August, we had a trip in a steamer on the river Severn to Tewkesbury and Stourport.

Some boys went to Canada to Marchmont House, Belleville in Ontario. They waited there until jobs came along. One or two did rather well. I could have gone to Canada when I left the orphanage but I decided not to. Charlie Mitchell's two elder brothers went there. In fact Louis Mitchell was the last boy that the orphanage sent there. He went with Ernest Jones in 1923; his brother John had already left for Canada in 1921. The very last boy to emigrate there from the orphanage was Walter Waters in 1925 but he went to Clymont PO, Alta.

There were walks on Thursday in crocodile ('crocodile file' meant walking in twos, 'Red Indian file' was walking one behind another), mainly into the country. We would leave at 2 o'clock for two and half hours' walk, come rain or shine.

At Christmas friends could send food parcels. We were allowed a week's holiday in spring and autumn. I went to my half-sister in Birmingham.

Saturday was sports day: football in winter, cricket in summer. Our other activities were in the gym which comprised dumbbells, parallel bars, vaulting horse and knotted rope which we went up, whether we liked it or not.

When leaving they rigged you out in clobber and gave you a cabin trunk. Some boys went to learn a trade. Some became cabinet makers. One left his job, went into the army and came out a major. Some boys eventually joined the navy. They found me my first job as a houseboy in Windermere. I left on 16 January 1923 [as is mentioned in John Brown's Diary] – aged sixteen.

There was no leaving ceremony. I just disappeared down the drive and through the iron gates. A couple of the lads helped me with my cabin trunk to Henwick Station.

3

THE 1920s

From the darkness and death of the Great War dawned a new age: the Jazz Age when the youth of the day danced from dusk till dawn the Charleston and Black Bottom.

The 1920s had their share of downs with the National Strike in Britain and the slump and Wall Street Crash in America.

The decade which became known as the Roaring Twenties was perfectly expressed in the life and writings of F. Scott Fitzgerald. He was the spokesman for the youth of the post-war generation. In his novels, and especially The Great Gatsby *is revealed the spirit of hope.*

The orphanage and life of these years is portrayed in the diary of John Brown. He went to the British Empire Exhibition at Wembley in the July and August of 1924.

JOHN BROWN (1916–25)

I quote from John Brown's last letter.

> *Dear Mr Hamblin, Thank you for your letter requesting information about the orphanage. I had been handed the cutting out of the local paper only a few days ago. I will be most happy to oblige. I go into hospital for an operation on Thursday 20th but will attend to it on my return. I had one brother and three sisters there. The period covers 1915–30 and I had kept some sixty years of diaries and have some photographs of staff. The building used prior to Henwick Road is still in use as a doctor's practice in St John's. I will take a photograph of it and send you a copy. I wish you all the best. Pity ciné cameras were not around then. Reminiscences to follow. Yours faithfully John Brown.*

Unfortunately John Brown died six days after writing this letter. He went into hospital on the 20th for a minor operation from which he did not recover. He died on the 24th.

The brother and sisters who shared his life in the RAO were Harold, Rhoda, Sylvia and Miriam. (His oldest brothers, Frank and Edward, did not go into the orphanage.) John entered the Royal Albert at the age of seven.

The following details are from his Scout diaries of 1923, 1924 and 1925 sent me by his daughters Susan and Marion.

Monday 1 January 1923 Had a good time. Rather cold. Had a game of football. Had a slide. Kind deed: helped Walter Waters with the chicken run. *Tues 2* Very rainy. Did the 'ash-hole'. Mr Wright came. Orange for tea. Dancing after tea. *Wed 3* Wet. Mother came. Dancing in afternoon. Gave cook her present. *Thurs 4* Wet in morning. Done nothing in morning. Football in afternoon. Good game. Transplanted strawberries. *Fri 5* Wet. Started path. Kind deed: picked up some raffia. Weighed. Height 4 feet 4 inches. Weight 4 stone 8 lb. Chest 28 inches. *Sat 6* Fine. Played Hylton Road, won 4–3. Had apples for dinner. Reginald Draper came back from home. *Sun* 7 Wet. Kind deed: picked up some peel. Went to Church. Orange for tea, nuts after. Burnley lost. *Mon 8* Wet. Started school. Football after dinner. Mr Lodge pruned trees. *Tues 9* Wet. Did raffia in latter part of school hours. Calendar put in schoolroom. *Wed 10* Windy. No school in latter part of morning. Did raffia. Went to see pantomime *Jack and Jill.* Came out at half past five. *Thurs 11* Dry, no wind. Holiday in afternoon. Whist drive for matron's friends. *Fri 12* Dug up parsnips. Two and a quarter pot hampers. Picked Brussels sprouts. Football after school. Had a slide. Kind deed: picked up paper. *Sat 13* Played Hollow on their ground. Lost 1–0. Had tea there, good time. I played. *Sun 14* Dry. Had orange for tea. Kind deed: told Walter Waters a date in history. Had new pair of braces. *Mon 15* Rather dry. Game of football after dinner. Started week of fowls. Had 2 eggs. *Tues 16* Bert Darby left and cook. Had Darby's locker. Orange for tea. Dancing after. *Wed 17* Went in carpenter's shop. Start cloakroom. Did the sticks. Went in the meadow. Committee Day. *Thurs 18* Rather wet. Went Scouting. Transferred to Wolves patrol. Nearly finished bandages. *Fri 19* Wet. Rhoda came. Went to play football. Kind deed: told Thomas Smith an answer. No eggs. *Sat 20* Played St Paul's. Lost 4–2. Rather wet. Orange for tea. *Sun 21* Wet. Went to church with William Longmore. Wrote to Mother. My best boots repaired. Had one egg. *Mon 22* Started doing mats. Went in meadow. Took chair to St Clements. Had a card. Did raffia. Sent letters. Sunny. *Thurs 23* Went in the meadow. No dancing. Fine. Harold's birthday. Started doing mats.

Wed 24 Went in the meadow to play football. Very fine. Went in carpenter's shop, finished 12 inch rule. Had drill. *Thurs 25* Fine. Played Co-op Circle. Won 4–0. I played for them. Sweets for tea. *Fri 26* Fine. Miss Bird ill. Played football. Went on with side door. Did raffia. Had golf ball and jack in box. *Sat 27* Played no match. St Paul's didn't come. Did side door. Fine. 'Zepp' had his outfit. *Sun 28* Windy. Dry. Reginald Draper left the orphanage but promised to write to me. Albert Clements had a new lace. *Mon 29* Wet. Had my old book mended. Did raffia. Practised that song. *Tues 30* Fine. Had dancing after tea. Had a game of football. Did no raffia. *Wed 31* Found my last *6d.* Co-op Circle gave us a good concert. Had a bag of sweets and an orange. Had a game of football. Told about the trip.

Saturday 3 February 1923 Played Wesleyan Guild, won 4–1. I played. Miss Lawton came up. *Sun 4* Went for a walk. The work was changed. Went on with front hall. Matron's friends came. *Mon 5* My birthday (14 years old). Had a post card. *2d.* in stamps. Fine. Had a card from Rhoda. Went in the meadow. *Tues 6* Scrubbed school room. Prepared for examination. *Thurs 8* Visiting Day. Mother came. Had drill in dining hall after tea. *Fri 9* Completed examination. No school in latter part of morning. Played football in afternoon. Had an egg for tea. *Sat 10* Went to the theatre. Saw *Country Girl.* Had orange after. Fresh exercise for boys upstairs. *Sun 11* Went to Church. Had a new pair of stockings. *Fri 16* King Tutankhamen's tomb opened. *Mon 19* Scrubbed top room. Mr Lockey took Alfred Mergan to Wales. School room scrubbed. *Tues 20* Had drill in dining hall after tea. *Wed 21* Rhoda came, had a banana and orange each. Rhoda had left the orphanage the previous July, she was three years older than me. *Sun 25* Finished week's sums and composition. Went for a walk after church. Cake for tea.

Thursday 1 March 1923 Did soup and damper. Had fire in playground. Mr Lockey gave all Scouts an egg. *Mon 5* Dug plot with Horace Weaver. Got my diary out of the sewing room. *Wed 7* Visiting Day. Mother gave me a penny. Co-op Circle gave us a concert. Collection £2. 5*s*. 10*d.* Good concert. *Thurs 8* Did raffia and picture in schooltime. Went in carpenter's shop. There is a great craze for marbles. *Mon 12* Started my week of fowls. Finished digging my garden. Set Bedfordshire Champion onions. *Tues 13* Had four eggs, most we've had this year. Two White Leghorn and two Rhode Island Red. Burnley beat Bolton 2–1. *Wed 14* Boys went in meadow after school. Pulled a tooth out. *Thurs 15* Dentist came, all right. The barber came. *Sun 18* Went to church. Had a new pair of trousers. Wrote to Mother. *Mon 19* No school. Scrubbed the Cottage. My turn on with the knives. *Tues 20* Spring cleaned the schoolroom. *Wed 21* The carpenter's shop was spring cleaned and scrubbed. Practised the concert. Committee Day. Helped the master with lawn. *Thurs 22* Annual Meeting Day. Rhoda had a nice sewing machine. Reginald Draper a watch. Had a concert. Mother came. Had an egg for tea. *Fri 23* Went to Public Hall to see 'Ideal Entertainers'. Grand. Went to bed 11 p.m. Miss Lawton came here. *Sat 24* The garden was wagged. Put some slippings in. *Sun 25 (Palm Sunday).* Went for a walk after church. Very fine. The plum trees in flower. *Thurs 29 (Maundy Thursday).* Set peas in plot. Boys bought seeds. Scrubbed dining hall. *Fri 30 (Good Friday).* Went to church. Went for a walk. Had two buns and an egg. *Sat 31 (Easter Eve).* Set Pilot peas. 1 trench. Played football in afternoon.

Sunday 1 April 1923 (Easter Sunday) Had an egg and bun for tea. Went for a walk in afternoon. *Mon 2 (Easter Monday)* Onions up in three weeks. Set radish, parsley and lettuce. Swimming bath door knocked down. *Wed 4* Visiting Day. Mother came, received 4*d.* Dug plot. Transplanted onions. Had dancing after. *Fri 6* Put shilling in St John's bank. Practised concert. Leant a new song. *Sun 8* Went to church with Scouts clothes on. Went for a walk. *Tues 10 Mauretania.* [Could this refer to the liner *Mauretania* crossing the Atlantic in record time and regaining the Blue Riband] Had a concert. Cathedral Choir. Scrubbed dining hall and class room. *Wed 11* Trained Charles Amphett for tenderfoot. *Thurs 12* Concert after tea. Successful. £2. 19*s.* 0*d.* Dancing after. *Sat 14* Fine morning. Caught an orange-tip butterfly. *Sun 15* Went to church with Scout uniform on. Sent boots to be repaired. Saw jackdaw by the hedge. *Tues 17* Had a letter from Rhoda. One shilling each. Meadow harrowed. *Wed 18* Rhoda came. Dug plot in afternoon. Went in carpenter's shop. Picked up stones off meadow. *Thurs 19* Scouting in afternoon, a good run to Broadheath. Dry, south-east wind. *Fri 20* Sang 'St George' in dining hall. Wrote it out. Meadow was rolled. *Sat 21* Went to the pictures in the afternoon. Very good. *Sun 22* Saw a bird's nest, two eggs. Went to cathedral. May blossom in bud. Had new neckerchief. *Mon 23* Saw a lesser spotted woodpecker and yellowhammer. Had seven new fowls. Made cricket pitch. *Wed 25* Had lesson about an egg. Very good. Mr Lockey let me listen to the chicks in the egg. *Thurs 26* The Duke of

York's Wedding Day to Elizabeth Bowes-Lyon. Set British Queen potatoes. *Sat 28* Cup Final Day. Bolton won 2–0. First at Wembley Stadium. Played cricket in afternoon. Heard the cuckoo. *Sun 29* Told about holidays and going to Malvern. *Mon 30* Birth of chickens. Reggie Williams and myself dug in between currant bushes. Put a few sticks on peas.

Tuesday 2 May 1923 Visiting Day. Mother came. Did cards for whist drive in afternoon. Many swifts about. *Sat 5* Won RSPCA 2nd prize: *Black Beauty*. *Mon 7* Started my week of fowls. Boys over fourteen played others. *Tues 8* Boys over fourteen lost cricket match. Found a chaffinch's nest. Three eggs in. *Sat 12* Came home. Went shopping with Mother. Nearly all the boys went home. Mr Lockey went away. *Sun 13* Went for a walk in afternoon near river with Teddy. *Mon 14* Went to see Mrs Matthews. A good time. Pig ringed. *Tues 15* Went to see Mrs Carleton. Had a ride in tram. *Wed 16* Went to Bromsgrove to see Rhoda. Missed 8 o'clock bus. Went to see Granny. Wet in Worcester. *Thurs 17* Went to see Mrs Carleton. Went for a walk. Saw a Peggy white-thrush. *Fri 18* Went to see Mrs Matthews. Made Mother's front garden tidy, set sweet peas. *Sat 19* Came back from home. Grand procession by Worcester Infirmary. *Sun 20 (Whit Sunday)* Went for a walk near Severn. Measles in St John's. *Mon 21 (Whit Monday)* Holiday. Played cricket all day. Received cucumber seeds from Edgar Mitchell. *Tues 22* Received 'pumps' from Frank Clarke. Played cricket all day. Bowled a lot. Master set turkey's eggs. Received frame off master. *Wed 23* Rhoda came to see us. Transplanted lettuce. Dug plot. Mr Lockey came back. *Thurs 24 (Empire Day)* Prepared clothes for Malvern. Dug in far garden. Did lawn. Mr Lockey gave me a handkerchief. *Fri 25* Three fowls killed. Prepared for Malvern. *Sat 26* Went to Malvern. Saw a turtle-dove and a whitethroat. *Sun 27* Went to the Priory, good sermon. Had a romp on the Malvern hills. *Mon 28* No ball-boying until 3.30 p.m. Saw a rabbit and a violet on the hills. Very windy up there. *Tues 29* Very busy on courts. Wet at night-time. *Wed 30* Master and matron came. Busy on the courts. *Thurs 31* I was cook. Successful. Washed towel. Received 2*d*. George Broadhurst was ill.

Friday 1 June 1923 Semi-finals played. Received 2*d*. *Sat 2* Finals played. Mr Leo Lyle won the cup. Received one shilling each. *Sun 3* Went to church. Had a ramble on the Malvern Hills. Reginald Draper, Cecil Tomkins and Leonard Hignell came here. *Mon 4* Took stove back to George's. Played cricket after tea. *Tues 5* Went for a long walk. Saw wild hops and forget-me-nots. *Wed 6* Great Agricultural Show here in Malvern. Had a postcard from Rhoda. Bought Mr Lockey a silver topped pepper box. *Thurs 7* Went to Agricultural Show. Very good. 'Abell and Smiths' were there. Our last night. *Fri 8* Came back from Malvern. 6*d.* in bank. Hoed plot. *Sat 9* Played cricket in afternoon. Bowled five boys out. *Sun 10* Went for a walk after church. Saw some sand-martins. *Thurs 14* Helped Horace Weaver to clean out master's fowls. Gave onions and peas a dressing of lime and soot mixed. Barbering day. *Sun 17 (St Oswald's Day)* Went for a walk. Saw honeysuckle, wild turnip and grizzled skipper butterfly. *Mon 18* Did matron's garden. Transplanted onions. Bought 1/2 lb of nitrates, 2*d.* Banked up potatoes. *Thurs 21* Scouting in the afternoon. Applied phosphorus to potatoes. *Fri 22* Transplanted cabbages. Many trees attacked with blight. *Sat 23* Went in the swimming bath for the first time. Had Scouting after tea. *Sun 24* Saw first sweet pea in bloom. Had pair of boots. Birth of five puppies to Chum. *Sat 30* Beans ready for picking. Propagated strawberries. Flag day for the infirmary.

Monday 1 July 1923 The meadow mowed. Played cricket after tea. Went in the swimming bath. *Wed 3* Visiting Day. Had a letter from Frank. *Thurs 5* Did hay-making. Cleaned out the swimming bath. *Fri 6* Received 3*d.* profit from the fowls. Settled accounts. Picked strawberries. *Sun 8* Went for a walk by river. Saw an aspen tree. Started week of fowls. *Tues 10* Smallpox. Boy vaccinated. *Sun 15* Vaccinated boys in bed. Wrote to Frank. *Sun 22* Went in the swimming bath. *Tues 24* Had a letter from mother. Put 9*d.* in bank. Transplanted tomato plant in frame. *Sat 28* Mowed and rolled cricket pitch. Played cricket. Sale of fowls.

Wednesday 1 August 1923 Sports Day. Very enjoyable. Won relay. Mother came. *Fri 3* President Harding poisoned in San Francisco. *Sun 5* Had a new shoe lace. 1*d.* for collection. Saw first mushroom. *Sat 11* Broke one of Mr Lockey's eggs. Swam three lengths learning to swim on back. Played cricket after tea. *Mon 13* Cleaned out swimming bath. Bert Darby came here. *Thurs 16* Picked egg plums all day. 45 sieves. *Fri 17* Went for a trip to Stourport. Received 5*d.* Had three handkerchiefs and tin of polish. *Sun 19* Had handkerchiefs marked. Collected leaves for naturalist badge. *Mon 20* No school. Did windows all day. One egg broke. Eggs sold. *Tue 21* Started school after holidays. Egg plums picked.

Saturday 1 September 1923 Came home at 12 noon. Went shopping. Went for a walk to see Mrs Matthews. *Sun 2* Went to see Mrs Carlton in afternoon. *Mon 3* Picked blackberries in afternoon at Crown East. *Tues 4* Picked blackberries at Groos Hills. *Wed 5* Went to see Auntie Fanny. Had grapes. *Thurs 6* Walked to Upton to see Mrs Jakeman. Helped in her allotment. Good time. *Fri 7* Went to see Grandma and Mrs Matthews. *Sat 8* Came back from home. Marrow had grown considerably. *Sun 9* Went for a walk by river in afternoon. Looked after Mr Lockey's fowls. *Mon 10* Helped in the wash-house all day. *Tues 11* Helped in laundry. Scrubbed scullery in afternoon. *Wed 12* Scrubbed scullery in afternoon. *Thurs 13* Scrubbed laundry and scullery. Played cricket in afternoon. *Sat 15* Scrubbed scullery in afternoon. Could not play cricket. Dull. *Sun 16* A new vicar at St John's. *Sun 23* No church in afternoon. A tooth beginning to decay. *Tues 25* Went to infirmary to fetch flags. *Sat 29* Played cricket in afternoon. Fine. Played baseball. *Sun 30* 5 eggs. 28 eggs this month. Harvest Thanksgiving.

Wednesday 3 October 1923 Visiting Day. Very wet. Cut marrow and picked beans for Mother. *Thurs 4* Scrubbed wash-house and laundry. Hygiene after tea. Interesting. *Fri 5* One cockerel put for fattening. Filled up literature book. Finished *Tempest*. *Sat 6* Started to play football. Enjoyed myself. Flag Day for RAO *Mon 8* Had hygiene and civics after tea. *Wed 10* Mr Lockey's birthday. Had dancing. *Mon 15* Men painted spire and railings, also spouts. *Wed 17* New boys came in. *Fri 26* Had lesson on confirmation. Drill in afternoon. Matron's birthday. Invited to Girls' Concert. Very good. *Sun 28* Collected coloured leaves. Went for a walk after church. Sent boots to be repaired. *Wed 31* Played football after school. Made decorations for concert.

Monday 5 November 1923 (Guy Fawkes Day) No bonfire. *Tues 6* Had draw ticket off master. Played football. *Wed 7* Mother did not come. *Fri 9* Master's birthday. Concert a success. Dancing after. *Sat 10* No eggs. Cleaned out the fowls. Put fresh straw in. Played Corner Angels, won 4–0. Boys went to the pictures. *Sun 11 (Armistice signed 1918)* Misty all day. Scouts went to the cathedral. *Wed 14* Rhoda came, had 8*d*. Put pot eggs in for the pullets. Cleaned the runs. Pullets' combs reddening. *Thurs 15* Dentist came. Concert by Mr Gregg's Party. Successful. Doris Clacton came. Scouting in afternoon. *Wed 20* Practised the concert after tea. A failure. Did programme covers. *Thurs 22* Successful concert. £4. 10*s*. Mother came. Had 3*d*. *Sat 24* Fine at mid-day. Went for a walk in afternoon. Got beech and sweet chestnut leaves. Saw a peewit. *Sun 25*

Had a lesson on confirmation in church. Had a slide. *Mon 26* I was confirmed at Holy Trinity, Worcester.

Saturday 1 December 1923 Went to see *A Midsummer Night's Dream*. *Wed 5* Visiting Day. Mr Russel came to see us and Claude. Had 2*d*. *Mon 17* Went in the meadow. Hygiene after tea. Wrote to Mrs Carlton. *Tues 18* Had dancing and singing. Learnt 2 carols for Christmas. *Wed 19* Rhoda sent us a parcel. The pigs were killed. *Thurs 20* Scrubbed the dining hall. Barbering day. Rhoda gave me a handkerchief. *Fri 21* Spring cleaned the schoolroom and passages. Helped in decorating the dining hall. *Sat 22* Played football in afternoon. Decorated the schoolroom. *Mon 24* Cleaned out the fowls. 4 eggs. 1 white, 3 brown. Had 3*d*. from Mr Lockey. *25 Tues (Christmas Day)* Frosty. Went to Holy Communion. Had a good time. Had a knife, dominoes and paints. *Wed 26* Had dancing and games after tea. *Thurs 27* Played Cinderella, lost 12–1. *Sun 30* Rain. Did not go to church. Had a tie off Horace Weaver. *Mon 31* Scrubbed the dormitory. Practised the concert.

Wednesday 2 January 1924 Visiting Day. Mother did not come. *Thurs 10* Stayed in the house all day. Snow rather thick. Did raffia and Scouting after tea. *Sun 13* Saw laurel catkins near Severn. Very high and muddy. *Mon 14* Had hygiene after tea. Sewed my basket together. *Tue 15* Did raffia. Put some decorating on my basket. Had drill after tea. *Wed 16* Finished my basket. Girls had diphtheria. *Fri 18* All the drains disinfected because of the diphtheria. *Mon 21* Railway strike. *Tues 22* Scout inspector came. Passed 'basket worker'. *Wed 23* A new Prime Minister (James Ramsey MacDonald). *Fri 25* Went Scouting. Fine. Had 2nd year star. *Thurs 31* Had games for Scouts in dining hall.

Monday 4 February 1924 Had hygiene after tea. Had drill. *Tues 5* My birthday (15 years old). Played cards with Morgan. Mr Lockey did not like it! There was laughing in dining hall. *Wed 6* Went in the carpenter's shop. Stained my 'toilet tidy'. Had drill in afternoon. *Fri 8* A fire at Needmans Stores. *Sun 10* Went for a walk to Hallow. *Thurs 14* Pulled up a tree in far garden. Fire. *Fri 15* Hail. Had Scout games in dining hall. Helped girls to wash up. *Sat 16* Went scouting to Callow End. Helped girls to wash up. *Mon 18* Had bandaging after tea in dining hall. *Tues 19* Schoolroom scrubbed. Went in dining hall after tea. *Wed 27* Started clothes horse in the carpenter's shop. *Thurs 28* Went Scouting in the afternoon to Callow End. Mr Lockey was ill. *Fri 29* No school. Worked in scullery. Went out for Mrs Lockey.

Sunday 2 March 1924 Went on Pitchcroft to see aeroplane. *Mon 10* Went on with the little dormitory. *Sat 15* Attended Court of Honour. *Tues 18* Spring-cleaned big room. Mrs Harrison left. *Wed 19* Went to Fort Royal Hill. Saw first wood anemone and many butterflies. *Thurs 20* Went to Perry Wood. Charles Parsons made a Scout. *Sun 23* Warm and rain. Saw a redstart. *Wed 26* Went over ambulance with Horace Weaver. Tram strike in London.

Tuesday 1 April 1924 Spring-cleaned new room. Practised concert for Annual Meeting. *Wed 2* Visiting Day. Mother came. *Thurs 3* Did posters for concert. Practised concert after tea. *Sat 5* Birth of 23 chicks. *Tues 8* Spring-cleaned top room. Practised first aid after tea. *Sun 13* Sent boots to be repaired. Harold came up. *Mon 14* Practised concert in afternoon. Plum trees in bloom. *Wed 16* New boys came in. *Sat 19 (Easter Eve)* Saw meadow brown and cabbage white butterfly. Started cricket. *Sun 20 (Easter Sunday)* Went to early communion. Went for a walk. Saw a red admiral butterfly and a chaffinch. *Mon 21 (Easter Monday)* Dug fowl run. Played cricket in afternoon and night. Pear trees in bloom. *Wed 23* British Empire Exhibition, Wembley opened by King George V. Saw a bullfinch. *Fri 25* Cleaned water fountain. Practised concert. *Sat 26* Lime leaves appearing. Saw a starling. *Mon 28* Went to town. Rehearsal of concert in Public Hall. *Tues 29* Fine in morning. Heard first cuckoo. *Wed 30* Concert at Public Hall successful. Sold programmes. Saw a blackbird.

Thursday 1 May 1924 Annual Meeting Day. Had three prizes. Concert a failure. *Sat 3* Arrival of swallows here. Played cricket in the afternoon. *Sun 4* Saw jackdaw by the hedge. Went for a walk. Apple trees in flower. *Mon 5* Started school after Easter holidays. *Tues 6* 10 eggs. 7 white. 3 brown. Cleaned out chicks. Did matron's garden. *Wed 7* Visiting Day. Mother came. She bought some rhubarb. *Sat 10* Mr Salmon came. Boys dug plot. *Sun 11* Saw a tawny owl. Got sycamore leaves. Birth of chicks. Lilac in bloom. *Sat 17* Played cricket against St Peter's, we lost. I was umpire. Mr Lockey sent chicks away. *Sat 24 (Empire Day)* Came to Malvern by train. Saw a pheasant. Practised display for British Empire Exhibition, Wembley at S. M. Moor's house. *Sun 25* Went on the hills. Harold came. Went to the Priory. Slept in Pavilion. Saw meadow trefoil and greater stitchwort. *Mon 26* Did not go on tennis courts in morning. Saw ground ivy and ox-eye. Inclined to be cloudy. Cleaned out rooms for Mr Ferris. *Tues 27* Rather dull. Matron and Miss Bird came to see us. Courts busy all day. Went to Post Office for Mr Salmon. *Wed 28* Very hot. I was cook. The master came to see us. Busy on courts. *Thurs 29* Intense rain at night. Busy on courts all day. *Fri 30* Up at gate all day selling programmes. *Sat 31* Lightning and intense rain. Harold came. Sir G. Thomas won the men's singles tennis cup.

Sunday 1 June 1924 Came back from Malvern. *Mon 2* West to see the flood. Three Counties Show flooded out. *Wed 4* Visiting Day. Mother did not come. Master has got some ducks. *Thurs 5* Weeded garden in afternoon. Wash-house and laundry in morning. *Fri 6* Weeded garden in morning and afternoon. Saw first poppy. *Sat 7* Some boys went home. Harry Webb came here. Holidays commenced. *Tues 10* Played tennis with Mr Lockey. Scrubbed new room. Worked in garden. *Wed 11* Played tennis at night. Worked in wash-house in afternoon. *Thurs 12* Cleaned and painted Mrs Lockey's bicycle. *Sat 14* Came home. Listened to band in afternoon and night on the wireless. Went on tram to Barbourne with Mother. *Sun 15* Went to see Mrs Carlton. Blossoms of ash in bloom. Listened to the wireless in the evening. *Mon 16* Expected to go for 14-mile journey. Went to Droitwich by bus. Saw Grandmother, took Claude. *Tues 17* Went to see Mrs Matthews. Played tennis after tea. Went to Pitchcroft to see show. *Wed 18* Mother applied for situation for me at Stanley Nye's. Went to see Uncle and Auntie. A red sunset. *Thurs 19* Horse chestnuts appearing. Went to see Mrs Carlton who was ill. Listened to wireless. Did carpentry for Ted. *Fri 20* Went to see Mrs Matthews. Very hot. Red sunset. Went for a walk on Merriman's Hill. Lovely, breezy. *Sat 21* Came back from home. Worcester Infirmary Carnival. Very wet and stormy at night. *Sun 22* Went in swimming bath for first time. Had my coat changed. *Mon 23* Told about Wembley. *Tues 24* Went to Malvern. Puncture. Saw first hay. Saw blackcap. Red sunset. *Wed 25* Played cricket after tea. Saw a hawk. Hoed my garden. Clarkia out. *Thurs 26* Cricket match against St Clement's. We won. Saw a dog rose. Strawberries ripe. *Sat 28* Went to Mayor Moore's cricket match. We lost. *Sun 29* Had a new collar and new pair of trousers. Flower Service.

Tuesday 1 July 1924 Went to Mayor Moore's to practise display. *Wed 2* Visiting Day. Mother came. Had neckerchief ironed. Practised cricket. *Sat 5* Played St Peter's. We won. Went to Mayor Moore's. *Sun 6* Warm and dry. Saw scarlet pimpernel and wild pansy. Birth of chickens. *Mon 7* Practised sports. Saw red clover. Mr Lockey had chickens from master.

Tues 8 Went to Malvern Wells to practice. Meadow was cut. Saw blacknap weed. *Wed 9* Mr Thomas brought bees. Played cricket after tea. Saw a seagull. *Thurs 10* Barbering Day. Practised surveying. Scouts sports. Saw marshmallow and succory and several moths. *Fri 11* Saw a hawk. *Daily Mail* printing in sky. *Sat 12* Played Cadbury's. We won. Went to Mayor Moore's to practise bridge building. A red sunset. *Sun 13* 12 eggs. Had a race. Harold came up. My nigella is out, also the marigolds and nasturtiums. *Mon 14* Rhoda came up but did not see her. Played cricket after tea. Committee meeting. *Tues 15* Went to Mayor Moore's to practise bridge building. *Wed 16* Was ball-boy for matron and staff. Played tennis until 10 o'clock. A red sunset. *Fri 18* Went to take wheelbarrow to Mr Thomas's house. Saw bees. *Sat 19* Cricket match against Celtic. Lost. Went to Mayor Moore's. *Sun 20* Went to Holy Communion. Wrote to Mrs Carlton and Mrs Matthews. *Mon 5* 21 eggs. Broody hen killed a sparrow. Went to infirmary to fetch boxes for Flag Day. Prepared haversacks for camp. *Tues 22* Marked Scout pole. Picked raspberries. Planted tomato. Scrubbed my room. *Thurs 24* Went to the cathedral. Saw bells. Went up the tower. *Fri 25* Went to town with matron about Flag Day. Had mugs. Scouting after tea. *Sat 26* Flag Day for RAO. Sold flags all day. £130 raised. Went to Mayor Moore's for last time. *Mon 28* Holiday in afternoon. Prepared kit for Wembley. *Tues 29* Prepared kit for Wembley. Had letter and 5*s.* from Mr and Mrs Matthews. *Wed 30* Went to Wembley (British Empire Exhibition). Pitched tents. Visited Nigeria, West Africa, Gold Coast and Palace of Engineering Exhibitions. Wonderful. *Thurs 31* First rehearsal of display in the stadium. Visited Malta, India, Burma, East Africa, Australia and Aquarium Exhibitions.

Friday 1 August 1924 Saw a falcon. First arena performance, took 9 minutes. Success. Saw Part 1 of *Pageant of Empire*. Good. *Sat 2* Went to Hong Kong, Palestine, Cyprus, New Zealand, South Africa, Ceylon and Poultry Exhibitions. Enjoyed the Amusement Park and Camp Fire for Prince. *Sun 3* Attended Great Scouts Service in Stadium. Prince of Wales and Baden-Powell present. Wrote a letter. Very wet in afternoon. *Mon 4* Went to London Zoo in the morning. Display at 3 o'clock. Successful. Went on Devils Bowl. Saw Battle of Zeebrugge at Government Buildings. *Tues 5* Film taken of our display in the morning. Went to Malay and Palestine Temples. Had a bath after display in Stadium at 6 o'clock. *Wed 6* Went around London. Saw Trafalgar Square, Buckingham Palace and Cleopatra's Needle, Tower of London and the Thames Embankment. Had lunch at the Hotel Ceigil. *Thurs 7* Visited Australian Cinema. Very good. Also its products. Two arena performances. Successful. Eight minutes. Mr Clues took our photographs. *Fri 8* Visited Madame Tussaud's Exhibition also St Paul's Cathedral. Returned to British Empire Exhibition, bought some souvenirs. Our photographs taken. *Sat 9* Came back from Wembley. Arrived 4 o'clock with Cathedral Scouts. *Sun 10* Had a new tube of toothpaste. Went for a walk after Sunday School by river. Saw a tansy. *Mon 11* Egg plums picked by garden boys. 2 eggs. All the chickens put together. Cockerel separated. Cleaned out the fowls. *Thurs 14* Scouting after tea. Made flag sticks for signalling. Started my first-class tests. *Fri 15* Went for our trip on steamer to Tewkesbury. Went in the abbey. Showers in afternoon. Bought views and sent them to Mother. *Thurs 21* Scrubbed laundry and washhouse. No school. Dentist came, one out. *Fri 29* Mr Lockey went away for his holidays. Fed the fowls. Nine eggs. Did weeding in the afternoon. Cleaned up the stoke-hole.

Monday 1 September 1924 Helped master with fruit packing. Busy all day. *Tues 2* 134 strikes. *Wed 3* Visiting Day. Mother came. Helped master with packing. Cricket after tea. *Thurs 4* Helped master with packing. Rhoda came to see me. *Sat 6* Went home. Went out with Mother. Fine. Did shopping with Mother. Listened to the gramophone after tea. *Sun 7* Went to see Mrs Matthews. Went to Ombersley on Ted's motor cycle. *Mon 8* Went to the Arcade Cinema to see *Wondrous Wembley*. Very good. Excellent. *Tues 9* Showers in afternoon. Went to see Mrs Carlton. She was not in! *Wed 10* Went to see Aunt Fanny and Mrs Matthews. Played tennis after tea with Mrs Matthews and Mrs Willmot. *Thurs 11* Went to see Mrs Carleton. Saw fowls. Met Doris in the evening. Helped Ted with his examination. *Fri 12* Killed fowl for Mother from Mrs Kendrick. *Sat 13* Came back from home. Went out with Harold to pay Ted's bill. *Sun 14* Went for a walk. Saw first honeysuckle. Bought two photographs of us at Wembley. 1*s*. *Fri 19* Did the laundry and washhouse. Matron went away. Did dormitory work after tea. *Sat 20* The Scouts went to the Arcade Cinema. Saw Jackie Coogan's understudy. They gave us a pencil each. *Tues 23* Went out for the master to fetch books from Mrs Lewis at London Road. *Tues 30* One egg. 1,872 eggs so far. 118 this month.

Wednesday 1 October 1924 Visiting Day. Mother came. 10*d*. in bank. *Thurs 2* Fowls given sulphate. Put up goalposts. Did Scouting after tea.

Sat 4 Played St Clement's Scouts. Lost 6–0. Harold came here. Helped Mr Thomas with the mending of the chairs. *Sun 5* Had waistcoat changed. Went to Holy Communion. Harvest Thanksgiving Service. *Tues 7* Put perch in for the pullets. Picked up the fallen apples. Scrubbed the 'New Room'. *Sun 12* Went for a walk after church. Finished pen and ink sketch of King Charles House. *Tues 14* Scrubbed 'Big Room'. Went in the dining hall after tea. *Thurs 16* Did cooking in the afternoon. *Fri 17* Did the beds on the lawn in the morning. Whitewashed the two coops in the afternoon. *Sat 18* Football in the afternoon. The coops were shifted. The five crossed breeds separated. *Tues 21* My dormitory scrubbed. Did card trick. Started to practise the concert. *Wed 22* After tea I read *The King's Pilgrimage* about the King's visit to the cemeteries in France. *Sat 25* Went to St John's Cinema. Saw *The Shadow of the Mosque.* Very good. *Mon 27* Matron's birthday. Invited to girls' concert. Very good. *Wed 29* General Election. Mr Greene successful for Worcester. Conservative 409 seats. Stanley Baldwin prime minister. *Thurs 30* No holiday because of the rain. Scouts had recreation after tea in dining hall. *Fri 31* Cleaned out the fowls. Scrubbed the coop. Cleaned crock eggs and drinking fountain.

Saturday 1 November 1924 Went to St John's Cinema. Saw *The Dancer of the Nile. Nov 3* British Empire Exhibition ended on Saturday. Attendance 17,403,119 at Wembley. *Wed 5* Visiting Day. Mother came. Had bonfire and fireworks. Splendid. *Mon 10* Had concert for the master's birthday. Success. Had dancing after concert till 10 o'clock. Harold came. *Tues 11 (Armistice signed 1918)* Had service in the dining hall. *Wed 12* Master read letter from Ernest Jones in Canada. Showed us his photographs. *Thurs 20* Went for run to Broadheath. All our patrol got through. 7 marks. *Sat 22* Played St Clement's. We won 6–4. Harold came and played for us. *Tues 25* Held concert in Co-op Hall. I was a 'Newsboy'. Success. Collection £2. 6*s*. 6*d*. *Sat 29* Played St Stephen's Scouts. We won 10–5. Harold played. *Sun 30* Held service in the dining hall in the afternoon.

Monday 1 December 1924 Death of Reginald Draper. He was only seventeen. *Tues 2* Mixed the Christmas pudding. *Wed 3* Visiting Day. Mother came. Mr Lockey sold his two Plymouth Rocks. *Sat 6* Went to Kidderminster to attend Reginald Draper's funeral. *Wed 10* Had drill in the afternoon. The King opened parliament. *Sat 13* Went to the pictures. Saw *The Kelly Gang. Thurs 18* Did cooking in the afternoon. We did porridge and roasted rabbit. Success. *Fri 19* Wireless poles and wires fixed up. *Sat 20* Played football in the afternoon. Other boys went Christmas shopping. Harold came here. *Mon 22* Boys were confirmed. Scrubbed girls' top dormitory. Christmas tree came. *Tues 23* Scrubbed dormitory. Decorated schoolroom and dining hall after tea. *Wed 24* Finished Edgar Tower picture for matron. Harold brought me a parcel. Listened to the wireless for first time. *Thurs 25 (Christmas Day)* Went to Holy Communion. Had diary and table tennis bat from tree. Harold came up. *Fri 26* Played football in the afternoon. Dancing, games and songs after tea. *Sun 28* Went for a walk in afternoon. River Teme flooded. *Mon 29* Went out. Saw Ted – gave me a shilling. Cleaned out the fowls. Played football. *Tues 30* Scrubbed dormitory. Bought celluloid balls for table tennis. Dancing after tea. *Wed 31* Concert in St Clement's Parish Room. Successful. Played table tennis.

Thursday 1 January 1925 Scrubbed wash-house and laundry. Dancing and games after tea. *Fri 2* Took down decorations in schoolrooms. Listened in to the wireless after tea. *Sat 3* Went to St John's Cinema. Saw *The Cowboy King*. Very good. *Sun 4* One egg from pullets. Went for a walk. Saw first hazel catkins. Reckoned up eggs – 2018. *Mon 5* Applied for situation at Mr Foss. Failed. Too small! *Tues 6* Had drill in afternoon. Dancing and singing after tea. Good. *Wed 7* Visiting Day. Mother came to see us. Listened to the wireless after tea. *Thurs 8* Barbering Day. Whist drive for matron's friends. Helped in afternoon. *Sat 10* Played football in afternoon. Harold came up. Had a game. *Sun 11* Went for a walk in afternoon. Saw first pheasant and rabbit. *Tues 13* Had dancing and singing after tea. Good. Listened to wireless while having tea. *Sun 18* Went for a walk. Saw first snowdrop. Service after tea. *Wed 21* Played football after dinner. Table tennis after tea. Had wireless on. *Fri 23* Went in carpenter's shop. Glued towel rack together. *Sat 24* Eclipse of sun from 2.30 to 4.00. Played the 'Porcelain Juniors'. We won 12–2. Harold came up – brought me the gloves. *Sun 25* Went for a walk to Bransford Bridge. Had a new pair of laces. *Tues 27* Had Scouting after tea. Kind deed – helped to scrub the schoolroom. *Wed 28* Boys listened to radio after tea. I didn't but continued my composition on Worcester. *Thurs 29* Did wood-carving of my canoe in American whitewood after tea. *Fri 30* Scouting in afternoon to Crown East Wood. *Sat 31* Went to the cinema. Saw *The Covered Wagon*. Good. 19 girls and 7 boys have got the influenza.

Sunday 1 February 1925 Went for a walk in the afternoon by river and Bath Road. *Mon 2* No school. Several boys in bed. *Tues 3* Went to town for Mrs Lockey and to Stewards the chemist for matron. Did not go to school. Helped upstairs. *Wed 4* Boys listened to the wireless after tea. I did not. Felt tired. Busy upstairs all day. *Thurs 5* My birthday. 16 years old. Had card from Mother. Had an egg from Mrs Lockey. *Tues 10* Did not go in school. Scrubbed my dormitory. Cleaned out Mr Lockey's fowls assisted by Ben Amphlett. *Thurs 12* Scrubbed dining hall, wash-house and laundry. No half-holiday. Scouting after tea. Concert by 'Odd Entertainers'. *Fri 13* Went to St John's for the master. *Sat 14* Played Porcelain Juniors. Lost 8–1. Cyril Draper came here. *Sun 15* Saw the first wild primrose and celandine. Also first lamb. My mistletoe seeds beginning to germinate in the trees. *Mon 16* King George ill. *Tues 17* Dancing and singing after tea. Scrubbed big-room. Prepared for examination. *Wed 18* Had examination. 5 sums right out of 6. No school in latter half of afternoon. Did well. *Fri 20* Scouting in the afternoon. Did damper and porridge. *Sun 22* Went for a walk. Saw a mole and water wagtail. Elm leaves appearing. Started to read *Early Explorers*. *Mon 23* Left school. Went out in the garden. Did drawing of table after tea. Helped in the wash-house. *Tues 24* Scrubbed the dormitory. Sawed up wood down stoke-hole. Singing and dancing after tea. *Wed 25 (Ash Wednesday)* Did not go to church. Painted my canoe after tea. Helped matron with brasses and warming pan. *Thurs 26* The hairdresser came. No half-holiday. Did digging all day by girls' playground. Games after tea. *Fri 27* Helped matron with cook's bedroom. Went in carpenter's shop. Mr Lockey gave me a writing book and pen. *Sat 28* Went to St John's Cinema and saw *Singer Jim*. Very good.

Sunday 1 March 1925 Went to Holy Communion at 7 o'clock. Went for a walk round Hindlip and Rainbow Hill. *Mon 2* Busy digging all day by girls' side. Did own work in writing book after tea. *Tues 3* Did digging all day. Practised three new hymns with Mr Powell. Singing and dancing after tea. *Wed 4* Visiting Day. Mother came to see us. Played football afterwards. Tried a crossword puzzle after tea. Did digging. Saw a robin and a woodpecker. *Thurs 5* Fine and sunny. Saw a blue finch. No Scouting in afternoon. Games, instruction and morse after tea. *Sun 8* Went for a walk by the river. Saw many pussies and primroses and violets in bud. A snow at night. *Mon 9* Snow at sudden intervals. Did scrubbing and cleaned windows upstairs all day. *Wed 11* Concert given by St George's Girls. Very good. Had dancing after concert. *Fri 13* Worked upstairs in girls' sick-room. Cleaned windows. *Sun 15* Went for a walk up the Ombersley Road and across ferry. Saw my first skylark. *Thurs 19* Went Scouting in the afternoon to Perry Wood. Saw a wood anemone and a partridge. *Fri 20* Madame Tussaud's burnt down in London. Much damage and losses. *Thurs 26* Annual Meeting Day and Concert. Had three prizes. Mother came, also Harold. Miriam had one prize. *Sat 28* Went to see football match in Worcester City's Ground. Boys did drill. Harold came. I bought *Birmingham Post.* University Boat Race. Cambridge won. *Sun 29* Had my school prize named *The White Feather* covered.

Wednesday 1 April 1925 Did spring-cleaning all day. Visiting Day. Mother did not come. *Thurs 2* Busy over in far garden. Concert after tea. Collection £2.15*s.* 0*d.* *3 Fri* Did hoeing on top patch all day. Saw first butterfly, King George. *Sat 4* Boys very busy with the gardens setting seeds. *Mon 6* Spring-cleaned my lavatory. Played football. Practised singing after tea. Busy upstairs all day. *Tues* 7 Spring-cleaned my dormitory. Upstairs until four o'clock and hoeing in far garden. Plum blossoms appearing. *Wed 8* Saw a humble bee. *Fri 10* Good Friday. Warm and dry. Went for a walk after church in the morning. Very wet in afternoon. Read *Black Beauty. Sat 11 (Easter Eve)* Played St John's Juniors. Lost 7–3. Harold and Bert Darby played. Very hot. Helped Mr Thomas with music stool. *Sun 12 (Easter Day)* Hot and dry. Went to Holy Communion. Did not go for a walk in the afternoon. Finished my book called *Black Beauty. Mon 13 (Easter Monday)* Table tennis tournament held. Harry Webb came up here. *Tues 14* Scrubbed the top-room. Went to see rugby match Worcester against South Wales. South Wales won. *Wed 22* Mowed and rolled the cricket pitch. *Fri 24* Busy mending gate until 9 o'clock. Rolled cricket pitch. Did digging in far garden. *Sat 25* Went to the pictures. Saw *Captain January*. Very good. Sheffield United won English FA Cup. *Sun 26* Attended Scout service in Worcester Cathedral. *Mon 27* Spring-cleaned my landing and stairs. *Tues 28* Spring-cleaned top room. *Wed 29* Invited to Arcade Cinema. Saw *Zeebrugge*. Very good indeed. *Thurs 30* Spring-cleaned matron's lumber-room. Scouting after tea. Went to church. Saw a thrush's nest. 4 eggs in.

Friday 1 May 1925 Went in the carpenter's shop. Master told me about situation as a chef. *Sat 2* Went to the theatre. Saw *The Gondoliers*. Mrs Knott came to see me about situation as a chef. Also Miss Piddocke. Very well. Gave seeds to Miriam. *Sun 3* Harold came up. Gave him gloves and scarf. Went to Holy Communion. Went for a walk. Picked bluebells.

Mon 4 Spring-cleaned the girls' landing and stairs. Went with master to get my outfit. He treated me to the Scala Cinema. *Tues 5* Scrubbed big-room. Did digging in far garden. Played table tennis after tea. *Wed 6* Visiting day. Mother came. Some new boys came into the orphanage. Played table tennis. *Thurs 7* Came home for my holidays. Had a good talk at night. Very wet. Stayed in all afternoon. *Fri 8* Met Teddy from work. Went to see Mrs Matthews. Listened to the wireless. *Sat 9* Wembley opened. Heard King's speech on the wireless. *Sun 10* Went for a walk with Harold by the river. Went to see Mrs Matthews. *Mon 11* Went to see Auntie Fanny. Also Mrs Carleton. Listened in to the wireless after tea. *Tues 12* Went to see Rhoda in the morning. Went back to orphanage. Had my box packed ready for leaving. Played last game of cricket. Last night at orphanage. *Wed 13* Hot and dry. Weeded some onions in the morning. Left the Royal Albert Orphanage to start work. Bert Darby met me in Birmingham. Had a look round. Came to Sutton Coldfield. Started work as houseboy for Mrs Knott at 1 Coleshill, Sutton Coldfield. Birmingham.

CHARLES JOHN PARSONS (1920–29)

Having left the orphanage so many years ago, my thoughts will be rather scrappy.

As you will see I entered the RAO in April 1920 and Mr David Whitehead and Mrs Agnes ('Aguss') Whitehead as she was known to the boys were master and matron. My only recollection of that day was standing on the main entrance steps and crying my eyes out whilst I watched my mother disappear through the main gates. I was not happy. I had had this experience before when I went to Kingham at five years old. I was there for twelve months, then back home for twelve months before coming to the RAO at seven. You weren't allowed to go in the RAO before you were seven.

Other members of the staff were Captain E. H. Lockey, head schoolmaster and a very strict disciplinarian. A Miss Williamson who was head teacher over the girls. She was subsequently replaced by Miss Larby and Miss Bird ('Dickey') who taught the youngest pupils. Sadly she died at a fairly young age. Miss Gwilliam was cook whilst we were there. And then there was Miss Atkins, a very pleasant person who was nurse and seamstress. My main recollection of her was attending to the POs (poor objects). Each morning after breakfast the cry would go out 'POs! POs!

And anyone who needed medical attention would turn up in the printing room (so named because there was an old printing press in there) and be attended to by Miss Atkins. I have very little recollection of Miss Bird; I can recall very pleasant lessons on sunny summer days under the old elm tree now sadly cut down.

I suppose Mr Lockey was the greatest influence in our school life, as he was involved in most of the school activities and instrumental in running a very efficient Scout troop. At school he was very strict and if you had the cane he certainly laid it on, on both hands and backside leaving a few wails into the bargain. He was very good at giving 'sermons'; if someone had committed a serious misdemeanour and hadn't owned up to it, he would lecture us for what seemed hours on end and we would pass the time in counting how many cigarettes he smoked in the process!

The Scout troop under Mr Lockey was one of the best in Worcester at the time. They had won the Barker Swimming Cup a number of times and we were the first troop to win the Spreckley Shield given for general knowledge and activities in the Scout movement. The very first competition was held in Perdiswell Park which was then a private estate.

Another feature of the Scout troop was the annual camp at Manor Park in Great Malvern. The park itself is made up of tiers of tennis courts and each year a pretty big tennis tournament was held and we would act as ball-boys. In these days a very young Dorothy Round would be competing and the men's final always seemed to be between a couple of characters named Sir George Thomas and Sir Leonard Lyle.

Of all the Jamborees the Scout troop attended I think the highlight was the Wembley Exhibition of 1924 when a number of RAO Scouts were privileged to go. I also enjoyed the week's camp at Wimereaux in France in 1927, all organised by Mr Lockey. Regrettably we had no photographic record of this camp as the camera was spoilt while trying to take snaps in the sea!

School-time was spent actually at the RAO. In later times the children went out to school but in my day classes were held 'inside' the orphanage.

Before school hours we were each allocated a certain area to be cleaned and scrubbed. The main steps were whitened each day and were really white. The ultimate in the cleaning line was being dormitory boy. Being in charge of one of the dormitories meant cleaning the wash-basins, polishing the taps and of course scrubbing the floors which were bare boards, but they were white as milk. There were four dormitories, the

Note the sparkling white entrance steps in the 1920s. The orphanage building is now listed

little dormitory, the long dormitory, the Wheeler Wing and the top dormitory. I'm just referring to the boys' side. Each week the four dormitory boys assembled to scrub one of the rooms. We would all kneel in a row with our buckets and scrubbing brushes while 'Aguss' sat on the bed, perhaps knitting or something, telling us when to scrub and when to wash off. But these dormitories were a sight to see.

Bath night was on Saturdays and feet-washing on Tuesdays. I can see David Whitehead now with his cane coming into the bathroom. Three bays bathed in one bath at the time. Whilst they were drying I can see him putting his cane under a boy's penis to see if he needed circumcising. I've seen him do that many times. One of the lads was circumcised whilst I was there. I believe my brother Cyril was.

Christmas-time was naturally a time to look forward to. One of the first signs of Christmas was killing the pig for Christmas dinner and looking out of the dining hall window and seeing the sides of pork hanging outside the dairy-room. The rooms were decorated with paper-chains and the old fashioned Chinese lanterns over the lights. A Christmas tree given by one of the nurseries was decorated and placed on the stage. Presents were placed around the base and each child received three presents. The feature of the Christmas dinner was the entrance of the Christmas pudding; when it appeared there was a tremendous din of banging of spoons on the tables. Christmas was the only time we were allowed to talk at meal-times. After tea there would be the distribution of presents and dancing, the old fashioned ones of course, one of the rare occasions we mixed with the girls. There was also what was known as the 'happy half-hour' when we were left entirely on our own; you can imagine what went on then – just bedlam!

Bedtime was 8 p.m. in the winter months and 8.30 p.m. in the summer-time. We always wore white nightshirts whilst I was there. I remember Howard Clements had the *Chip* comic and in this comic there was a serial called 'Cragadoon' and after we had gone to bed old Howard would relate this story to us while we lay in bed. Every time this comic came out, once a month, I think it was, Howard would continue with this story, 'Cragadoon'. And old Lockey used to get outside the door and spy on us!

Mealtimes were heralded by a big bell kept near the dining hall. There was 'first bell' and 'second bell'; first bell was telling you to get ready and second bell was to tell you to form up in proper order in the 'play-shed' and then we would march into the dining hall. Meals were taken in silence, Mr Lockey on the stage overseeing the proceedings and a teacher at the end of each table. I'm afraid I can't remember much about the actual meals. In the early twenties tea comprised one thick slice of bread about an inch thick with perhaps jam or treacle. On occasions when I first entered the orphanage one had to pocket half a slice for the older lads.

When Paddy Drew was in the orphanage, towards the end of my time, the Committee let Scouts camp in the field and sleep there at night. I don't know whether it was older Scouts or who it was. Some of the lads used to get out of the dormitory at night and raid these people and let their tents down!

Plays and songs were arranged for concerts in the dining hall. The boys always gave a concert on Mr Whitehead's birthday and the girls gave a concert on Mrs Whitehead's birthday. We always had a jam turnover on those days. The concerts were always under the direction of Mr Lockey who at times would get most exasperated if we couldn't sing a tune properly. I've know him bang his baton on the floor and it would bounce right up to the ceiling!

We did on occasion give concerts in the Public Hall in Worcester in aid of the orphanage. I remember performing there in *A Midsummer Night's Dream*.

We attended church every Sunday morning. When I first entered the RAO we went to St John's Church in St John's district. The Rev. Waugh was the vicar and the Rev. Benison was curate. In 1928 we changed to St Clement's Church owing to the alterations of parish boundaries. We would all parade in the playground for inspection, a look behind the ears and then were ordered to form fours military style and then march to church like a regiment of soldiers! At St Clement's the Rev. R. F. Diggle was rector and chaplain of the RAO and he was also involved in the Scout troop. Thinking about church, if we misbehaved Mr Lockey would make us learn the collect for each Sunday and recite it. Canon Diggle would also arrange for St Clement's choir to go across the road and sing carols in the main entrance of the orphanage on Christmas Eve. He was also known to dress up as Father Christmas and go round the dormitories filling stockings after we had gone to bed.

In my time at the RAO cricket and football were the main boys' sport under the direction of Mr Whitehead. He was reputed to be an ex-Hampshire cricketer. There used to be two meadows: the 'big meadow' was used for football in the winter and cricket was played in the other field. A wooden pavilion was in between the two. I had the privilege of playing in the football team usually at half-back and Mr Whitehead would be the referee telling us what to do and what not to do. The RAO colours were red and black. The highlight of the football season was the annual match against the Cinderella team (employees of Willis's shoe factory) played on their ground in Bransford Road. It always took place at Christmas time, usually on my birthday, 27 December. We always looked forward to it because we had a good 'bun feast' afterwards with fun and games.

I rarely played in the cricket team. My earliest recollection of cricket was being hit by a cricket ball just above the left eye and being taken to Dr Bunting's surgery to have some stitches put in.

Referring back to football – each year a competition for the Orphanage and Infirmary Cup was held and the final was always played on Worcester City's ground, St George's Lane. During half-time the orphanage boys always gave a PT display under the direction of Mr Lockey: one of the few occasions in which he was involved in sport.

I have a pleasant cricket recollection of going out to Kenswick Manor at Wichenford near Mortley, the home of the late Colonel Britton. Pleasant Saturday afternoons and having refreshments in the open air. That was an annual event.

On leaving school the boys usually spent the last twelve months in the garden under the watchful eye of Mr Lodge ('Lodger') and the stock-man was Mr Coombes ('Monty'). There was quite a large garden with lots of fruit trees. I remember a pear tree called 'the bendy' because of the shape of the trunk and another one called the 'hard iron' because the pears were always hard. All the cultivation was done by hand.

There was a stretch of land between the 'big meadow' and the railway line called the 'far garden', quite a number of acres and there would be seven or eight of us stretched across the patch digging it with spades and 'Lodger' telling us not to take too big a 'weft'. When we worked over there we always looked out for the ten past five express coming through with a van on the back marked Palethorpe's sausages. We always enjoyed fruit picking of course! I recall Mr Whitehead in the garden shed packing sieves of plums and apples to be sent by rail to Birmingham and Liverpool.

Hay-making was a pleasant time too. During the summer the 'big meadow' was closed for haymaking and when ready a Mr Heath would bring his horse and mower to cut the hay. We would have the job of treading down the hay in the barn. There was a cowshed with a stall for three cows, pigsties and fowl houses, all of which have now gone. With all the apple trees around of course, there would be a lot of windfall apples. They would be collected up and three or four apples would be on our tea plates, which to us was quite a treat.

In the front of the buildings are lawns which were immaculately kept when we were there. Mr Whitehead would be responsible for cutting them and one of us would have to pull the mower along while he directed it. The older boys had their own little patch of garden at the side of the building by the playground, and we would grow the annual flowers and perhaps a bit of lettuce and a few radishes. We used to have quite a nice show during the summer and then would come along 'Aguss' and cut them for her floral arrangements. She really liked her flowers. She would spend all Friday mornings arranging flowers in her lounge and sitting room.

The playground brings back memories of the boys walking round in twos and threes waiting for the first and second bell for meals. Just imagine sixty-odd boys walking round the playground just like prisoners exercising!

The outside toilets were next to the playground. They were called the 'petty' and we used to mark the wall to represent a wicket and bowl against the 'petty wall'. We'd play tennis with wooden tennis bats and play football with a paper ball and a lad named Joe Home was the expert at making these balls with paper and string. In the winter time we would throw buckets of water down the playground to freeze and make a slide. The mad point about it was the slide used to run into the railings!

Once a month our parents could come and see us. That particular day was called 'visday' – short for visiting day and the lads would congregate in the corner of the playground to see if their parents would arrive.

Another summer event was the river trip. We would go to Stourport one year and Tewkesbury the next. The steamer was called the *Belle*. There would be boxes of sandwiches and apples to be eaten on the way and on the return journey we'd have a sing-song. On reaching Worcester bridge while the boat was manoeuvring for us to disembark there would be three lusty cheers in appreciation, bringing crowds of people on to the bridge.

Other outings arranged were trips to the theatre and cinema. These trips were only occasional, perhaps to the theatre to see a pantomime or a musical. *San-Toy* was one I seem to recollect seeing at the theatre. We were always seated on the 'jam shelves' right at the top. If a Saturday afternoon was wet we would sometimes be invited to St John's cinema

Trips up the River Severn in the 1920s

by the proprietor, Mr Godsell. I remember seeing the silent film star Pearl White and the film *Go Get-em Hatch* among others of the silent days.

Another annual event was the annual meeting of the governors and the prizegiving when once again the children would give a concert and receive school prizes. In fact I still possess the books I received, not that I was very brilliant but always managed to be in the top three of the class.

On leaving the RAO I received a silver watch and chain which I still have and it is keeping fairly good time. If a boy or girl was of good behaviour during their stay at the RAO the boys were given a watch and the girls a sewing-machine when they left.

When I left the RAO in February 1929 I was apprenticed as a cabinet maker at G. T. Rackstram's and I was fortunate to receive a complete set of tools valued at over £20 which was a lot of money in those days. I still have most of them. Children stayed at the RAO until they had a job to go to. A lot of the girls would go into service and some of the boys went to Canada and Australia.

We saw very little of the outside world during our sojourn at the orphanage. When out walking we had to walk two and two and keep in sight of whoever was taking us out, usually Mr Lockey. We were allowed two weeks holiday a year if we had somewhere to go, one week in June and one week in September. I always remember having a lump in my throat when it was time to go back. I think that is how I learnt to tell the time by continually looking at the clock and counting the hours before I had to return.

When I first arrived at the RAO we used to wear the old Norfolk jackets, with no collars, and a belt around the waist and a stiff wide collar over the coat. The girls used to wear straw boaters.

We had a woodwork shop and woodwork classes were held on Wednesdays and Fridays by a Mr Thomas. I think the first thing we had to make was a ruler and then on to a soap box and jam spoon. I remember Mr Thomas was a keen bee-keeper and during the First World War he used to tell us how he worked on aircraft propellers.

Another little incident I recall. When a new youngster arrived he was taken down to the 'stoke hole' or boiler house to see the 'white elephant' and of course when you got down there someone was behind the boiler bellowing away and frightening the daylights out of you!

The swimming pool was an open air affair with a cubicle in each corner of the surrounding wall. I have recollections of cold water on cold evenings in the swimming pool. One of the pleasanter episodes was swimming for a life-saving certificate. We hadn't time to complete all the exercises required so we finished them on Sunday mornings. I can recall looking up at a clear blue sky swimming the back-stroke and thinking of the trip to France the following day. I have still got the certificate signed by the Chief Constable of the day, Chief Constable Cole.

The orphanage was equipped with quite a good gymnasium with a vaulting-horse, parallel bars, a horizontal ladder and various ropes. I haven't any recollection of using it that often.

Before going to school, apart from scrubbing floors we had to help prepare vegetables for dinner. I remember baths full of potatoes being scrubbed and washed before being boiled in their jackets. I remember having to write 'It is a crime to waste food', for some reason or other, a hundred times.

In later years the boys had to help with the washing up in the kitchens. Your name was on a rota and if you failed to turn up you could have a good caning.

I have a faint recollection of the laundry with huge long clothes-horses on wheels which were pushed into large airing spaces. One of the characters was 'Elsie' Hardman, a small person with glasses who used to talk with a lisp.

As you may see I spent nine years at the RAO. Some times were happy. Some times were unhappy. But we were taught to treat people with respect and accept discipline, and we had a fairly good education for those times. On leaving I was kitted out with clothes, a suitcase which I still possess and a complete set of wood-working tools which I still have. So I had a lot to be thankful for.

Charles is mentioned in John Brown's diary on 20 March 1924 when he was made a Scout.

HOWARD WILFRED CLEMENTS (1920–30)

A few memories of the Royal Albert Orphanage. I was admitted on 20 October 1920 and left on 3 March 1930: nearly ten years.

The numbers were 63 boys and 32 girls. When I arrived aged seven years, the staff then were Mr and Mrs Whitehead, master and matron. Mr Lockey was schoolmaster of the boys; Miss Bird was the girls' teacher. Miss Atkins was the sewing mistress and sickness officer. Mr Lodge was the gardener and Mr Coombes the cowman.

We slept in three dormitories for boys with twenty in each. The girls were quite apart from the boys and you were forbidden to speak to them, even if you had a sister in residence.

We were called at 7 o'clock in the morning. We made our own beds, washed and parted our hair for breakfast at 7.30 a.m. to the second! Out at 8 o'clock after prayers and scrubbing floors from 8 to 9.15 a.m. School was held in the orphanage from 9.30 a.m. to 12 noon. Dinner was 12.30 to 1 p.m. Gardening if fine took place from 1 to 2 p.m. We went back to school from 2 to 4.30 p.m. Tea was 5 to 5.30 p.m. Bed was 7 o'clock in the winter, and 8 o'clock in the summer.

We had the best Scout troop in Worcester. Joining was compulsory and practised most nights from 5.30 p.m. until bedtime. Mr Lockey was Scoutmaster.

A bit about food. Breakfast was 8 oz bread and margarine and 1 pint of cocoa in mug. Dinner was vegetables, mostly potatoes in jackets and cabbage, steamed, not boiled. A small amount of meat, sausage or liver. Tea was 8 oz bread and marg. with 1 pint of tea. No supper. These meals never altered in ten years!

Unless you were very bright and stayed at school, you were sent out gardening at fourteen years of age from 8 a.m. to 5 p.m. and had the same amount of food as a boy of seven years of age, who only picked up paper from around the playground!

There were prayers and hymns every evening after tea and church on Sunday mornings. What they called a country walk on Sunday afternoons was a march in fours all the way. If you got out of step on the way, you had to march around the playground when you got back, to teach you to keep in step.

There were fifty or sixty fowls running about the playing field, but the eggs were sold in St John's. We had two eggs a year, one on Good Friday and one at Easter Sunday teatime. People were very good at Christmas. A Mrs Payne at nearby Pitmaston Lodge sent two huge slab cakes made by her cooks. A Mr Mason sent two or three boxes of oranges. I mention this because our tea was cut in four slices of a square loaf and when you got a slice of cake or an orange you lost half a slice of bread and marge!

You were allowed a visitor (if you had anyone) on the first Wednesday of the month from 3 to 4 p.m. You had one week's holiday away from the orphanage in August, if there was a relative to have you.

Our caps had RAOW on the front – 'Royal Albert Orphanage, Worcester'. But if asked we used to say it stood for 'Rob All Old Women'!

We had a good football and cricket team, partly because Mr Whitehead insisted on being referee at all football matches and umpire at one end at cricket. I understood we played all football matches at home and most of our cricket matches.

When I left the orphanage I met Mr Lockey and his lady wife in the Winter Gardens, Great Malvern.

After cleaning the main steps Charlie Mitchell was congratulated by a member of the Committee, who said, 'They look good.' Charlie answered, 'I should bloomin' well think so – I've spent three hours on them!'

The difference between children at public school and children at an orphanage is this. Children from a public school come from money, therefore 'no stigma'. Children from an orphanage don't come from money, hence 'the stigma'.

In closing, I must make this observation. I must say that the staff lived on the fat of the land and the lives of the orphans never varied!

The Mayor of Worcester granted the orphanage two flag days a year but if they collected £200 or £2,000 we never got an extra piece of anything! They said it went to keep us.

I have so many vivid memories of my ten years there.

MIRIAM ALEXANDRA BROWN (1921–30)

I was born in Alexandria, Egypt. My mother had eight children. I was the youngest. My father was in the Boer War and when my father died his pension died with him. You either sank or swam in those days. So it was under stress that my mother had to do something. They were very, very hard days. My mother did dressmaking to earn a living, with a large family to look after on her own. No allowance was made for children. My mother was a very smart intelligent lady and through circumstances was forced to let go of her children. She was in the army as a soldier's wife and had to travel out in the far east and elsewhere. So being in the Worcestershire Regiment she had plenty of discipline. My father was a regimental hair-cutter and chiropodist.

I was about seven years old when I entered the Royal Albert Orphanage. I remember I was so frightened that I didn't take much notice of the vast mansion I was going into.

I remember having little jobs to do at an early age, before we had our breakfast, like shaking the door mats and cleaning the door knobs with

Brasso. We were given jobs to do such as cleaning all the corridors and classrooms. Everybody had a job to do. The children did most of the work; the boys were the same in their department. In the evening it was sewing and mending and darning socks. The shoes were all cleaned on Saturday afternoon. We took it in turn to do that. As we got older we would have to lay the tables for the staff – it all had to be done correctly – then wait on them at table.

The staff consisted of the cook, the sewing mistress, the cowman, the gardeners, the teachers and one or two in the laundry room. The master and matron were Mr and Mrs Whitehead. They were Scottish and extremely strict. The matron would go round to examine our work.

In the dormitory one of the girls would put a sheet over her head, pretending to be a ghost. The teachers would come up and ask, 'Who's walking about up there?' but we pretended to be asleep. We all had a wash before going to bed at 8 o'clock. All the lights were out by 9 o'clock and there was no laughing. Later a teacher would come through the dormitory to see if we were all in bed, and lock up. We had a bath and washed our hair with carbolic soap every Friday night.

In the morning the bell would ring to get us up. We would strip and make our beds before we came downstairs to start our jobs. Then the bell would ring again for breakfast and we all walked in line to the dining hall. The tables were very long. The older girls sat at the top and you knew where you had to sit in order of age. The boys and girls never mixed under any circumstances. They kept to their own department and the girls the same. We had grace before each meal, 'For what we are about to receive may the Lord make us truly thankful.' We said grace after each meal, 'For these and all other mercies may the Lord make us truly thankful.'

We used to run round the corridors, they were so big and endless, until you ran into one of the teachers and that was the end of it!

All the girls and boys were given a number. Mine was 66. We were called by that number. Our clothes, hats, stockings, our lockers, everything belonging to us personally, including underwear possessed this number.

In the recreation room we would do puzzles, play snakes and ladders, do sewing and knitting and play with our dolls.

Once a month we went to St John's cinema. It was all silent films with stars like Charlie Chaplin and Pearl White. Everything was so orderly, even the way we walked in and out of the cinema.

We played in the playground with big iron railings all the way round. We went to the swimming pool in the summer. We liked that. Then on Sunday afternoons in the summer we would take a walk around the extensive grounds in an orderly manner with one of the teachers.

Strict discipline was our way of life. I suppose with about a hundred children, boys and girls, to look after there had to be a code of conduct. Everything was done to a plan. A very high respect had to be given to the master and matron and the teachers. You only spoke when you were spoken to first. There was no familiarity.

The cane was administered to the girls as well as the boys. Sometimes we were given a hundred lines to write out or to go to bed early as a punishment.

I think my brother Harold and other boys climbed up onto the roof which was a very daring act. It was such an unusual building.

There were big fields where the boys and girls played, always under supervision. The girls played rounders and hockey and the boys cricket. Our big treat was going on the steamer on the river Severn to Holt Fleet, Tewkesbury or Stourport. We never went to the seaside at any time. We had one week's holiday a year to stay with our mother but we had to be back by 8 p.m. the following Saturday.

The orphanage employed outside gardeners but the boys helped in the garden after the age of fourteen years, helping with the chickens and collecting the eggs, looking after the pigs, doing some digging in the garden and picking the fruit in the late summer. We all had a little plot of ground where we would plant seeds. Fourteen years was the age you left school. The only egg we ever had was Easter Sunday for breakfast, so that was a real luxury.

Every Sunday morning we went to St John's Church or to St Clement's which was in Henwick Road. We all wore our best clothes, walking in crocodile. We were confirmed at about fifteen years of age.

School was on the premises. The teachers were very strict. It was all red and blue ink and blotting paper. We had the ruler or the cane if we didn't behave ourselves.

Usually on Sunday afternoons we went for walks in crocodile style. We picked wild flowers on the way, it was lovely. We were given two pennies a month to buy sweets. I would buy two lollipops and two bags of sweets. You could get a lot of sweets for one penny.

All the girls wore exactly the same style of clothes. We knew our clothes by our number. The boys were the same, they wore short trousers until about fifteen years of age. They always wore caps with RAO on them. We had good clothes. Long black stockings with garters, serge dress and jumper in the winter and gingham dresses in the summer. On Sundays our shoes had to be well polished. The matron would inspect our clothes before going to church. We wore velour hats for the winter months and thick navy coats. In the summer months we put on our 'straw brimmer' hats. Sunday was the day when all clean clothes were put on.

Well, I think in my experience the orphanage didn't equip us properly to face the outside world. It was dreadful. I think you felt afraid and very shy. You knew nothing about the real world.

We knew every day what we would have for food. Pork on Christmas Day with Christmas pudding. One egg only on Easter Sunday. I remember pea soup and corned beef and potatoes on Saturday. If you were thin by nature, they would give you more food to fatten you up: plenty of roly-poly suet pudding and stews. We only had cake on Sundays. We never had jam and cake together. There was porridge in the winter. There were no cereals years ago. Every now and then we were given as medicine 'brimstone of treacle'.

Once a month we would write to our mothers or fathers. All letters were read and checked by matron before posting. We had our family up to see us once a month. That seemed a long time when you were young.

My brothers joined the Scouts. They would go camping in Malvern, having to walk in line all the way to their camp site. The boys used to climb trees. My brother broke his collar bone climbing one. When the tennis tournament was on in Malvern the boys would act as ball-boys during the camping session. They would walk to Malvern and back.

The girls joined the Girl Guides. We went to Hewell Grange near Bromsgrove. It was a rough affair but we liked it. We filled a pillow case full of straw and had a ground sheet to sleep on with a blanket over us. The cows came round the tents during the night. We would get up in turn to get the wood and light the fires and cooked the breakfast about 8 o'clock. It gave us all a bit of freedom.

We all left the Royal Albert at the age of sixteen years. The girls worked in the house and the boys in the garden for the two years prior to leaving the orphanage. We had a sewing mistress who made all our dresses and did all repairs.

Dances were held in the main hall. We danced the lancers, waltz and foxtrot. The boys asked the girls to dance but went back to their seats after. We staged plays like *A Midsummer Night's Dream.* We sang in front of our parents and staff. The only music in those days was the piano.

On Christmas Day we would have a nice time. In the evening there would be dancing and we would go and collect our Christmas presents from the Christmas tree. The matron and master would call our names out and we would go and fetch our presents. The girls had to curtsey and the boys salute.

Two pets we made a fuss of were a spaniel dog called Chum and a cat called Smut.

I just remember all these things but an awful lot of things happened which float back to me now and then!

MURIEL MAY DAVIES (1921–30)

I was born on 23 April 1914 and admitted to the Royal Albert Orphanage on 19 October 1921. I was seven.

Well, I can't say my days in the orphanage were too disagreeable. It wasn't too bad really on the whole, you know. But of course I can't remember the day I went there. But I must have been very upset.

I had two stepsisters who were in the Royal Albert and one sister who was never admitted. They live in Malvern somewhere but I don't know their address – I think it's near Dines Green. Though they were in the orphanage they never let anybody know they'd been there. That's how they are. They don't want to know. I don't know why!

I can't say that I wasn't happy there. But you made the best of it. We were taught to swim, something which perhaps we wouldn't have done outside the orphanage. We were well taught in the school and I used to have to wait on matron and do other jobs.

I was a favourite of the matron, Mrs Whitehead. I was a very delicate little girl with blonde hair and big blue eyes. Perhaps that's why she tended to look after me. Once Mrs Whitehead told me that since the first child was admitted to the Royal Albert Orphanage in December 1862, I was No. 657. To think that over six hundred children had been in the orphanage before me.

Life in the girls' dormitory was quite good but we were never mischievous. Nothing like that. We were very quiet. We had to go to bed very early but then we were very young.

The orphanage was all discipline. There was a not very nice master there, Mr Lockey. The teachers weren't all that bad. It was just this one teacher. I used to think he was very cruel. He's dead and gone now, though, so it's no good talking about it. He died here in Malvern. The master and matron, Mr and Mrs Whitehead, however were very good people.

Once I wore a teacher's watch to go swimming. I used to play up a bit!

At Christmas time we always had to eat our dinner and if we didn't eat it, we couldn't have any Christmas pudding. You couldn't have your pudding if you didn't eat your dinner! Well that's only what you're taught, I suppose, when you're young.

I hadn't got a father; he died and had served in the army. But I'd got my sisters there, so of course I was happy. They were older than me. My mother took me into the orphanage. My sisters were already there. I met them once we were inside the building. So all the time I was in the Royal Albert I had the company, love and friendship of my sisters.

On 1 May 1930 I was discharged from the orphanage. I entered the service of a Mrs Hinds, 11 The Lees, Malvern.

MURIEL NELLIE PARSONS (1922–31)

I don't remember getting there and I don't remember being taken into the Royal Albert Orphanage but I do remember that the first people I saw were two of the older girls. I remember standing there in the middle of the playroom with these two girls, and they turned round and cut my hair. Just trimmed my hair at the bottom. They were about fourteen. I was put under their charge and the first thing they did was to do my hair, because you had to have it very straight and level at the bottom. That's the only thing I can remember on the first day. I was only seven.

We were in the playroom with the great big dolls house on the one wall and the lockers on the other, where you kept all your little bits and pieces. I don't remember crying at all. No, I didn't see my brother Charles that day.

I know when Cyril went into the Royal Albert they sent for me to sit with him in the infant school so I remember him going. Cyril was my younger brother, he's dead now. I think it was my grandmother who brought me. I remember going with my grandmother to take Cyril into the orphanage at Kingham. I didn't go into Kingham but I went with my grandmother to take him. We lived with my grandmother.

We had seen the orphanage building so many times before because we lived in St John's, only half a mile away and we went to St Clement's

School when we were children. We had seen it – it was called the 'The Royal Albert Orphan Asylum', a refuge for young orphans. It was not a 'mad-house', it was a refuge! The sign was taken away at a later date and the world 'asylum' deleted but it was on there when I went in. There used to be an Asylum Lane. They took the sign down and put another in its place. The colours of the new sign were green and yellow. The letters were white or yellow on a dark green background, reading 'The Royal Albert Orphanage'.

The first jobs we had to do when we were quite young, about eight, were to clean the knobs, taps and basins. Later on we would polish the knives and forks. We had to clean the shoes. I don't know whether we cleaned our own shoes or other children's! There was a little greenhouse where we cleaned the shoes – a little round glass building. It was a properly built thing, like one of those cab-men's hutches, popular before the war with glass all the way round. It was in the centre of the building, the side of the centre anyway, because the dining-hall was in between. You see, there was a yard as you came through the front-hall.

The front-hall was kept in beautiful condition and the steps were whitened by the boys. We did our own jobs in the orphanage.

The dormitories were scrubbed every week and there would be a row of girls on our hands and knees scrubbing and you had to do one patch and then the next patch had to be done half-way over the other one so that you wouldn't have a blank mark. The matron or one of the teachers were always there watching you. You had to scrub so many times and she would tell you when to stop. So much time spent on one patch!

In the mornings we had to get the cocoa for breakfast and stoke the boilers. There were two boilers in the kitchen where they washed up, beyond the cook's kitchen and the scullery. I don't know what the two big boilers were for, but we had to make them up. The one was to heat the big urns. We had cocoa in one and porridge in the other and the porridge always came out lumpy, with great big lumps as big as my fist, sometimes. I kept saying, 'I don't think Oliver Twist would come for a second helping!'

We had to do the vegetables in the play-shed. With new potatoes we put them in a big bath and brushed and scrubbed them. They were home-grown in the gardens. The orphanage employed a gardener. On one occasion we peeled the potatoes too thickly and we had to write out a hundred times, 'It is a crime to waste food!'

The matron used to tell us a story, 'Now there was once a gentleman who wanted to engage a servant and there were three questions he asked: "What do you do: do you eat the rind of the cheese, do you scrape it off, or do you cut if off?" To cut it was waste, to eat it was wrong, but to scrape it was right!'

The washing up was done in the scullery on a rota basis. We looked after the milk. We used to skim it. The staff had the cream off the top and we had the rest. We had to make butter as well. The orphanage had three cows, several pigs and chickens – that was a boy's job though.

The dormitories were good and large. We went to school about 9 o'clock in the morning. There were three classes: infants, middle and senior. The teachers had their own school classroom. Sometimes they took us for walks on a Thursday afternoon. Visiting day was the first Wednesday in the month. Any money we had given was put into the bank. Miss Bird, one of the teachers, collected it from us.

We were left to our own devices after school. Sometimes the matron would invite us into the boardroom to play rummy. Instead of money we used buttons.

We always had two in a bath at bath time. It was smashing because it was really hot water and to have a real bath was lovely. In those days you didn't have baths so much. There wasn't a proper bathroom in most homes. Most families would use a tin bath. Friday night was our bath night and we had to wash our hair as well. The teachers were there to supervise. They were nice big baths though, not these little baths you get today. The bathroom was really nice, it was very well kept. On bath night we just undressed and got in. Other girls were waiting in the dormitory. When we came out they went in, carrying their nightdress and their clothes to get undressed in the bathroom. We went into the bathroom in twos. I can't remember whether the next two came in whilst we were out of the bath drying ourselves. They could have done. I only know that it was a treat to get into a nice hot foaming bath with carbolic soap, and afterwards dry ourselves with big bath towels.

The girls had a little dormitory and a big dormitory. The boys had the attic as well, but we didn't use the attic because there were only 32 of us, whereas there were 60 boys. We didn't use our names either. We were called by our number. Mine was 76 and I think my brother Charles was 25. All our clothes were marked by this number.

When I first went into the orphanage we wore long navy-blue serge dresses with a lace collar and a straw boater, black stockings and boots. But I don't think that lasted very long. Then we wore velour coats and felt hats and we were quite modem for the time. In the summer we wore printed dresses, but they were different colours with the same design. It wasn't too bad really.

We went for walks on a Thursday, Saturday and Sunday. On Saturday we went to the pictures at the local St John's cinema. The Godsauls who owned it let us go in free.

At Christmas time we went to the pantomimes. When we visited the Scala cinema in the city we used to come out with a packet of sweets and an orange.

At first we went to St John's Church but when Canon Diggle came we went to St Clement's. I reckon he got it altered. We would march to church in crocodile fashion. The choir was upstairs at St Clement's Church and so were we and the choir boys would 'give the eye' to the girls. Later the choir boys came along Henwick Road and the girls were up at the windows waving to them. The boys would come up Orphanage Lane and cut across over the fence into the playground. The girls would be in the sickroom sending down notes to the boys and the boys would send notes back, with paper tied to a pebble with a bit of string. It was great fun. The girls let the string down from the sickroom then pulled the notes back up again. This went on for quite a while. One of the girls eventually married one of the choir boys.

This one night the girls from the big dormitory came into our little dormitory. They were all in there facing Henwick Road looking out for the choir boys when the master came round with his dog, walking his dog last thing at night as was his custom before locking up. He went by and of course the girls were all up at the windows and he saw them. They were sent for and all had to go down for the slipper. So I went down with them. All the dormitory had to go and they all had the slipper but the girls said that Muriel Parsons wasn't one of them, so I was allowed to go back upstairs. I didn't get the slipper because I wasn't among those up at the window. One of the choir boys, a chap named Alf Wood, married my friend Rosey Miles. My other friend was Rosemary Fitzer. Rosemary went into the orphanage after me as she didn't go in until she was nine. Rosey Miles and Lucy Miles went in later as well.

Miss Atkinson used to do the POs, the 'poor objects'. If you had anything wrong with you, she'd do the dressings. She made the clothes as well including all the coats. We had a Miss Severn helping in the sewing room when the coats were being made and the dresses and we worked in the sewing room after a certain age. I think it was from about fourteen. We made all our own clothes in the sewing room.

We had school examinations in the orphanage and gained prizes. But the only trouble was that there were no scholarships. In the school there were a lot of clever ones. It was sad they never had a chance.

Our nightdresses were made of white calico and the knickers were the old fashioned ones. The nickname for the knickers was 'drawers'. We had long dresses down to here! The drawers came half-way down your legs. The dresses came down to just above your ankles, because we wore boots. We had to embroider both the drawers and dresses. We did feather stitches on them all. The clothes we made in the sewing room, we wore when we left the orphanage.

Miss Hardman, a friend of Mrs Gwyn, did the washing. We helped out in the laundry. There was a row of big wooden tubs to do the washing in. They also had a clothes-horse on wheels to dry out the clothes and sheets.

The boys wore those Eton collars and hacking jackets when I first went into the institution.

At Christmastime and New Year concerts were held in the dining hall on the stage. *A Midsummer Night's Dream* was put on. People came to see us perform.

We were talking just now about Visiting Day and the money we got. We had to put it in the bank. If we had any odd coppers we kept it.

When we went out for a walk, we walked miles. We walked as far as Powick, to Powick School. Then we ran back in time for tea. We were dismissed after a while as we weren't in crocodile file then. We ran a long way in front of the teacher until we reached the shops. Then we spent our pennies in the shops in Bromyard Terrace or in St John's but the teacher never got to know about it at all. We were supposed to give all our money in – we used to keep it!

In the dining hall there was a pianola. Sometimes when Lockey had his day off Mr Whitehead, the master, would entertain us, peddling away with this pianola, whilst we had our meals. The teachers would be on the stage overseeing. I remember the first time we had a wireless. It was a great big thing on the table, on the platform. It was quite a novelty.

We ate hash on a Monday but it wasn't like the cook book. Everything was mixed up together with the barley. It was thick stuff and put me off hash for a long time. The cabbage was black. It was horrible. It put me off cabbage for life. I still don't eat it!

The tea was sometimes greasy after the other cooking had been done in the urns. It was horrid! There were two urns, which were used for everything and they weren't cleaned out very well. We had porridge and cocoa in the morning, then it was washed out ready for dinner. Soup first, then potatoes and the vegetables. Then greasy tea for tea-time!

I don't know where the meat got cooked. We had roast on a Wednesday and on a Sunday. I think we had bread and cheese on Saturday. Very meagre and lentil soup with chunks of bread and cheese. The soup was clear and you could see the lentils in the bottom. Ugh!

I can't remember nice meals – only Christmas. We were all right then. They were lovely Christmases in there. On Christmas Day we had pork and Christmas pudding. After dinner we opened our presents which our parents had brought us – you know, the family. At night-time we all gathered around the Christmas tree. It was a huge tree with all the presents underneath. We all had three presents each off the Christmas tree. I've still got one of mine that I had after I'd left, because you could go up after you'd left the orphanage at Christmas time and you were quite welcome and you had a gift off the Christmas tree. They used to shout your name out. All the gifts were donated by benefactors. New Year was just as good. We had dancing. Well, of course they used to keep up the New Year, David Whitehead, because they were Scottish. It was all like Christmas again. We had a good time then.

I don't think we had much punishment really. I don't remember getting punished a great deal. It happened of course. I managed to avoid it – I was a bit backward in coming forward. I kept my nose down. I'm a bit like that now. My brother however had weals on his hands and bottom.

We had to cook the staff suppers some nights. That's when we were learning to cook. I wouldn't say they had better food – they had the cream of everything – but still! We made their puddings and dishes – quite simple really.

On Sunday we had to go to church in the morning. We didn't go at night. We had to line up with our hair all plaited. They didn't like you having curly hair. If you had curly hair you had to brush it straight back: the girls, anyway. We plaited it over Saturday night and if you hadn't done it you'd be told off. We didn't have our hair cut; we had long hair, they didn't allow short hair. I don't remember wearing ribbons. We wore straw hats or felt hats. We had to line up on a Sunday morning to see if our hair was tidy to go to church. We had it trimmed now and again.

We used to take Epsom Salts about twice a year.

The milkman came round with a churn in the morning. A boy used to help him. The milk churns had taps and we would turn the taps on and run away! We used to go for a loaf of bread just round the corner and pick the crust off all the way round!

We played truant under the railway bridge because my grandfather was a signalman at Henwick Station – only 5 minutes walk away. My brother Cyril played under the Henwick subway with others for weeks and my grandfather hadn't seen them until one of the other signalmen told my grandfather. He got the slipper. Oh, he was a tartar! Cyril wouldn't have gone to the orphanage – Grandma would have kept him at home.

You see, my grandmother wanted to adopt us all but my mother wouldn't let her. If she'd adopted us we wouldn't have gone into the orphanage. It was a big house, there was plenty of room but she was very strict. My mother was like me, a bit backward in coming forward. She wouldn't speak up for herself and my grandmother was really the boss. But as regards the adoption my mother put her foot down with a firm hand!

In the morning the girls used to try and wake you up when you were in bed. Some girls talked in their sleep. I think I slept well, I was a good sleeper.

When we first went into the Royal Albert we wore long drawers but I don't think it was for very long. The drawers had a split down the front by the crutch. We wore a liberty bodice and a long petticoat and a thick blue serge dress.

People don't like it being known that they were brought up in the orphanage. Rose, a friend of mine, didn't tell her family that she was brought up there. I don't know whether they know to this day. They won't know now, because she's passed on.

Thinking back we had a jolly good education. It was up to us to learn at the time. I was no good at school. The only thing I was good at was sewing and knitting. But I could write and I like drawing. I could draw maps. I didn't like arithmetic, and very often I had to stand on the table when I didn't know anything. Lockey made us stand on the table! I learnt more after I left the orphanage. We were very sheltered really.

We played hockey and netball and rounders. We were good. We didn't play matches, though, not like the boys. We used to do cartwheeling round the playground and leap-frogging. Wouldn't do it now! We also went into the fields to play. We didn't do any gardening, but we picked up the apples and windfalls. The boys dug the far garden and years later it was done with a tractor.

We had a good bonfire night. I don't know where we got the wood from, I suppose it was from around the grounds.

The orphanage ground was thickly populated with trees. There was an orchard right down to Oldbury Road, right up to the railway. It all belonged to the orphanage. I mean they were wealthy by the time they sold all the produce. I don't know what happened to the money!

We went for a long walk along the river down Hilton Road, to the Dog and Duck Ferry and along the riverside, along the river right up to Hallow. There must be a little footbridge somewhere there because we went over this little footbridge and I fell in the water and my straw hat went floating down the brook! They took me into Mary Aphlett's aunt, one of the girls' aunts in Hallow Road, because I was all wet and they kept me in bed for nearly a week. Whether it was a punishment or not I don't know. They thought I had a cold. Charles and I were a bit weak when we went into the orphanage and they gave us Brimstone and Treacle and Codliver Oil and Malt. That was funny because the straw hat went floating down the brook. Whether they ever got it back I don't know. Trust me to fall in. I couldn't have hurt myself. I wasn't very old – about eight I expect. I must have cried. It wasn't very deep.

The Misses Cane used to be on the Committee, and they had a very big house in Hallow Road where they lived. We went there for afternoon tea parties in the grounds. Their country house was very much like a stately home boasting white columns at the front. Fountains played in the grounds cascading sprays of water. We had a wonderful time playing in the maze – we often got lost. The gardens were beautiful with lots of rhododendrons of various shades and colours and grass and yew hedges stretching away as far as the eye could see. For tea we always had strawberries and cream. It was all so different from being in an institution.

One of my best friends was Miriam Brown. She had lovely red hair. I liked her very much. She was John Brown's sister. They weren't all nice – the children up there.

Everything looks so big when you're small. I remember the big yard where the dairies were. The stairs in the orphanage building were wide. They were wide enough to get two or three across. You came up the stairs and went along a little corridor before you got to the dormitory where there was a bedroom on one side and a room on the other. Miss Lowby had one room and the cook had the other. There was a window overlooking the dormitory. It had a curtain where they could check upon us all.

When I left the orphanage they sent me to Hillstone School in Great Malvern. I was employed as a kitchen-maid, and I didn't like it. I stuck it out for ten months and then I ran away. My grandmother sent me back but she brought me back again. I didn't like housework, anyway. I'd had enough of it in the orphanage!

GEORGE ALFRED CHARLES SIMMONDS (1924–32)

I have just read your letter in the *Worcester Evening News and Times* – I am an orphanage 'Old Boy'.

I entered the Royal Albert Orphanage on 16 April 1924 – I was just seven years old – and stayed there until 1932. The master and matron at that time were Mr David Whitehead and his wife Mrs Agnes Whitehead. The head teacher was Mr Lockey and the two lady teachers were a Miss Bird and a Miss Darby. The gardener was, if I remember rightly, Mr Lodge or Lodger, and the chief cowman was Mr Coombes. We had our own Scout troop.

Discipline was harsh but very fair and we were a self-contained unit. The big change came when we left St John's Parish and came under St Clement's. The rector of St Clement's, the Rev. Diggle, was one of the finest men I ever met. Incidentally, he later became Bishop of Oxford. He changed a Poor Law Institution to a Home. Boys were allowed to speak to girls and we participated with outside teams for football, hockey and cricket.

The grass in front of the institution was cut regularly by the boys under the supervision of the headmaster Mr David Whitehead. When finished it looked like a bowling green!

It was a hard time but looking back I found companionship, which later stood me in good stead when I was called up for the army.

I left the Royal Albert Orphanage on 4 June 1932 and was apprenticed in carving to Mr Rackstraw, Castle Street, Worcester.

Some years ago two or three of us 'Old Boys' arranged a dinner and fund raising activities for all old boys and girls we could contact, some being in Canada and Australia.

ROSA MAY THOMAS (1928–36)

I went in the RAO in March 1928. I cannot remember who took me in but I was quite happy as I had left another home with lots of children, called the 'Cottage Homes' at Worcester, up the Droitwich Road. The Royal Albert Orphanage was a very large place. I got lost in it, but made friends very easily. I was nearly eight years old.

The oldest girl worked in the parlour. Her main purpose was looking after the master and matron. Every morning without fail she took a cup of tea up to the matron in bed. Then she laid the table in the office for the staff breakfast. The dormitory girl made the beds and cleaned the bathroom. Another girl scrubbed the passages which were made of red tiles. The toilets and wash basins were the next job. Then the girls had their breakfast! Afterwards the playroom was cleaned, the brass knobs on all the doors were polished. Other rooms in the orphanage were likewise dealt with including shaking all the mats, then sweeping the playground.

Mr Lockey looked after the boys. He was Scoutmaster and taught the oldest class. Miss Bird was the girls' teacher. We called her 'Dickey Bird'. She taught the youngest girls and Miss Darby taught the older ones. Miss Atkinson was the sewing teacher. When we left school at the age of fourteen, we went in the sewing room to make all the boys' shirts and girls' frocks and darn the boys' socks. I hated it.

The master's brother had three children. They came to the RAO for holidays to be with their aunt and uncle. They were Muriel who has since passed away and Dorothy who I still write to after many years. She now lives in New Zealand and has a big family out there – some in Australia. Muriel was staying with us and slept in the big girls' dormitory. She was doing the snake dance up and down the dormitory when Miss Bird came up and caught her. Then she took off her high heels and gave us all a whack on our backsides, even the ones who were asleep!

When King George V died we all had to go into the dining hall. They played 'God Save the King' that many times on the wireless and we had to stand up every time! Matron got fed up and gave up in the end and we sat down for the rest of the National Anthems.

One day someone said the world was coming to an end. We girls all sat round in the playroom and said goodbye to our best friends and waited for the end to come – but we are still here!

We had two dormitories. The boys were on the left of the building and the girls on the right. There was only a locked door between us. The little girls slept in one dormitory and the older girls in the big dormitory which was along a passage up two stairs. A bathroom, toilets, wash basins were at the top end. Bath night was two in a bath on a Saturday night and hair was washed until you could do it yourself. The cook's bedroom was next to the little dormitory. There was another bedroom up a set of stairs but it was never used only to store things in.

The living room was our playroom. We had a locker to keep our things in. We collected all sorts of things, mainly rubbish. Every now and again matron would come along and tip everything out on the floor! Then we had to find our own things and put them back, not all of it, as we were supposed to throw a lot away.

The dining hall was a very large room with a stage. The boys had three long tables and the girls two. Dinner was served from a long table at the top by the staff. Older boys and girls had to go up and take the food to the others. For breakfast and tea we had one and a half rounds of bread and Mayo margarine – one inch thick. We called them doorsteps. Every other Sunday we had jam or rock buns. Dinner was roast, stew and at Christmastime we had liver when they killed the pigs. We used to hear them squeal then we knew! Puddings were rice, sago, tapioca, semolina and spotted dick. Pancakes for the day were cooked in the big kitchen on a flat electric stove. We always had Christmas pudding – the mixture was done in a pigs' trough – clean mind you and we all had a stir and a wish. Great. Everything was cooked by steam, vegetables as well.

We had a big fire in a room next to the kitchen which we older girls looked after. It heated the water for the whole building and was fuelled by coke. The washing up was done in this room. We girls used to pinch bread and margarine for a midnight feast. We had quite a few of those.

The corridors were made of long red tiles which we had to scrub. I was cleaning the corridor towards the kitchen one morning, leaving the sides of the corridor untouched. When I had finished matron was standing there. Did I get a telling off. 'Go back and start again!

The open-air swimming pool was behind the cottage where Mr Lockey lived. A gardener had it after him. We swam there often and went in for badges for the Girl Guides. I got my badges. If you didn't have a costume you went in naked but you had to go in. The boys would climb the walls to have a look at us. Then the squealing started. All good fun though. We were no angels!

Discipline was strict in some ways, doing this and that. There were a lot of home rules which was right with so many children. I pretended to run away once but I was only in the playground hiding. Miss Gossit was looking for me. I could hear her in the corridors as she wore high heels. She went to the master and told him I had run away. He said, 'Don't worry, she'll come back when she is hungry.' I didn't get very far and fortunately I didn't get punished!

Most punishment was standing in a corner. When they started to put electric pylons on land, they put one in the orphanage grounds and some of the boys climbed up it. People from across the road had phoned in to tell the master about it. He went and waited at the bottom for them to come down. At dinnertime he came into the dining hall and they had the cane across their backsides on the stage in front of us all.

We went on the roof through the bedroom window! On top of the wardrobe was a big bag or something like a sledge. We would get it down, put it out of the window, then get into it and slide down. It was to use when there was a fire. We had great fun. Once they left the window open and the master called for me, 'Rosa Thomas!' thinking I had opened the window. My friend Barbara Cook had done it but I got the blame. I had to go down to the office. As I stood there matron came and asked me why I was there. Then she told me to get back to the playroom before he came back. I went mighty fast I can tell you!

We girls played hockey and cricket in the summer. The boys played football and cricket. A hockey ball hit me in the left eye the Saturday before I left the RAO so I left with a black eye. I played for the orphanage team after I left, mostly as a goalie. I loved the game. We had Scouts and Guides. We did our badges for swimming, cooking and all sorts.

The boys did the farming and gardening. We had lots of fruit trees. We girls used to go scrumping the fruit. There was really no need, as they gave us plenty of fruit. We carried them in our knickers as they had elastic bottoms.

It was St John's Church we went to when I first went in the RAO. Then we went to St Clement's. I don't know why. The vicar was the Rev. Diggle; we called him Father Diggle. He was later made Dean of Worcester Cathedral. He gave me confirmation lessons. I was baptised at St George's, Worcester and confirmed at All Saints, Worcester. Later I was married at All Saints in West Bromwich. We were going to lessons one night and matron halted us, saying, 'Someone has scent on.' We said, 'No, it was scented soap.' Matron said, 'Fetch it.' But of course there wasn't any!

We only went to school in the RAO, not outside. There were three classrooms – the older ones' was down the boys' end. So we had to walk through the front hall to get there from the girls' end. After Mr Lockey left a Mr Parry came.

One day six of us were coming out and matron stopped us by the front door. 'Halt,' she said. 'You go and fetch me a pair of scissors.' When we'd got them she said, 'Now lift up your shirts.' Then she cut off all our pockets and there was a little pile on the ground! (Maybe they had been smuggling food to the boys?). You see the older girls had been carrying on with some boys in the lane that ran along the girls' playground – they got through the railings. Someone had rung the orphanage. While they were with the boys we younger ones did their scrubbing for them, so that was the end of that. Mind you we did our share, as we had a dark passage in the laundry and the big driers that pulled out and we used to meet the boys there to have a kiss or two. I cannot remember ever being found out!

We always walked in crocodile as we went for a very long walk, about ten miles on Saturdays. So we used to pray for rain so that we could go into St John's to the pictures. Nevertheless I didn't like the pictures either. So I said they hurt my eyes and I got away with it!

Once a year we went up the River Severn on the steamer called the *Belle*. Another year we went to Barry Island. Someone gave the money for it. We travelled on the Midland Red bus. It was great. We went for a ride on a donkey. Margaret Fletcher, Dorothy (matron's niece) and myself. Two on one donkey. Margaret fell off between the two donkeys. What a laugh. They gave us money to spend.

We wore high laced boots and grey thick coats with a sailor collar when I first went into the RAO. Hats were a soft material, rain proof, I guess. There was a tunic with blouse, vest, combinations, knickers, and if you were older, stays with bones up, which we took off and put under the mattress, till the matron had a raid for anything hidden. We also wore black stockings and shoes. Sunday was the same. In the summer after many years we had frocks made of Miss Muffet print, really nice, with straw brim hats.

At Christmas we had three presents, ludo, snakes and ladders and tiddley winks if you were a Girl Guide. Scouts had a diary. Christmas Eve we had a present on the foot of our beds. The night before the people of St Clement's came round and gave us a present on our beds. We called that night Christmas Adam – it was the day before Christmas Eve! I had a chocolate turkey. Never seen one since but it was good.

On New Year's Eve matron had a dance for all her friends, all dressed up in evening dress. We used to watch through the skylights. Of course

Rosa Thomas in 1936, the day she left the orphanage, taken in the laundry washroom

the master and matron were Scots. We danced the old fashioned dances – foxtrot, waltzes, lancers, military two-step and the polka. We had great times.

When the time came to leave, we were fitted out with all our clothes, some we had made ourselves. We had a trunk to put them in. On leaving we had to go to the vicarage for talks with a Bible class teacher. The day I left matron took me to Tardebigge. They sent a car for us. Even though I was nearly sixteen I cried all the way. I didn't want to leave; the big world was frightening. Matron told me the do's and don'ts about the boys of the world! The first job they gave me as a kitchen maid, was to peel the potatoes which I still hate to this day. I had £1. 3*s*. 0*d* a month. Mrs Macdonnell got me a bike, it was £3 and I had to pay ten shillings a month until it was paid. I did some miles on it.

As you see I am not a good writer. My best at school was history and geography. But please don't pity me for being an orphan child. I have had a good life, a happy life. There were bad moments but I am still happy.

GOD BLESS ALL, ROSA.

MARGARET HARRIS (1929–36)

Article quoted from the Worcester Evening News:

Reading your 'Memory Lane' article about life in the Royal Albert Orphanage brought back memories of my years there from 1929 to 1936.

I must say we had better times than seems to have been the case with our successors in the late 1940s. [*See 1940s 'Reunion Reminiscences'.*]

We were never given left-over food to eat meal after meal.

The master and matron then, Mr and Mrs Whitehead, were a devoted couple and very kind, but also very severe at times.

We had very happy times at Christmas and were usually given three different games plus sweets, an orange, nuts and apples. There were also New Year parties as the Whiteheads were Scots.

At Easter we used to go over to the Rectory to the Rev. Diggle and hunt for Easter eggs. It was great fun and he also made sure every child had one, even if we weren't lucky enough to find one.

Outings were a trip on the river steamer *Belle* either to Stourport or Tewkesbury and we went long walks on Saturdays or to St John's cinema if it was wet. We always hoped it would rain so we could see a serial called *Hero of the Flames.*

We also went on holiday to Barry Island. While we were there we were given good conduct marks and when we came to leave, if we were lucky, the boys had a bicycle and the girls a sewing machine. I am still using mine today!

My brother had a bicycle. He was also in the choir at St Clement's and I hated the time when I had to leave.

4

THE 1930s

Adolf Hitler dominated this decade and the decade to come when he was appointed Chancellor of Germany in 1933.

The abdication crisis rocked Britain and the Empire. In 1936 we had three kings: George V, Edward VII and George VI.

Then at 11 o'clock on 3 September 1939, Britain declared war on Germany.

In the orphanage the years of Mr David Whitehead's headmastership came to an end in 1937. He had been at his post since 1907.

Mr C. Parry became headmaster and Miss E. Gossett, matron: positions they were to hold till 1940.

VIOLET BERTHA WILLIAMS (1930–37)

Referring to your recent letter in the *Worcester Evening News* I write to tell you that I was in the RAO for eight years from 1930–37. I was admitted at the age of eight after my father died from TB brought on by his service in the 1914–1918 war. My mother was left with seven children and another baby on the way, due seven months after my father passed away (my father died in the January and my brother was born the following August), and she was left literally penniless.

I vividly remember my first day at the RAO. We were taken up by my mother and an aunt and I felt very sad, but my mother told me it would not be for long; as soon as she could get a bigger house and some new furniture we would be going home again and I sort of believed that. I went into the RAO with my younger brother, Sidney. Little did I realise I would be in the orphanage for eight years. I felt homesick most of the time I was in the RAO. We were able to go home for two weeks a year, one week in June and one week in September. I always felt terribly homesick after spending the two weeks at home and wished I could stay with my mother and never have to go back to the RAO. I do not think I had much feeling for the place. I just felt very scared and did not know what to expect.

The older girls were very bossy, I remember one being very nasty to me because I held my knife in the left hand and the fork in my right hand.

The master and matron at the RAO were named Mr and Mrs David Whitehead. They were Scotch and very Victorian. The teachers were Mr Lockey who was also Scoutmaster, followed by Mr Smith and Mr Parry. The female staff were Miss Darby followed by Miss Bates, and I remember a Miss Doyley who didn't seem to stay very long. Also a Miss Bird who died from cancer and I remember attending the funeral. Miss Bird, to my mind, died rather suddenly. She was at the orphanage one day and about a week later she died. This was in 1933 or 1934. I remember very, very plainly going to the funeral and walking down McIntyre Road behind the cortège to be buried in McIntyre cemetery, and for some reason I didn't feel terribly upset. I don't know why because I was very, very fond of Miss Bird. Our Girl Guide captain at one time was Miss Spreckley. The assistant matron was Miss Atkins; I thought she was very motherly and when she left we had a Miss Gossett in her place. When Miss Atkins left she went to live somewhere round the Ross-on-Wye area, where she originally came from. I always feel when I go to Ross-on-Wye that that's where Miss Atkins lives.

I quite enjoyed school and I think we had a reasonable education. There were three classes but I do not remember how long we stayed in each class but probably about two years in each as we left school at fourteen years old.

I was put into the orphanage kitchen to learn my role as a kitchen-maid when I was fourteen. It was very hard work, black-leading the cooking grate, cleaning large tea-urns (copper and brass) and scrubbing the kitchen and part of the scullery floor which had red tiles.

We had to scrub the playroom floor frequently and the teacher used to tell us to scrub, scrub, scrub, then gave instructions to wipe, I also had a period when I had to scrub a long corridor every morning. My very first chore when I was about eleven years old was to clean all the door knobs round the girls' area of the building.

I was never impressed with the food. I think we had the same meals every day for the whole eight years I was an inmate. Breakfast was always porridge which was like gruel with golf balls in, very insipid, and with that we had two rounds of bread and marg.

The lunches were as follows:

Monday:	cottage pie, rice pudding.
Tuesday:	pea soup, suet pudding (currant or treacle).
Wednesday:	roast mutton, potatoes and veg.
Thursday:	hash, made with fatty mutton (very greasy).
Friday:	sausage and mash.
Saturday:	pea soup, bread and cheese.
Sunday:	roast meat and veg.

On Tuesday it was our favourite pudding, treacle duff or spotted dick. If there was any food over you were picked at random for a second helping. i.e. little boys, little girls, older boys, older girls. As soon as you had finished your helping you turned round with your leg half over the wooden form hoping it would be your turn to go for 'seconds'. Miss Bird would say, 'Any of the little boys off the bottom table, any of Miss Bird's little boys would like a second helping?' You turned hoping it would be your turn for a second helping, with your legs over the bench so you'd get up quickly. 'Any of the big girls, any of Miss Bird's little boys, any of the middle boys?' – and so they went on. Oh! I wonder if it'll be my turn today. Oh! I hope it's me. You used to scramble up there. I'm sure a lot of old boys and girls can remember that incident because it really was something to look forward to on a Tuesday.

Sometimes the rice pudding was made with milk just on the turn and I hated it but you were not allowed to leave anything so I just swallowed it, trying not to taste it. For tea on Friday we had dry bread and treacle. I remember the bread used to go very dry and it was hard to get the treacle to stay on the bread. On Sunday for tea we had jam or cake, and one egg per year on Easter Sunday.

Life in the dormitory at times was very amusing. Friday night was bath night and when I was about ten years old I considered I was a bit of a favourite with the teacher, Miss Bird, who supervised bath night. We were bathed two at a time; the same bath water was used for six of us. On this particular night Miss Bird was very attentive, helping me dry after my bath and eventually coming round each bed and tucking us in. As she tucked me in she felt something under my mattress which was a girls' annual book. We were not allowed to have books in the dormitory so instead of having a tuck-in and a goodnight kiss I ended up having a spanking which upset me very much.

We were up in the top dormitory when the staff had gone into dinner around 8 p.m. We used to dress up in the concert clothes which were stored in the dormitory. No doubt we made quite a noise and suddenly someone heard footsteps so we all dived into our beds, still dressed up, shaking with fear, in case any of us was asked to get out of bed.

Every Sunday morning we went to church and when I got older we attended Bible Class in St Clement's Parish Hall. Our instructor was a lady called Miss Rogerson; she was very kind and I remember we went to tea at her house which was opposite the RAO in Henwick Road. We had lovely hot pikelets which were delicious. The rector of St Clement's Church was Rev. Diggle; he lived in the rectory in Henwick Road. One Easter time we went to the rectory garden to play 'Hunt the Easter Eggs'. (Sadly the rectory is now demolished and replaced by flats.) The Easter eggs were hidden all around the garden in hedges, under flower pots, in buckets, under flowers and you kept all those you found. I never found any and felt very disappointed. We sometimes sang anthems in church and I remember one Sunday morning singing Parry's 'Jerusalem', and some old gentleman in the congregation said it brought tears to his eyes.

Punishment was always in the form of the cane, and there was plenty of that.

Most Saturday and Sunday afternoons we had to go for long walks; we walked for miles during the time we were out. We obviously got very hungry and all we had when we got back was two rounds of bread and marg. and at about 8 p.m. we had half a slice of bread and dripping and a cup of watery cocoa.

Our parents were allowed to visit us once a month and they usually brought a few goodies. If we were lucky enough to have bananas we always ate the skins as well!

At one period, I suppose I was about fourteen years old, we spent part of the day in the sewing room mending the boys' socks. The socks were put in the middle of the table and you just picked a pair at random and had to use a darning mushroom and do a really neat darn. Some of the socks almost had a foot worn away, but they still had to be mended.

Some Saturday afternoons if the weather was bad, and we could not go for a walk we went to St John's cinema which was really exciting, or we walked around St John's and were able to spend 2*d.* on sweets. We spent ages choosing the sweets which lasted longest. Miss Bird kept the cash books and providing you had a few pennies in your account you could draw out just 2*d.* No more.

Christmas was quite an exciting time. On Christmas Eve we had just one present left on our bed. We went to church on Christmas Day. I don't remember if we had a real Christmas lunch; I think we may have had roast pork and Christmas pudding. After lunch they used to bring round a big clothes basket with presents from our parents, relations, and friends. This was quite a nice thing. After tea on Christmas Day we had a party with dancing, games and another present off the large decorated Christmas tree. That was really the highlight of the year.

In the eight years that I was in the RAO we had one day's outing which was on a Midland Red bus and we went to Barry Island in the summer of 1935. That was the first time I had seen the sea. I was probably fourteen years old then. I had never travelled outside Worcester before this. It just seemed like another world to me to see the seaside and the donkeys and it was a very nice sunny day. I remember we stayed on the beach for quite a while and then towards 4 o'clock we were taken into a café and had tea.

One incident which never fails to amuse my family happened when I got to about twelve years old. I used to help in the scullery to slice and put the margarine on the bread. With 96 children to be catered for it was quite a chore. Occasionally my brother would call round from the boys' playground which was quite near the scullery and I would put two slices of bread and marge just inside my 'bloomer leg' (they reached just below the knee and were elasticated) and I would just lift my skirt and hand it to him.

One thing that always sticks in my mind is the fact that we only ever had one egg each year, which we had on Easter Sunday. While I was working in the kitchen, I would be fourteen, I got on very well with the cook (Miss Morris) and the laundry mistress (a lassie from Lancashire called Miss McGrath). So on one or two occasions when the master and matron and teaching staff had gone into breakfast Miss Morris would let me sit at the kitchen table and have an egg and bacon breakfast which was really something. Also I remember they asked Mrs Whitehead if they could take me to the pictures one afternoon.

I was the fourth eldest in our family and I had two younger brothers with me in the RAO and we were not allowed to mix with them, only on a social evening when matron brought along her wind-up gramophone and we were taught a few dances: polka, waltz, the lancers and the military two-step. One lunch time one of my brothers came round to the girls' playground to show me some little toy which he had bought on our Christmas shopping expedition. He had bought a little accordion from Woolworths for *6d*. The master caught us chatting and we had a real good caning. My brother had to touch his toes and he had six of the best.I had four strokes of the cane, two on each hand. It didn't hurt that much but I felt very upset because this was the first caning that I'd had.

We had these little social evenings when the boys and girls could mix together under supervision. My brother Sidney absolutely hated the orphanage, so much that when everything was in full swing he'd get off over the fields and go and visit my mother who lived just a little way away. It was a regular thing that he did on these occasions, to get over the fence and go there for the evening and get back in time before the social finished. The strange thing was that nobody ever missed him. It was funny really because I knew where he was and you'd think the master and matron would have wondered why the three Williamses weren't together.

One of the highlights of our time in the orphanage was to go and see 'Miss Gertrude Fisher and her Dancing Pupils' at the Public Hall in Worcester. This was a very good concert and well worth going to. Just a few days before the concert we were playing and larking about up in one of the dormitories. I got on top of one of the high wardrobes and was jumping down on some mattresses. Whilst we were larking about and making a noise matron came as she very often did very, very quietly along the corridor and up the stairs and caught me on top of the wardrobe. The girls were shouting, 'Go on, jump, jump.' I was really absolutely frightened because it was a long way down from the top of this high wardrobe onto these mattresses. I was terrified to do it and my friend kept saying, 'Go on, just jump.' But as soon as I saw matron I didn't think about it twice, I just jumped. So for our punishment the three of us weren't allowed to go to this wonderful concert. So I plucked up courage to apologise thinking perhaps that she'd let us off and we'd be able to go. I said, 'Oh excuse me, Ma'am, I'm very sorry for what I did yesterday,' thinking that she would be very nice to me, but she said, 'Oh don't come humbugging round me, you just get off and tomorrow night whilst they're at the concert you'll go and clean all the out-houses.' We didn't go but cleaned these store houses out, where they kept bread and great chunks of margarine and some vegetables. Amongst the vegetables we found some sticks of rhubarb. We didn't have any sugar but we took them back into the playroom and started to eat all these big sticks of rhubarb which were very tasty.

My youngest brother, Leonard, came into the orphanage about two years after us. He was about eight and after he was established and put in amongst all the other boys he dashed down the Henwick Road and across the railway level-crossing and went back home again. On his return he got into awful trouble. The matron was very, very cross with him.

As regards my best friend, she had the job of doing the waiting on the tables for the staff, and she had access to the storeroom. One evening she said, 'I know what I'm going to do, I'm going to go in and get a tin of peaches' – and it was quite a big size tin of peaches. She went into the kitchen and got a tin opener and we went into the toilets and opened this big tin of peaches and we had half each and drank the juice out of it. I just can't remember what we did with the tin – that was the biggest problem – how could we discard the empty tin?

We had an RSPCA writing competition and we had to write about animals. I wrote an essay and won first prize in the Worcester schools. I went down to the public hall in Worcester and had my photograph in the *Berrows Journal* with the mayor of Worcester handing me the prize. I remember the book, it was called *Band of Mercy*. I have often thought how I would have loved to have kept that book but my sister was one of those people forever tidying the house and it went the way of all flesh!

I went into service at Severn Stoke on leaving the orphanage. I was there for only 11 months. We did an awful lot of washing up and used a great amount of soda. We didn't have washing up liquid like they have now. I was the kitchen-maid amongst a big staff at the home of Mrs Gresson. I had to do all the washing up and I've got ever such sensitive skin, so using all this soda I contracted eczema. I went to the doctor in Upton-on-Severn and I said to him, 'Well it's only just a little problem but I don't know what it is,' and he said, 'Oh, yes it's a little problem, but if you don't look after it, it's going to be a big problem!' I went back to where I was in service and the cook there was really horrid to me for some reason because the doctor had said, 'You won't be able to put your hands into water, with that on, you've just got to keep it dry.' And I remember the next morning she said, 'Oh! well, you'll have to get up and black-lead the grate.' Even though I'd got these great big bandages on! And so I had to see Mrs Gresson, who was the lady I was working for and she suggested I went home to my mother. So I left after only 11 months which was a shame because the rule of the orphanage was that if you stayed at the job they put you into for 12 months the orphanage gave you a sewing machine. And I missed out by one month. I tried ever so hard to say that I couldn't stop because I was sick, thinking they might let me have the machine! It was such a nice thing to have, especially in those days because we were taught a bit about sewing and mending. However, I just missed out by a month and that was that!

I would say when I left the RAO and was put into service aged sixteen years, I was nowhere near being ready to face the outside world. My life had been too sheltered and we never had any instructive talks, so really it was like living in a cage for eight years and suddenly being released. It certainly gave me an inferiority complex which has stayed with me all my life. I never ever felt happy whilst I was in the orphanage and always envied everyone who had a normal home life, however meagre. But that's life!

COLIN GORDON BAKER (1931–38)

I entered the RAO in 1931. Walking up the orphanage drive I thought back to the Dickensian days. I was just eight years old. The front steps were scrubbed white and the building looked like a haunted house! Mr and Mrs Whitehead were waiting there to greet me. It was like a chapter from *Tom Brown's Schooldays* – a place I will never forget. During my time there I was nicknamed 'Spud' and my orphanage number was 22.

The orphanage building was a landmark for miles around. There were playing fields at the back for football, cricket and hockey and an open-air swimming pool. The institution had extensive orchards. It was quite self-contained with a barn for the cows, a pig sty and numerous poultry. We all had different duties to perform such as 'spud boy' and 'boot boy'. We cleaned the toilets and washroom. All the passages, hall and dormitories were scrubbed. We sat on benches for our meals; they were hard as iron. If you were caught scrubbing big patches of floor or helping anyone out, you received six of the best. Funnily enough, I got caught helping my future wife out, as we used to meet the girls half-way. Girls were made to have their hair in a bun at the back.

Mr and Mrs Whitehead were in charge when I joined, followed by Mr Parry and Mr and Mrs Jenkins. We also had a Scoutmaster called Mr Lockey – a real right nasty piece of work and German by birth. Maggie McGrath was in charge of the laundry. Mr Grovner and Mr Winders were head gardeners.

We had a clothes drying green and coal house where we used to see who got the most kisses in with the girls. My 'pash' was Dorothy Allison who is alive today, living in Broom, near Evesham. We had folk dancing and pushed ourselves against the girls' lockers to see if they would break open. Once a month we had mixed swimming in the open pool. We played hockey with the girls. Each boy and girl had their 'fancy bit'. We had some good laughs really and some good hidings!

I made a date with Kath Gurney in the sewing room. We had very big laundry baskets so I hid in one under the socks that wanted darning. I got to the sewing room, waiting awhile; the door opened, I popped my head out of the basket and who should it be but matron. She gave a loud scream and fainted! I suffered for that!

We went to the laundry to see who wore the biggest knickers! It was a girl by the name of Iris Graves who was a real bully. Someone told Maggie McGrath, the lady who did the laundry, so we jumped on the dryers to annoy her. As she pulled one out we jumped on the next one. She couldn't catch us and was worn out and pouring with sweat. She said, 'I know you're in there!' Anyway, we thought it was fun.

Lights were always out at 8.30 at night. Bath night was three in a bath at a time. They scrubbed you clean so that you came out like a glowing ember. They felt your toothbrush to see if you had cleaned your teeth and if you broke wind at night, you had to stand at the foot of the bed for an hour with a book on the top of your head.

We had one egg a year. Breakfast was mostly porridge and if they asked, 'Did you want any more?' it reminded me of Oliver Twist as you got knocked over in the rush! Discipline was very strict. We got our hands and ears inspected before every meal. We said grace but you had to keep one eye open in case someone pinched a piece of bread off your plate. Punishment was the cane on your hands or bottom. I had plenty. I played up a lot but still no regrets.

One night a girl came across the flat roof to see Neville Roberts who was my dormitory boy in the little dormitory. I asked him why girls did that – he hit me so hard I ended up the other end of the dormitory and he said, 'You should be seen and not heard.' Later the windows were all nailed up.

Mr Grovner taught me how to play hockey, as he had played in India for a number of years. It really came in handy in the Navy, as I played for the Navy and the fleet.

You became a garden boy at about ten or eleven years of age. Seven of us in a line would dig a field in a day. It was really hard work, feeding the pigs and hens and milking the cows. I was shown how to strangle a fowl. I had to pluck one down in the coal house one day. I plucked it with no head, put it down to clean up the mess and the fowl stood up and walked away! I ran out of the coal house – it put the wind up me!

Every Sunday we marched to church at St Clement's. The Rev. Diggle was our vicar; he was a very nice man. It was a lovely church. I had the pleasure of going back there to my niece's wedding. It brought back memories.

The thing I remember mostly about school was a lot of rug making. We used to walk miles, to Whittington Tip, Rainbow Hill – we walked all over Worcester. As regards clothes the less said the better!

I'm afraid the orphanage didn't equip me to face the outside world. They just said, 'We have put you in the Navy for sixteen years.' I have known my wife Doris most of my life, also her sister Phyllis and husband Raymond, who were with us in the RAO. We have been married many, many years and I can honestly say Doris has been one in a million. We brought up three sons, so you can't wish for better than that. The orphanage taught you discipline and respect which never did us any harm. My wife's two sisters, Joyce and Phyllis, came through well but I'm sorry to say we lost Joyce, it was very tragic to us all. Well, that's about it.

I left the orphanage on 30 August 1938 to join the Royal Navy. I was fifteen and half years old.

Colin Baker married Doris Davies (see page 178).

JOAN MILLICENT POOLE (1931–41)

I recall only a little of my first impression of the Royal Albert Orphanage. I remember a little of the walk up the driveway to this very, very big place. I thought then, and still do, that it was such an ugly building. I walked up the driveway with my grandfather, two of my brothers and one sister. I was six years old. There were lots of children there and when anyone new arrived everyone came out to stare.

When I was older there were many jobs for us to do. Washing floors, sweeping and dusting were never ending chores. We found work in the laundry very hard, but we did have fun putting the many sheets through the mangles. Our arms were tired after turning the big handle but we had fun making the rollers on the mangle bang loudly. We would get into trouble for making so much noise but, when the teacher left the room, we would once again bang the rollers.

We would love to hide in the long, dark passages and jump out on someone. However, I always got a friend to walk with me down the darkened corridor.

There were lots of apple, pear and plum trees on the grounds. All around the playground were bars. I don't know why. We were not prisoners, at least we thought not. We would find a small girl and get her to go through the bars and get us what fruit she could pick up off the ground.

Then in cold weather, when there were no staff around, we'd get buckets of water to put down on the playground. The next morning we'd run out hoping that it had frozen and that we could slide around.

I did enjoy the grass hockey team, also the one quarter of an orange that we received at half time. In fact, maybe the orange was the attraction to the game, as we did not usually get oranges!

Well now, I did get my share of discipline at times. The boys seemed to get the cane more than the girls. We were very sad when that happened as the caning was always done in front of everyone.

I never did enjoy the food, but suppose it was hard to cook for so many. I remember big steamers in the kitchen and the cabbage that they cooked was not one bit appetizing. Anyway, it did prepare me for Army food in the later years.

Now, a few teachers' names that I remember. Mr and Mrs Whitehead, the master and matron, were very good people who I and many of the old boys and old girls (as they called us after we left RAO) went back to visit. They were very strict indeed but did their job well. I remember a special going away party for the Whiteheads. Lots of old boys and old girls were invited – some came from as far away as Canada. We little kids climbed onto the flat roof and looked through the skylight at everyone dancing below.

There was another master and matron later on whose names I know, but don't want to mention. They were not good people. Names of teachers that I remember were Miss Atkins, sewing teacher, Mr Parry, Miss Gossett, Miss Bird and some of course I can't recall. If we got all our work done Miss Bird would read us some of Charles Dickens' books – *David Copperfield*, *The Old Curiosity Shop*, and so on. This was a real treat.

We also learned to knit socks for the boys and how to mend socks and other clothing. We were never allowed to knit on Sunday.

I enjoyed going to church but sometimes we went three times a day. It was down the street and so it was a change for us from the orphanage.

If we had a penny for the collection we'd ask if we could have two half pennies instead. Then (you guessed it) we'd put one in our pocket and one in the collection. I'm sure that God forgave us!

I think about how we'd laugh at night in our beds. The teacher would yell at us and then we'd be quiet for a while. Then, we'd start laughing again.

At Christmas time we would all line up and go into the kitchen. Each child would get one stir of the big pot of Christmas pudding.

We had nice panama hats in the summer and felt hats in the winter. Both had the RAO emblem on them. We'd line up at the beginning of the summer, see how much we'd grown and then pass the clothes along to the next child. We had two different kinds of dresses – one with a buttercup pattern and one with forget-me-nots or violets. I liked the buttercup dress the best. When George VI was crowned we all got a navy blue serge dress with a white collar with blue and red dots on it. We called the dress our coronation dress. To this day I do not like navy serge dresses.

When I was sixteen years of age the orphanage got me a job as a kitchen maid at Hallow Park in Worcester. It was very hard work. Up early, off one whole day a month and one half day a week. Then at seventeen years of age, I left the service and went into the Army. So, the strict discipline and life in the orphanage helped prepare me to take orders in the Army.

RAYMOND JOHN DIGGER (1934–41)

My father took me into the Royal Albert Orphanage. I was eight years old. I remember the big door opening at the front. I'm sure we went through the big doors at the front, although there was a side door as well. Then we climbed up the big steps. I think it was matron who came out to meet us. Now I was always called 'Little Digger'. We had to go and see Dr Bunting to be examined – we had a full medical. I was given a number 2 and fell in with the routine. Naturally, I was upset on my first day there but that was only to be expected – so were the rest of the lads. You soon got in with the swing of things. And of course being the newest one there you had the lowest job to do. Then as one of the oldest left you moved up till you came to the top.

Visiting day was once a month but I can honestly say that in the eight years I was there I don't think anybody ever came to see me. Of course

Dad was always at work but I had a sister at Studley. My uncles and aunts could have come – they only lived on the doorstep.

I always remember Dad saying that if any of our relatives would have us, so well and good but nobody wanted us, so that was that and the orphanage was the last resort!

I have no regrets whatsoever. In fact we were better off than a lot of people in the 1930s. At least we always had a meal and good clothes. We certainly had some good times there.

My first recollection of going into the orphanage building was like entering into a New World; it seemed like something out of Dickens. The building was vast to a mere eight-year-old. It had three floors with a dormitory at the top. The orphanage was on a massive piece of ground – some sixteen acres, though sadly it's nearly all built on now except for a football field. The grounds went right out to the railway – we called it 'the far garden'. There were spiked railings all around the orphanage. We dug the gardens ourselves and looked after cows, pigs and fowls. I did the milking of the three cows and used to go and fetch the milk churns.

Except for the very young, everyone had some job to do before school, mostly scrubbing and polishing. The boys scrubbed the dining hall. I can't remember the girls doing it. We used to draw lots. If you got the bigger number you scrubbed where all the muck was but if you got number one you cleaned right against the wall where nobody walked. We were fetched back no end of times to do it again, especially when there were tide marks.

Mr Parry was in charge of the boys. You could tell what sort of mood he was in by the clothes he wore! He was pretty fair.

Funny incidents were plenty. We were watching a German bomber circling around on a gloomy day. When it came in very low we all started yelling and waving at it. Then it came round again and dropped bombs on the Meco and started machine gunning – we suddenly disappeared!

Life was not too bad. We took turns in telling stories in the dormitory – some were quite good and you always had a nice bed to sleep in.

When I went in the Army in January 1944 that was nothing to me because I knew all about discipline. I know it was a little stricter in the Army and you couldn't answer back, but with one thing and another it was nothing new to me although I know with some young men it used to break their hearts. I enjoyed myself in the Army. I was released in September 1947 from National Service.

We would climb up over the roofs. If you fell you'd break your neck but you never saw danger at the time. We would climb down the drainpipes but not the very top ones – we daren't do that! As far as I remember nobody ever climbed to the top of the orphanage building.

Sport was very good. Mr Tyler was the best for us. He managed to get the Worcestershire cricketer Reg Perks to give us coaching. Cricket, football, hockey were the main games. Indoors was table tennis which was most popular. We had plenty of good players – I was average.

We had a lovely time at the Manor Park Lawn Tennis Tournament at Malvern. It was held over a week or a fortnight once a year. The older boys, about fifteen or twenty of us, used to go ball-boying there. We even had competitors from the Argentine. I remember one Argentine player – all the kids were round him every time he arrived on court each morning. They had some good stars there. Then you had the college girls. They used to say, 'Pass the ball, sonny.' We would throw it into the next court, much to their dismay! But what we liked about it was that the tennis club supplied meals like cake and rolls and much, much more. There was always plenty to eat. We had a really good time there.

Leaving school at fourteen years you went into the garden for your final two years. There was always plenty to do. You were known as the 'gardening kids'. There was plenty of ground and it was all dug by spade. I really enjoyed my time as a 'gardening kid'.

Church was quite a bore at time. Three times a day was enough for anybody!

In the school at the orphanage we made a lot of carpets and mats. When the war came we went out to school. The finest freedom we had was going outside the orphanage to school at Christopher Whitehead's in Malvern Road. The younger ones went to St Clement's. We marched down as far as the level crossing at Henwick Station but this became too much for the staff so we were inspected and made our own way to school. They let us go on from there on our own thinking we would continue to march. Well, once we got through those gates we ran hell for leather! We were far from saints, I can tell you. We would sting the legs of the girls on the way back from school. It used to make them run! Oh, we had some fun, there's no doubt about it! Stale cakes we bought from the baker's. They were lovely and very cheap.

Four or five of us would pass by Tandy's fruit stall on our way to school. He would give us an orange and an apple as we went by. Tandy's son was in our class. He's dead and gone now though.

Clothing was pretty grim: black coat and shorts; red and black tie and stiff white collars. If you had a dirty collar you got a clip round the ears. With the war here we had a new rig-out. Grey suit, grey shirt and cap, yellow and green tie, which was very much better.

Leaving the orphanage in 1941 I was sent to Broadheath as an under-gardener to an old RAO boy. I really enjoyed myself there with plenty of freedom. I was there two years. As I mentioned earlier, in January 1944 I was called up for National Service.

At Christmas we didn't want for anything. When George VI was crowned King we had quite a feast. I only wished there had been more coronations!

Every other Sunday we had a rock cake for tea. We always looked to see who had the biggest bit and the following Sunday we'd have a daub of jam. And the porridge – you could put the wallpaper up with it! Oh, the Epsom Salts, Mr Parry used to watch you get them down you! He lapped it up. We had stewed rhubarb – then you had to have some more. You just couldn't have what Mr Parry gave you the first time. 'Right ho,' he'd say, 'Have some more, come on, you lot.' And you all had to have some more. I like stewed rhubarb but not when it's forced down you like that.

We would crawl through the space by the central heating system. We would go through the grating in the passageway, crawl all the way through and come up into the girls' playroom. It was very tight in there and very dirty!

The stairways seemed massive when we were there.

There was a place where we kept all the buckets, mops and one thing and another. The 'togger' we called it. When a new boy came into the orphanage we would take him in there and chuck all these buckets up in the air and he had to dodge them. If one hit him it was just too bad. More often than not they got out of the way all right. It was only for a couple of minutes. Oh yes, they were steel buckets! Sometimes they hit the new boy but nobody was really hurt. But that initiated him!

The playground was all fenced off with iron railings. At night especially when it was cold we would throw buckets of water up the playground which was slightly on the slope. If it did freeze over, in the morning we would slide towards the railings. Nobody ever got hurt.

We had some good times on bonfire night. We pinched the spuds and threw them into the fire and they would come out black. We soon got them down us.

I always remember David Whitehead when he came to the end of saying the Lord's Prayer. He would make a point of pronouncing each letter for the word 'w-o-r-l-d' without end in a strong loud Scottish accent.

We had some characters up at the orphanage. One was Howard Clements. He had left before I went there. But he was a good cricketer and he played for our team as an old boy. We called him 'Cow Clements'. We would say when we were kids watching him. 'Here he comes, no pads, no centre, one, two, three, bang!' Oh yes, he was quite a character! There's a heck of a lot I forget, you know!

Did you ever hear of a committee man by the name of Greswell Williams? He owned a big house. It was called Broadwas Court and he ran us out there for the day. Sometimes we went in Mark's bus but usually it was Burnham's. There was a huge maze in the grounds and big marquee stood on the lawn. We had a lovely feed. We thought a lot of our day out there. We couldn't wait to get into the maze.

We went to Bristol Zoo but I can never remember going to the seaside. Bristol Zoo was a very pleasant day out.

The first bike I had, had only got a back light and when we cycled to Broadheath the copper up there, Constable Eastbury, used to catch us. He said 'I shan't tell you again. Get a light on your bike or I'll clout you.' He never caught us again but it was the good old copper in those days. The estate was all fields then.

I won a book prize: *With Drake on the Spanish Main* but what became of it I'm not sure. One thing I can't do is read a story.

My interest now is railways. I had ten years on the track. Oh, I had a good time there, lovely job! I also spent twenty-nine years at the Worcester Porcelain Works.

But all in all I've no regrets whatsoever.

Raymond Digger married Phyllis Davies (see page 179).

RAYMOND TURNER (1935–43)

I've always regretted through not knowing it, missing the Royal Albert Orphanage Reunion which they held many years ago. Meeting others who were there (1935–43) would no doubt have jogged my memory on other events.

Strangely enough today is the birthday of my sister Olive, the eldest of five children of the Turner family who through Mother's death in

January 1935 found ourselves housed in the Royal Albert Orphanage – a long way to go back!

Recalling my first day is no problem. When mother died on 6 January 1935, Olive, Ralph and I were first put in the Cottage Homes, which I believe was either in Midland Road or Stanley Road, transferring on Wednesday 13 March 1935 to the RAO. The first upset was being parted from my sister who, being three years older, I quite looked up to. I was just seven and half years old, Ralph was nine and Olive ten and a half.

The place looked massive and spotlessly clean and the gardens and fields were immaculate. I was soon to know who kept them that way! It was a bitter raw day and snowflakes around as someone took Ralph and me to a field where the lucky ones were the ones kicking a football about, while about thirty boys gathered along the touch line tried to keep warm. I was to find out later the staff preferred you outdoors to indoors and only heavy rain or nightfall would give you the warmth and comfort of being inside.

Eventually, the sounding of a bell heralded tea time – the boys would march in from their end and the girls from their end of the home. Grace would be said and the 90–100 children would be seated at three long tables. Talking wasn't allowed and one folded one's arms once all food had been consumed. Tea time was the last meal of the day where we all assembled; this I believe was at 4.15 p.m. (though for supper we had bread and dripping!).

Bed I'm sure was 7.30 p.m. – around that time the boys would assemble in the cloakroom, and one of the bigger boys would go round to the kitchen and come back with the required number of half slices of bread and dripping. There never was, for some reason, any supervision at this last meal of the day. Like a ritual night after night as soon as the boy appeared with the tray someone would kick it out of his hands and a mad scramble for the slices of bread and dripping took place. It was a forlorn hope of the little ones getting any – certainly a waste of time queuing up. Proceeding to bed one passed the elderly matron's office where with the door open and sitting in some high chair she awaited your call, 'Night, ma'am' – woe betide you if you forgot; years later I compared it to Queen Victoria reviewing her subjects! Once lights were out which was as soon as one had washed and changed, silence was demanded for the rest of the night. Often, once the master had departed, someone in the dormitory would tell a story, but with an ear listening out for the master's office door opening or footsteps on the stairs.

A bell ringing at 6.30 a.m. heralded a new day. Beds were uniformly made and each boy had a cleaning task to do – be it toilets, bathroom, passageway, hallway, and even outside steps. This would take up to breakfast time at 7.30 a.m.

After breakfast there was a bit of a break, but at about 8.30 a.m. a whistle was blown summoning anyone with illnesses to report to the dispensary. It was known as POs' time. I remember asking one of the lady assistants one day what POs stood for – 'Poor Objects,' she replied!

Up to September 1939 school was held inside the three classrooms – infants, juniors and seniors and here you did get mixed classes; alas, Olive being three years older was in a higher class all the time and to me there seemed to be an unwritten rule, one only spoke when spoken to. When we went in early in 1935, the master and matron were a Mr and Mrs Whitehead, while a Mr Parry, the senior master seemed to rule in all but name – the Whiteheads were elderly and eventually left in 1937.

Now looking back over all these years I can think of no one I loathed more than this Mr Parry and I'm sure many children, well boys anyway, of that era would agree with me. He was such a bully, administrating the cane or his right hand at the slightest thing. He left eventually on 1 April 1940. I just couldn't believe it, after all it was 'All Fools Day' – it was several days later I accepted with huge relief he had gone out of my life for good. Our gain was Borstal's loss because that's where he went to.

Strangely enough there's little from the schooling I remember but one thing sticks out vividly. Miss or Mrs Wilcox taught the juniors, Parry the seniors. One day Parry came in and set about one boy with the cane and continued to thrash him when the lad went down on the floor. Mrs Wilcox fled the room and we were screaming and shouting for it to stop but we were powerless, he was such a big man and it went on and on. The lad was a bit backward so whether it was to do with exam results I just do not know.

We had an outside swimming pool – my first memory of it is Parry picking me up in the shallow end, throwing me through the air to the deep end and in a few strokes getting down to the deep end and throwing me down the opposite end – this seemed to go on for eternity with me screaming and hysterical. I expect I gained by learning to swim quite early, but he certainly didn't gain any respect from me or countless others who endured his sadistic brutality.

Parry was a bachelor and lived on the premises and any affection he had for anything living was solely devoted to his cat David. They say cats have nine lives; I'm sure his had many more! The only way we knew of getting back at Parry was stoning his cat whenever the opportunity arose. I expect in this day and age he would be termed sadistic, perverted perhaps, but I can't recall anything happening untoward to any of us, well certainly not me.

I recall one Christmas Day evening and boys giggling at this person in lady's clothes, and couldn't understand why and someone saying, 'Don't you know who it is, it's Parry!' And being young and not understanding that perhaps he enjoyed dressing up in women's clothes.

Mentioning Christmas – it was the only time I felt we did well compared with the rest of the year. You were actually allowed to talk and laugh and joke at table. After Christmas tea, the dining hall was cleared of all tables and made ready for the entertainments of the evening which was generally games and then dancing. Parry didn't believe in anyone standing around on the side, you had to dance even with another boy if no girls were available, and he would say, 'Off to bed if you don't find a partner!'

Saturdays, when there was no school, meant a bigger workload – work then would commence after breakfast and besides your Monday to Friday job you would have such places as the large dining hall, recreation room and swimming pool to scrub out which could and did go well into the day.

Occasionally on a Saturday afternoon if it was raining and not being taken on a walk (in line two by two) we were treated to two or three hours at St John's Cinema where we watched enthralled Hopalong Cassidy or some other Western film. There were occasions too when a Mr W. H. Austin who lived nearby and had a music shop in town, would come along and put a film show on. These would be rare occasions. I still remember the dismay when the film stopped while a new reel was put in and we waited anxiously for the restart.

Sundays were different altogether – once you were in your early teens you had confirmation classes leading up to being confirmed by the Bishop of Worcester. Although St Clement's was our regular church, they with St John's and All Saints took it in turn each year to hold the confirmations. Once you had been confirmed it meant you had to – no choice – attend communion at 7 o'clock on Sunday mornings at St Clement's and not allowed to eat and drink beforehand. There was bible-study, morning service at 11 o'clock, Sunday School at the Church Hall in the afternoon and what was called 'family worship' at the orphanage after tea every evening. In the early part of the week we practised the hymns which were due the next Sunday but practised other hymns too. There were 779 hymns in the *Ancient and Modern Hymn Book*. I'm sure by the time we left that building for the last time most of us knew quite a percentage of that 779!

I recall one master and matron kept us at it for ages. They took a great delight by saying, 'The next hymn will be sung by all those with the surname starting with the letter . . . (then a pause as they scanned the anxious children) . . . T' – well, it wasn't so bad for us; at least there were five Turners and three Tandys. We had quite a little choir – not that we had good voices though. I felt so sorry for Ken Kendrick struggling through five verses blushing his head off while we all stared watching him, relieved it wasn't us! For all the religious mania that we had to put up with I still enjoy watching *Songs of Praise* on television of a Sunday evening!

When I went to Worcester recently I fulfilled a long cherished ambition to go to morning service at St Clement's. The hymn book was different – the tunes different and of the five hymns I only knew one and thankfully they played it to the tune I remembered so well – the hymn 'Just as I am without one plea' – what wonderful words, what marvellous music; at least I sang that with gusto!

Looking at your list of guidelines I see 'funny incidents', but I have to scratch my head to think of one – one found so little to laugh about, any that came so easily! I do recall one Christmas Eve 'Father Christmas' had been in and out of the dormitory – one lad woke the rest up and although we were never allowed to put the lights on, we rummaged in the dark to see what we had. One boy was violently sick in the early hours of Christmas morning and when they checked his stocking apparently he had eaten some rubber toy which he obviously thought was jelly!

During non-school hours in the daylight you were left most times to your own devices – if we didn't have a ball to kick round the playground we made one by wrapping a stone in lots of newspaper and tying it up. They never lasted long but we always had several in reserve.

During the pre-war summers the older boys would go to Malvern when the big tennis tournament was held at Manor Park. Several of the well-known stars of the day including Dorothy Round, twice a winner of the singles title at Wimbledon, were there – we were used as ball-boys and to sell programmes. From watching the experts several of us got hooked on the game but with no money we made our own rackets, an apology for one really because it was a piece of wood about twelve inches square with a piece of wood nailed to it to act as a handle. Surprising the games we could play with bits of wood and stones!

Discipline was hard; I recall boys being caught scrumping and for three days having for their meals three or four grubby little apples to eat. All children need discipline but it was to excess here. I don't think affection was ever in their repertoire: the very first week I remember falling heavily in the playground and with my knee bleeding I remember going crying to the woman supervising us, throwing my hands out to her and her shouting, 'Don't you dare touch me!' The worst part was the segregation, so brothers and sisters only met at mealtimes and they were taken in silence! Birthdays were not celebrated there at all; in fact I can't ever recall seeing a birthday card all those years!

As regards the farming and gardening, the older lads of fourteen to sixteen attended to that supervised by a head gardener and a couple of staff – they produced enough to feed a hundred children and staff and in December three pigs would be killed for Christmas and New Year. I believe the orphanage and grounds were 32 acres. The gardens and fields were kept immaculate and on school holidays or other times the school children up to fourteen years were used to weed and keep tidy.

The war in September 1939 did us a good turn because someone in authority had the good idea of letting the evacuees from Birmingham and such places use our schoolrooms while we went out either to St Clement's or to Christopher Whitehead School. You found your own way which did at long last give you a chance to get acquainted with the girls, so many one just couldn't put names to as contact and talking had been taboo. At that time the school leaving age was fourteen and here I felt we did lose out, because whereas the outsider began earning then we were still committed to the RAO until we were sixteen years of age which meant the boys did two years in the garden and farm, while the girls were working either in the kitchen, the laundry or the sewing room. I was lucky in that I took the examination at thirteen and a half for entry to the Worcester Junior School then housed in the Victoria Institute and by passing the examination spent two years training for office work.

As regards clothes worn daily: generally shorts and shirts, but on Sundays we, well the older boys, wore long trousers though at school it was shorts – not so bad for me, I was a mere 5 foot 3 inches, but a bit humiliating for the tall lads. I remember in the early part of the war the shorts and jackets were made of corduroy and were a ghastly colour!

Then, of course, going to the Commercial School I obviously stood out being the only one in short trousers till I left at nearly sixteen. Of course, there was a war on, shortages regarding clothing coupons. I don't think we did too badly really in that way. I expect with the uniform everyone was the same.

One very unpopular couple we had during the early part of the war were the Carters but fortunately we only had them for twelve months. Mr Carter, I believe, was an ex-Marine and he strutted around and expected us to march just like soldiers. After his first church attendance he expressed his disgust at the way we walked, he wanted us marching, and each Monday evening he put us through our paces not only with marching but with PT too. I can understand Parry going to Borstal: they were inside for being in trouble, we were inside through loss of one or both parents. Incidentally Carter got the sack as he got caught in his office with a teenage girl on his knee. Parry was probably the right type for a Borstal Institute, not an orphanage – the way we were treated you would have thought we were criminals. The last master and matron I had were certainly an improvement on Parry and Carter. I had respect and affection for the Tylers.

The outcome of the war certainly changed our lives as we had a sight of the outside world. We met more children, made new friends and when we left at sixteen, we felt you were two years behind children who had the chance of work at fourteen. In some ways I felt equipped to face an outside world perhaps more independent not relying on others for help. On the other hand I felt cheated of a normal family life – little or no contact with a beloved sister – to see her enter the dining hall three times a day and not even allowed to speak to her – this was to me inhuman.

Anyway, these are my main memories of life in the Royal Albert Orphanage.

DENNIS TURNER (1935–45)

I only wish I could give you the exact feeling of what it felt like to be brought up in the Royal Albert Orphanage but I think all sense of feeling was driven from you. I've always noticed over the years that it's been difficult for me to show real affection.

I went into the RAO on 8 April 1935, although I don't remember the first day. I know my sixth birthday was in February of that year. I only know you had no mother or father to run to, if you fell over and cut your leg or something similar. You never ran to anyone. I think there must have been a lot of damage done to our minds, and by different attitudes of the staff. My brothers Raymond and Ralph and sister Olive went in the RAO in March 1935. My brother Ken went in on 21 December 1937. I was number 14.

I feel sure that it was at the age of seven or eight years of age you started scrubbing the floors and corridors. You did your work before breakfast in the winter about 6.30 a.m. In the summer it was done when you finished school at 4.30 p.m. You finished your scrubbing duties when you left school at fourteen. I left school in April 1943. You were then what we referred to as a 'gardening kid'. You worked in the orphanage gardens with the gardener and stockman until 4.30 or 5 p.m. Later in the summer, after tea till about 6.30 or 7 p.m. Bedtime was 7 p.m. for the little kids. The time for the remainder was 7.30 p.m. until you left at the age of sixteen.

I was too young to know what impression the building or that sign 'The Royal Albert Orphanage' gave me at first but slowly as my ten years began to pass by, I knew as long as I live, I would never forget this place!

As I've mentioned you started scrubbing the floors around the age of seven or eight. During the winter months at 6.30 a.m. and in the summer after school each boy had a particular part to scrub Monday to Friday. The same on Saturday except that after you finished your everyday work, you reported to the matron or other staff members for more work, such as scrubbing the dining hall, dormitory (boys' side), little dormitory, big dormitory and top dormitory. In the summer on Saturday after dinner you scrubbed the swimming bath out with long handled wire scrubbers with powder, so as to get all the green off the bricks, and side walls too.

Normally at one time there were about four to six 'gardening kids' and you took your turn, making sure the fires (boiler fires) in the kitchen and laundry room were kept stocked up. The gardener who had the cottage in the grounds at the back of the orphanage had to service the main boiler fire next to the boys' playground. You also made sure the firewood box was always full up for the girls who worked in the kitchen, as they had to light the masters' fires and staff members' fires. If you were on the fires, after teatime you wheeled a barrow round by the girls' playground for coke to bank up the kitchen and laundry room fires and push the damper nearly all the way in. Next morning you de-clinkered it and stoked up with damper out ready for kitchen and laundry girls.

You yourself must have seen the orphanage in Worcester. Well, while I was a school kid, at one time my job was scrubbing the front steps. You must have seen the main concrete steps. Can you imagine me on a winter's morning at 6.30 a.m. scrubbing concrete steps with my long scrubber flannel and soap and bucket of hot water? It's laughable now, but it wasn't at the time.

When I first went into the RAO in 1935 the master and matron were a Mr and Mrs Whitehead. He was a tall upright man from Scotland with white hair but seemed to walk with his head and shoulders a little bent forward. When he was watching us play football he used a walking stick, which opened at one end with a small seat for him to sit on. He was very strict and used to cane a lot, but he had a good side, sometimes he would appear from the archway with a tray of cakes and hand them out to us kids in the playground. Also he would throw apples from a basket for us. Mrs Whitehead was a small plump woman. I never came into contact with her much but at bedtime when you walked in single file from where your lockers were and along the hall and corridor passing their sitting room near to stairs leading to the dormitory, they would have their door open and as you passed by, you would say 'goodnight mum'. (ma'am). This I remembered only happened with Mr and Mrs Whitehead. When they left, I think they had done thirty years as master and matron – well that is what they say.

The assistant master was Parry – I can describe him by one word 'bastard'. I think he left in 1940 or 1941. My brother Ray would know the exact date. We have both been surprised that no one has ever written a book on the RAO, Worcester. It was bad enough in 1935 but what it was like when it was first opened in 1868? God knows! Parry was the one to be feared. In the swimming bath, he enjoyed throwing the little kids in the deep end – I was one who couldn't swim either. He would come round the dormitory about twenty minutes after lights were put out at 7.30 p.m. He switched the lights on and called out for us to stand at the foot of our beds. He would then walk past each one of us and whack anyone with dirty feet with the cane he was carrying, across their leg – then they would have to go and wash them. We often got our own back as Parry had a fluffy white cat called David. If we saw the cat in the playground we would beckon it towards us, by calling out, 'Come on David,' then soak it with water from a can or bucket someone had rushed to get.

One of the school teachers was a Miss Wilcox. She had a go at Parry one day, as he was laying into one kid for some minor thing he had done wrong, and Ray my brother often recalls this. When we are chatting about the orphanage Ray would often say to me that I remember much more than he does himself.

One winter's night after tea – it was always dark then, and you played in the classroom till bedtime at 7.30 p.m. – Ray and I went over a red side gate, or was it a panel, with barbed wire running along the top. We trotted down Henwick Road, down Church Walk and over the Severn Bridge to our Aunty Winn in Lychgate, near the cathedral. We would have something to eat and a sweet and get back for 7 p.m. We did this twice and weren't missed, but the third night as we got near the Severn Bridge, the Scoutmaster came along on his bike and on seeing Ray and me, said, 'Where do you think you are going?' Ray just shouted, 'To buy a postcard for my Aunty,' and we carried on running. On getting back Parry was waiting for us. I got the slipper on the bare backside. When Ray's turn came he was kicking and screaming for all he was worth and kicked Parry's glasses off! I will always remember this as on that third evening it was raining. The Scoutmaster's name was Mr Parsons. Although Parry was hated, he was the one who used to make us write occasionally to our relatives. My brother Ray said that when Parry left he went to a Borstal Centre.

I think the next master and matron were a Mr and Mrs Carter. He was a small man, with a well tanned face, unless it was his permanent colour. Looking at him, he looked like an ape but he seemed a very fit person. He used to give the older kids PT every Monday evening. He too was over strict. They say he was an ex-Marine PT instructor. If he came in the playground and shouted to a kid at the other end, the kid would double down to him and spring to attention, saying at the time, 'Sir!' If you were walking in the corridor and you knew he was behind you, you would rush to the swing door and hold it open for him standing to attention.

Until 1939 we used the classrooms in the RAO. When the war broke out, the evacuees from Birmingham and elsewhere came to Worcester and were put into digs and to keep these children altogether they used the orphanage classrooms for their schooling. They put us kids to outside school. Up to eleven was St Clement's just down Henwick Road and over eleven years went to Christopher Whitehead School. This gave us orphanage kids some very welcome freedom. One day as we were marching down the drive swinging our arms, we were going past the side of the RAO where there were sand bags up against the little classroom window. Carter came from behind, and belted me across the head knocking me flying about six feet against the sand bags. He then shouted at me, 'I can see daylight through your arms!' I don't know who was the worst, Carter or Parry. Carter came from Coventry. Mrs Carter was always telling us about the bombing there, especially on bath night which was a Friday. There were always two or three of them bathing us kids – three in a bath at a time. They would give you a good going over, then you would duck your head under the water and get out. Then the next three would get in and bath in the same water! Most Friday nights Carter's wife would help. She was a big woman and wore glasses. She always talked of the bombing in Coventry.

At mealtimes they had a very large brass bell. One of the kitchen girls would ring this bell a quarter of an hour before a meal, so that you washed your hands. The second bell would then go a quarter of an hour later for you to fall in outside the dining hall. Then one of the mistresses would open the door and you walked in single file and stood up in your place at the long table waiting to say grace. In the dining hall there were three long tables made up from short tables. There were two outside long tables, one for the boys and one for the girls. The shorter one in the centre was for the little kids. You were not really allowed to talk during mealtimes and got away with this most times, but some days the mistress in charge at mealtimes would send any boy or girl talking out and round to the master's office. You either got two strokes of the cane or were sent to bed straight after teatime for a week. Sometimes both.

I can't remember much about food. Saturday morning was always porridge and half a cup of Epsom Salts. You didn't sit down until you had drunk it. Teatime was three and a half rounds of bread and scrape (margarine). Some times you had jam, always a 'stone' jam – take the stones away and you had not much there! Cake once a week on a Sunday: a little rock cake plus your three and a half pieces of bread and marge. I can always remember some of us kids would take our time eating our bread so that you could be the last eating your rock cake and making the other kids jealous! There were no tablecloths, just a plate and cup, no saucer. Supper time was half a piece of bread and dripping and a cup of cocoa. It was the usual dinner, meat, fish and so on and you had a pudding but sometimes the dinner was horrible. As I got older I used to take some paper in my pocket and scrape the lot into it and put it in my pocket!

On Sundays you had no scrubbing and after breakfast you messed around until 9.30 a.m. or 10 a.m. then got ready for church. Once you were ready you walked slowly round the top of the playground in pairs, just chatting together, until it was time to fall in. We all wore our Sunday best suits. The master or whoever was taking us kids, inspected us. After 1941 he would give us all a halfpenny each to put in the collection. When I went in in 1935 it was a red and black striped tie and cap with RAOW just above the peak. There was a big white celluloid collar on the shirt. You were always losing your front or back collar stud and had to buy them from Parry. He used to sell tie pins, combs and so on. You came by money from Visiting Day which was the first Saturday in the month from 2 p.m. to 4 p.m. in the dining hall.

During the war, about 1942 or 1943 they changed our colours to green and yellow ties. After the church service you fell in outside St Clement's Church, then walked back to the orphanage. We had Sunday dinner, then from 2 p.m. to 3 p.m. we went to Sunday School. After that one of the mistresses would take you for a walk from 3 p.m. to 4 p.m., always up the riverside and back, never round the town. After teatime we would be messing around in the classroom in winter and in the playground in the summer. Family worship was held in the dining hall from 6.30 p.m. to 7.30 p.m. Then bed! Most of us had to go to confirmation classes when aged twelve at the vicarage across the road from the RAO. I was confirmed on 12 December 1942. So it was then I went to Holy Communion from 7 a.m. to 8 a.m. besides the rest of the Sunday routine!

When you talked between yourselves you referred to the women staff as Ma William, Ma Cooper, Ma Tucker and so on. I think the worst part of my ten years was until the age of eleven or twelve. I think by then you were hardened to the routine. We had our good times. Sometimes someone treated us to the pictures on a Saturday afternoon. There were steamer trips too, up the River Severn, but not very often.

Christmas we all looked forward to but it seemed always to be over too quickly and back to the normal routine. I remember when we were at the outside school during the war – if we had any money left over from Visiting Day we would race up to the cake shop, 'Burdens' in St John's, on a Monday for a penny bag of stale cakes left over from the weekend, and after school at 4.30 p.m. if you had a few pence you bought a two and half penny loaf and a penny worth of scratchings! You ate the lot before you got to Henwick Road as you were always seeing people who knew us orphanage kids and we had to doff our caps or touch them when we passed by.

I could go on and on, but I won't! Good luck.

DORIS EVA ELLEN DAVIES (1935–39)

On 23 April 1935 I went into the Royal Albert Orphanage with my two younger sisters Joyce and Phyllis, after losing both our parents only two months previously and still feeling their great loss. Speaking for myself, this day 23 April was, I think, the saddest day of my life. I was twelve years old. Entering this great cold building with its strict rules and regulations and to be parted from my two younger sisters at bed time really made me sad and resentful. I was put in the older girls' dormitory where I remember sitting on my bed feeling very sorry for myself, when an older girl came to me, with a lovely smile to cheer me up, saying it wasn't such a bad place, that I would soon settle down. Those few first kind words spoken to me meant a lot. It was reassuring. Maybe the staff were not allowed to do this.

The impression of the RAO building was that of a workhouse – very Dickensian. Mr and Mrs Whitehead were the Victorian matron and master.

Duties started from the age of eleven years up, with more to do as one got older, even to being responsible for a younger child in the ways of hygiene, hair and keeping clothes and socks repaired. Staff usually did play duty and meal duty. During my stay school was held on the premises so staff were teaching also. If one hadn't done cleaning and scrubbing properly we were fetched by matron from class to do it again. We also did a lot of rug making in school which were put on exhibition and sold afterwards. Most of what I learned was before 1935.

Discipline was very strict and regimented. No talking in dining hall, everything had to be eaten, like it or not. Grace was said before and after meals. The teacher was on duty at the end of the table and Mr Whitehead liked boxing your ears quite hard.

I missed going to the circus for being cheeky, by saying I had earned my seat. I was then handed a few more pairs of socks to darn and sent to bed without supper (a piece of bread and dripping). My sister Joyce sneaked it in her knicker pocket and I ate it gratefully, when she came back from the circus. Another time I had the slipper on my backside for a noisy pillow fight in the dormitory.

Girls played hockey for the RAO against outside schools, also 'friendly' cricket against boys which I didn't much like being afraid of the hard ball. We also played in the mixed hockey team sometimes. Girls did not do gardening; we helped in the sewing room, mending and making summer dresses which were all the same style – cotton prints. I liked helping with the spring cleaning with the daily helps as Mrs Grosvenor (the gardener's wife) often gave us a few sweets.

Every Sunday morning we attended church, after inspection by matron to see if we were well groomed. Friday night was bath night and our hair was washed and had to be put into rags on Saturday night ready for Sunday, when hair was in ringlets or plaits. Hair was grown long at that time, which matron took credit for from the congregation in church. We always walked in twos to church and on our walks on Saturday and Sunday afternoons. If it rained on Saturday we went to the matinee performance at the local St John's cinema. We loved the pictures very much.

Our relatives were allowed to visit the first Wednesday or Saturday in the month, the only time we had sweets or goodies. We had old clothes for work. We wore black stockings with our summer and winter dresses and were all dressed the same, with another dress for 'Sunday best'. As we grew dresses and coats were passed down – I hated that. We were not really equipped for the outside world; except that we knew we had to work and be honest, and knew right from wrong.

I don't think the staff were allowed to show too much feeling, but I do remember how kind Miss Gossett was with everyone. She became Mrs Jenkins and was temporarily matron when the Whiteheads retired. My husband Colin Baker was also in the RAO and we have been very happily married. Having kept in touch on and off, we tied the knot in 1944 and have had many a laugh looking back on the RAO. We used to wait for the teachers to go into meals to see the boys on the drying green for kisses (which we called 'smackers'). I remember one boy nearly strangled himself on the clothes line when he tripped and fell after a signal someone was coming!

However, life in the orphanage didn't do us any harm as we're here to tell the tale!

Doris Davies married Colin Baker (see page 158).

PHYLLIS CLARA DAVIES (1935–41)

It all happened at the beginning of the year 1935. I was the youngest of five girls and we lost both our parents within two months of each other. By 23 April, St Georges Day 1935, the three youngest were admitted to the Royal Albert Orphanage.

My elder sister and aunty were taking us to the orphanage but first we walked up Henwick Road to Dr Bunting's house for examination, only to be told we had to walk back down into St John's to Dr Bunting's surgery. After the examination we walked back up to the orphanage and I remember a figure of a buxom woman standing on the door steps, as we turned into the driveway. She clapped her hands, shouting, 'You're late, you Davieses.' Before I had ever reached the steps to the entrance I felt a lump come into my throat as big as a golf ball, which remained with me for many days to follow.

Then we were shown our routine of going into age groups. I was only eight years old. I was separated from my dear sisters straight away which upset me very much. I think I cried for about a month. We did not even sleep in the same dormitory and I was very upset about that as we had always slept together in our two bedroom council house. Neither could I sit by them for our meals. We were only together in between meals and when not working.

The building seemed massive to me. It looked tremendous. But looking at it now, it's like a doll's house. But in those days it looked huge. Frightening! Yes! And the drive seemed endless. We never knew what it was like to sit on a soft seat, for in the playroom you sat on a wooden bench and in the playground you sat on the ground. We always had to stand up when staff did their daily round, especially to matron and say, 'Morning, mum' (ma'am).

Your duties as you got older were mending, laundry, kitchen work and especially cleaning a corridor every morning after rising at 7 a.m. You did this before you had a bite or drink. You were timed to scrub and wipe each patch as you cleaned these corridors. The staff looked after our tongues – we were never allowed to make much noise and if you were caught talking, especially when you had gone to bed and lights were out, the teacher would creep up the wooden stairs and give you the slipper on your bare backside and you knew when you'd had it!

I do remember an amusing incident when a very tall boy came round to the laundry one dark winter's evening hoping to see his girlfriend, and ran into a clothes line on the green and had a nasty mark to show for it on his neck. I don't know whether he ever got to see his girlfriend!

I had a great time jumping along the row of beds, right down the dormitory. We thought this was great fun especially as we were supposed to be asleep as lights were out before 8 p.m. We had baths every Friday night – two in a bath at a time. You helped bath the younger ones as you grew older and rubbed their hair with towels until dry.

I was punished and put to bed for getting into the classroom and playing the piano and had to go without my supper which was half a slice of bread and dripping, but it did grieve me having to go without.

Our sports included hockey, rounders and swimming. The boys played football and cricket.

We went to church two and sometimes three times on a Sunday and marched to and fro on every occasion and it was 'God help you' if you were out of step!

Usually weekend afternoons we went for walks which nearly took three hours. If wet we went to the pictures at St John's Cinema. I was one who used to pray for it to rain!

We had hard material for our winter dresses and nice cotton for summer. We wore navy hats for winter and panama cream hats for summer. Both had bands on them on which were stitched RAOW.

Our food didn't vary much. Usually for breakfast we had porridge and bread and margarine. Marmalade on a Sunday and cornflakes. Boiled egg every Easter Sunday! We had fruit cake one week and coconut cake another week. The boys had crusts – the girls couldn't have them. They had one piece more than us. We had three halves and they had four. Epsom Salts was the worst thing we had to take every Saturday morning, half-a-cup in hot water. Ugh! If it was anything nice you didn't get asked for a second helping – the favourites had it!

During my time at the RAO there were several matrons and masters, whose names were Mr and Mrs Whitehead, Mr and Mrs Jenkins (née Gossett), Mr and Mrs Carter and Mr and Mrs Tyler. The Whiteheads were lovely people, really, in their own way. They were the nicest couple there. The teachers were a Miss Bird, Miss Pearson, Miss Jones, Miss Wilcox, Miss Griffiths and not forgetting Mr Cecil Parry. When we went there on St George's Day 1935 there were 98 boys and girls altogether. Both my sister and I met husbands there and have lots of happy memories. When the four of us are together we go through the old times which we can laugh about now. The cook's name was Nellie Blye and the laundry maid was Margaret Magraff. The gardeners, who in turn lived in the bungalow, were Mr and Mrs Windons, Mr and Mrs Grosvenor and Mr and Mrs Little.

As soon as we got in the queue for our meals, the bell went and you got in this queue in the playroom to go into the dining hall and matron looked at us new ones straight away and we had a fringe. She came across to me and said, 'You won't need that,' and brushed it all on one side. We couldn't even sit together for meals. We had to go in age groups.

My number was 94 and my sisters were 91 and 92 so you can tell how many of us there were.

Visiting day was the first Saturday in the month. On visiting days when you went into the dining hall to see your visitor, you were called by the girl on duty. We saw them enter the front door and the girl shouted, 'The three Davieses!' and you'd go into the dining hall and see whoever had come to see you. We always looked to see if they'd got a carrier bag, because we got some goodies! But despite this fact we had a girl there who used to take them off my sister. We hardly had any. You see we were bullied! I could name the girl and I will. The bully's name was Iris Graves. We used to call her Nigger. Mavis was her younger sister. She was a nice kid, Mavis was.

Now we were lucky, we've always been a very close family despite the fact that we were put in an orphanage. And we always had a visitor. I had two older sisters who were not in the orphanage. My brother-in-law brought my eldest sister over in his little Austin-Morris but he never came inside the building to see us because it upset him too much. He'd sit out in the car and read his newspaper and wait. He'd drive his wife – my sister – all the way down from Birmingham to come and see us but he wouldn't come inside. Never. No, he was much too upset to see us in there.

We had this particular girl who was friendly with a choir boy at St Clement's Church and my sisters and I were bullied into taking notes to this boy who lived in Bromyard Terrace. His name was Cyril Thomas. A lot of bullying went on in the orphanage.

Well, I did a deceitful thing myself when I gave Ray (my future husband) an Easter egg one Easter. I gave it to another girl who was working in the kitchen (because it was near the boys' end) who gave it to the boy who stoked up the fire and he got caught. Ray was punished by having to sit next to me at Easter teatime on the girls' table which was a bit embarrassing. Then we both went to bed after tea without any supper and we were upset by this. I gave the Easter egg to Ray because I knew that he had nobody. My sister had given it to me before she left. It was a lovely Easter egg with little ice rosebuds on it.

We had lovely Christmases at the orphanage. They used to shine a torch in our face to see if we were asleep on Christmas Eve. We would keep our eyes shut tight. In our Christmas stockings were little things like nuts, an apple, an orange, a pencil, a rubber and a notebook. We were most grateful. At Christmas dinnertime we always banged our spoons on the table when Dr Bunting brought in the Christmas pudding. Christmas Day and New Year's Day was the only time the boys and girls really got together. You could get up and dance with them if you wanted to but we were too shy, then. Ray said he spotted me the day we walked into the dining hall for the first time!

We had two weeks' holiday a year but it was very upsetting when we had to return to the orphanage. In fact travelling back on the buses, you were ill because you knew where you were going. You felt really bad. I don't think I've got any tears left now. I shed them all there.

Going to school outside the orphanage was one of the best things that happened to us, by letting us go out into the world, so to speak. We met outside people and made friends. The boys used to sting the girls' legs with stinging nettles on the way home!

I can't ever remember being tucked up in bed. Never! We would wave to each other when we went to bed, if we happened to go to bed at the same time. I would look down the other end of the corridor to see if I could see Ray and he looked down to see if he could see me. If he didn't wave I thought, 'What have I done?' We went to bed in a team, looking through the keyhole of the bathroom at bedtime to see what we could see – see if we could see each other!

We would slide down the drainpipes onto where the stores were. That was the lower roof. We would come down the top storey to the second storey then get through the skylight.

In the kitchen we would scrape the saucepans out when we worked there. We didn't have to let the cook see us doing it or she went mad if she saw us scraping. If she'd made custard and put the saucepan on the table to be washed, we were there with our fingers in it.

I don't think the orphanage has hurt us but it does mark your life somewhere. I think you appreciate the little things of life because of the life we've had. It's like something has been done to you. I suppose I feel it because I lost my parents so young. When I hear people in the town saying 'Mum this' and 'Mum that' it makes me think I've had a great chunk cut out of my life! But you do appreciate life much more and you're willing to help other people much more.

We made 'apple pie beds' for some girls. You know what an apple pie bed is? You double the bottom sheet underneath the pillow and bring it up halfway so when you get into bed, you think you can shoot your legs down the bed. You can't because there's that stoppage of the sheet being folded over. The girls would remake their beds – but I guess they moaned!

In the little backyard we had a little sunhouse – it was a very small round building where we would clean our shoes. This was outside the dining hall.

We had bonfire nights there too. We would burn the old mattresses and whatever else we found. We had great fun around the fire. The orphanage committee gave us a good display of fireworks. The shop 'Soames' did a lot for the orphanage.

You were reckoned to be well off if you had a wireless in those days. After all it was the 1930s – the years of the depression. We even had a huge wireless in the orphanage.

I well remember Mr Parry coming over the girls' side to see if the girls were up and my sister (she's dead and gone now) was still in bed and he came straight up to the bed and stripped it off. Just like that. That was Parry! Mr Parry could play the piano – he was fantastic. He would play the piano while we were having our meals if he felt like it. But if he was in a bad mood you knew you were in for a game that day, didn't you! He always wore a green polo-neck jumper and tan plus-fours.

Mr Carter was dismissed for giving gifts to girls. It was during the black-out because we had no shelter. When we had air-raid warnings we had to come down out of bed, down the stairs and sit in the corridor. Below the stairs was the safest place. He used to put the gifts behind the piano, in the lounge, such as chocolates, a gold watch and tell these girls where to find them, because he knew these girls went into these rooms as it was their duty as a maid to go in there, to make either tea or coffee. Three girls were alleged to have found these gifts.

Mrs Carter had a niece, a ginger-haired girl who used to come and stay there from Liverpool. I was fascinated how Mrs Carter would say, 'You put your B-O-O-K-S away!'

We never went to the seaside. As far as we went was Bristol Zoo. We looked forward to that. A nice ride out – a good day's outing.

We remember the time when Queen Mary travelled through Henwick by train and we went to the bottom field to the edge of the railway to watch her go through. We thought it was great to be able to see her.

We were given special mugs for the coronation. I'm deeply upset about mine because I sent them to an aunt (my mother's sister) to look after them for me but she died. They were left in the hands of my uncle and he died. And his son-in-law claimed them. In fact the son-in-law took everything!

The most boring job I ever did was cleaning a coconut-mat on a Saturday. It came out of the sewing room. You had to turn it and put it outside in the yard and pick all the bits of cotton off it. With a Hoover today you would do it in five minutes!

When you look back you think where has all the time gone and yet when you were in the orphanage, you thought, aren't the days L-O-N-G! Especially when you were shut out on a Saturday in the playground till dinnertime.

We had prizes for rug-making. There was a Committee Day once a year in March when our things were put on show. I had a book prize *The Lost Girl* which I still have. I've also got my Communion Book which I had when I was confirmed by the Rev. Barnett.

When you finally left the orphanage you were set up with a domestic job. I went to The Blue Coat School, Stourbridge as a kitchen maid. I was very upset when I left. It was like a homesick feeling to leave the home and go into service.

Having written all this, some good came from it: I met my husband there!

Phyllis Davies married Raymond Digger (see page 162).

ALFRED HORACE ROY DIGGER (1935–45)

I was only four years old when I entered the Royal Albert Orphanage. I was admitted on 15 May 1935 and as my birthday is 18 June you can see that I was very nearly five years old. My memories of that day are lost in time! I never knew my mother. I was placed in the RAO with my brother Ray because my father could no longer bring us up on his own.

The building itself didn't make much impression on me; after all I was only four years old! But as I grew older I came to realize the size of the building, its rooms and passages, the whole structure of the RAO.

Work duties! There were plenty of those, scrubbing the floors and cleaning out the toilets. We would come back from St Clement's School in the afternoon, and get down on our hands and knees and scrub the orphanage floors. Then, before tea, we had to go and wash our hands thoroughly and clean behind our nails. Two bells rang at tea-time, one to tell us to get ready and the other to go to the dining hall. Our hands were inspected as we went in and, if our hands or nails were found to be dirty, we were sent to stand outside the office and usually got the cane.

On Saturday morning, some of us boys had to spread out, six in line, on the floor of the orphanage's outdoor swimming pool and scrub it before it was refilled with fresh water. This was always backbreaking – we only had carbolic soap and a scrubbing brush to do the job.

We were tucked up in bed in the dormitory by eight o'clock when lights were out. In the morning you were up by seven o'clock, to make your bed and stand at the bottom of it and wait for inspection before you went down for breakfast.

There was plenty of discipline – they were very strict. If you did something wrong you had six of the best and went to bed. I had plenty of it – the cane I mean!

The sports activities in the orphanage were very good – there was football and cricket. I played both cricket and football for the orphanage. There were also Scouts, Guides and Cubs. We would go camping once a year to different places.

From St Clement's School, I went to Christopher Whitehead's before leaving at fourteen. For the next two years before being sent out to get jobs at sixteen, the orphanage boys had to work in the extensive grounds, where there were orchards, gardens, grazing cattle, pigsties and two wartime brick air raid shelters. We were brought up to do both farming and gardening. There was plenty of ground to cultivate; two fields; the top one was for haymaking. We were always busy doing something: cleaning out the pigs and chickens, feeding the animals and milking the cows.

On Sundays, there were always church parades from the orphanage to St Clement's Church for morning service and then back in the afternoon for Sunday School. In the early evening, a Sunday service was also held at the orphanage in the dining hall. Prayers were said before and after every meal throughout the week.

We had two sets of clothing. From Monday to Saturday we would wear our weekday working clothes but once a week we would put on our best suits for church on Sunday, all pressed and looking smart.

At Christmas time the food was very good indeed, exceptional, but for the rest of the year food in the orphanage was rubbish, if you'll excuse the expression!

When you left the RAO at sixteen years of age they sent you down to the outfitters in the Shambles in Worcester. 'Maggs' was the place we went to. They gave us quite a lot of clothing. I went to live with my father in Buck Street, who had by that time remarried. I was apprenticed as a motor mechanic at Norman's Garage, in St John's, Worcester. We had some hard times and some good times.

MARJORIE EILEEN JONES (1935–41)

We went to the Royal Albert Orphanage in May 1935. We were three sisters – our mother had died three years previously. Our grandfather looked after us until our little sister was five, which was the youngest age they took children. Our vicar from the village where we lived took us to the orphanage in a car which was a great treat for us. I thought I was only going there until someone could come and look after us! I was nine years old.

We had new clothes – a navy serge dress each, very scratchy, and boots. These boots would just not wear out and seemed to last forever! We had a stores which we went to get either new shoes or someone else's which they had grown out of. As I had small feet I nearly always had someone else's, but we did have new sandals every year and to this day if I go into a shoe shop and smell new sandals it brings it all back. It must have been a Friday when we went into the orphanage as Mary, just five, told everyone in a loud voice – much to my embarrassment – 'I don't like fish!'

The matron and master were a Mr and Mrs Whitehead. They had been there a long time as they celebrated thirty years of being there in our first few years. They retired and we had a lovely party. We always had parties on their birthdays and at Christmas and lovely ones for New Year as Mr Whitehead was a Scot and we stayed up to see the New Year in – that's only if you were eleven or twelve years or older.

In that time we didn't go out to school but had an infant teacher, Miss Pearson. Our junior teacher was Miss Wilcox – she was Welsh. Mr Parry was the senior master. When I was in his class I don't think we did such a lot of actual school work as he was a great story teller and we made lots of rugs – I don't know who for? – while he read or told us stories. It sounds wonderful down on paper but we had to work hard. The older boys and girls had to scrub floors – great long corridors. Everyone had something to do before breakfast at eight o'clock. Even the little ones dusted or shook the mats and everyone had to be finished and in line when the bell rang.

We did have a woman who looked after the laundry – a Miss or Mrs Magraph but the older girls helped with the washing and ironing and there was a lot from about a hundred children and staff. We all had numbers which were on all our clothes. We had to learn sewing and the sewing mistress was Miss Gosset who made all our dresses and helped us with our mending. We had to mend the boys' clothes as well, great piles of socks to be darned – some of them more darns than sock!

Miss Butler was cook in the kitchen and the older girls helped. While Mr and Mrs Whitehead were there we had plain food, bread and margarine for breakfast with porridge, extra on Tuesdays and Thursdays. Bread and margarine for tea with a treat on Sunday – with jam one Sunday and rock cake the next. We always had a good dinner with a pudding to follow. Each day of the week we had a different menu but that was repeated every week except for a short while in the summer when the large gardens were full of lovely raspberries, gooseberries, blackcurrants, plums, apples, cherries and pears – the girls helped to make lots of jam.

We had to go through the gardens to the playing fields where we passed plum trees and apple trees laden with fruit or fallen on the ground but woe betide anyone caught pinching any. Many times we put an apple or plum up our knicker leg to eat when no one was looking! We had a swimming pool and it was a lovely treat to be allowed to go in. The boys scrubbed it out once a week.

The boys were separated from the girls except for classes and meals. We went for long walks all over the Worcester area, always in twos in a crocodile and had to stay that way. If it rained on a Saturday afternoon we all went to St John's cinema. We used to pray for it to rain. We went to church at St Clement's every Sunday morning and Sunday School in the afternoon. We wore panama hats in the summer and felt ones in the winter.

On the first Wednesday of each month we had visitors. But our family didn't have many as it wasn't convenient to be there between 2 p.m. and 4 p.m. After a while visitors were allowed to come the first Saturday in the month but some children never had visitors. We used to look out for our own family to come and were very disappointed if they didn't turn up.

We were sent to bed for punishment before tea if the teacher thought the crime warranted it. I once said, 'Sod!' – I didn't know it was a swear word – and had to go to bed for a week without any tea. It wasn't so bad if it was summer as you could smuggle a book up with you but in the winter you weren't allowed to have the light on and with twenty beds in the dormitory it was very scary, and you were glad when everyone else came to bed. Many times we all had the slipper for talking. I should think the mistress who doled it out must have been worn out when she got round us all! If it was cold in the night we used to get into each other's beds but we got into trouble if we were found out.

One day one brave girl decided she was going to go to a shop which was up the road from the RAO. She dressed up in the most unusual clothes out of our dressing up clothes! She must have been spotted just outside the gate and brought back. I was never brave enough to do anything like that!

When our old master and matron retired we had Miss Gosset and Mr Parry to take their place and we went out to school. The infants and juniors to St Clement's and seniors to Christopher Whitehead's in St John's. It was lovely to mix with other children. It was a school where boys and girls were still separated but we often walked to school with our boys and brothers and sisters saw more of each other. We always clung together as a family if any disputes arose.

We still had our chores to do before we went to school and on Saturdays we had to scrub out our playroom which was huge. About eight or ten of us scrubbed a strip each and others would be doing the same in our old classrooms. We had more variety in our menu at this time – more on our plates and sweets occasionally, unheard of before.

Miss Gosset got married and we all went to the wedding. Our sister Mary and Ethel Moule, being the youngest girls, were bridesmaids. We were all very excited as we had never been to a wedding before.

Mr and Mrs Carter became our new master and matron. I left school at fourteen and I was in trouble from then on. I couldn't do anything right. We were given *2s. 6d.* pocket money a month but I nearly always had some of mine stopped as I had broken something or hadn't done something right. So my last year at the RAO wasn't very pleasant and I went into service at a rectory looking after twelve evacuees.

We really didn't have a bad time considering the time of the century when there was so much unemployment about and families were living on next to nothing. In fact I have spoken to people with families about that time and we were well off compared with them – except for LOVE.

NORA ELIZABETH JONES (1935–44)

On 15 May 1935 we entered the Royal Albert Orphanage. Mary was the youngest at five, I was just over seven and Marjorie was nine years old. We went through the big iron gates, up the wide steps to the double doors. They were opened and we went into a large hall, pictures hung on the walls, including one of Prince Albert, also large dark notice boards with names on them lettered in gold.

Later in the day we were taken to the infants' classroom and Mary and I joined with the others in singing May Day songs and songs of Empire Day.

We had quite good schooling there until 1938 when we started going out to school at St Clement's Church School (since pulled down) and Christopher Whitehead Secondary School.

The orphanage playground was enclosed by iron railings which were taken down in the war with the gates for the war effort in 1940. We were not allowed to go into the gardens and orchard around our playground but we used to sneak through the bendy railings to get our ball back.

The playroom had lockers at one end to keep our personal things in; cupboards down one side for coats and a bench seat over the central heating pipes. We played all our table games and puzzles in there, also table tennis. The woodblock floor was swept every day and scrubbed; also the long passages. The washroom and toilets were up the side passage by the playground with the big girls' dormitory and bathroom on top of the playroom and washroom.

There were a lot of staff when we first were there but fewer after 1938. There were teachers for infants, junior and senior classes, also woodwork and sewing. There was a large collection of books to borrow so we all became bookworms. The kitchen had staff, also the laundry and some who came in daily. The sewing room ladies who made a lot of our clothes, taught us as well.

Older girls and boys did a lot of the cleaning after they left school at fourteen, for two years before leaving the orphanage. They got a small wage that was paid to them once a month with stoppages for any breakages. When I was old enough, I had *7s. 6d.* a month. The staff had a book to keep a record if you had any money (not many had) but you could use it for stamps when you wrote home or for Christmas presents to send home, mostly all bought for pennies at Woolworths – making us very thrifty in later life.

During the first year there we were not able to go on holiday. One outing I remember going to was a day coach trip to Bristol Zoo. Our holidays at home were the highlight of the year. We had two weeks in June and two in September.

The boys had their own side of the building although we had lessons together. We ate our food in the dining hall at separate long tables; in later years we sat together at smaller ones. Breakfast was lumpy porridge and one slice of bread and margarine or dripping. We had a roast dinner on Sundays but the rest of the week was stews, corned beef, hash, sausages or cold meat with potatoes and cabbage from the gardens. We had pudding: rice, sago, spotted dick, treacle pudding, stewed fruit and custard. Often it was the same thing, week in, week out. Tea was two slices of bread and margarine. On Sunday we had jam and sometimes a cake. In the war we had butter as well as it was in our rations. I don't remember having bacon or cheese but I expect we did have some at some time.

Visiting day was a Saturday afternoon once a month when we could see our relations in the boardroom. Once a month, on a Sunday before tea we had to write home.

Christmas was a happy time as we celebrated it in the usual way – a stocking with an orange, apple, packet of sweets, a gift like a pen wipe, or a pencil or a needle case. Only one year did we miss having a stocking! We went to church in the morning, then we had our Christmas dinner. Our doctor who lived across the road always came and carved the meat. The Christmas pudding was brought in all flaming while we banged our spoons on the tables. In the afternoon we had our presents from relations brought in the playroom in the big laundry baskets. Those who didn't get a parcel from their relatives had one from the orphanage.

We started getting ready for Christmas about October, practising for the concerts. We wrote our Christmas cards that went round each year, written in pencil so we could rub them out ready for next year. If you fell out with someone you rubbed out their name and sent it to someone else – the card went on for years! We kept the ones from relations or used them to cut up and make into calendars. At teatime we had a party with games and dancing. Boxing Day was the time the Salvation Army came to play hymns in the front hall. We called them the 'mince pie naggers'!

After school and Saturdays we had to be outside in the playground unless it was raining. We were given some small gardens at one time to grow flowers if we wanted to. I think we had a competition for the best – this was when rules were a bit more lax.

We had gym equipment and practised very hard to give demonstrations – in the war we went to local football matches and other events to raise money for the war effort. We had teams for table tennis, football and hockey to complete with children from outside – in later years we went to their sports grounds. We had a Scout troop and Girl Guides, which brought us into contact with children outside the orphanage.

On the fields at the back of the gardens we played sports. The fields were also used for growing hay and for cattle grazing. The cows were kept for milking. The railway line from Worcester to Malvern ran alongside our fields – one year we went to watch Queen Mary go past in the Royal Train.

We went to church on Sunday mornings and Sunday School in the afternoon. After we were confirmed we went to the 8 o'clock service. On Saturdays and Sundays we went for walks – miles and miles to outlying villages. We picked blackberries for jam and flowers when we could for our window sills in the playroom or for the tables in the dining hall.

Most of the year we wore gym slips and blouses, but in the summer months we changed into flowered dresses with puffed sleeves (the princess line). In the early part of the year we wore straw bonnets with flowers on them but later we changed into summer straw hats. We had navy mackintoshes for everyday but grey coats for best. We had black shoes for winter and sandals in the summer. We cleaned our shoes in a round building in a yard outside the walls of the playroom.

The cane was given for punishment. Other disciplines imposed were being sent to bed and lines. Sometimes all the girls were writing lines. We had not been there long when one boy was caned for kissing a girl in the boiler house – they married in later life! We were also made to stand in line for ages if no one owned up when things had been broken. We lined up for meals and for going to bed or to go anywhere else.

At fourteen we left school but had to work in the orphanage for two years before we left. The girls wore caps and aprons over striped dresses. If you were working in the staff rooms you had an afternoon apron and cap with a black dress. We were allowed to stay up later and the last years I was there we had a sitting room for our own use.

The laundry was hard work as all the washing was done there. We changed jobs once a month so you learnt everything. We had washing machines but most was done in the big tubs round the sides of the room. There were drying rooms – we put the washing on rails with wheels on and pushed them into the drying room. We worked there all day with only about an hour off in the afternoon. All the ironing was done next door but there was a roller iron for sheets and flat irons that fitted on a stove for all other ironing.

The kitchen was quite good work in that you had your dinner there, but it was still hard work as you had to clean it as well. Scullery work was terrible – all pots and pans and all washing up was done here and the preparation of vegetables. We did have a potato peeler but the eyes had to be taken out too, piles and piles of cabbage and root vegetables were prepared as well. The large steam ovens were in here, also a coke boiler for heating this part of the building. In the yard outside was the dairy to separate the cream for the staff.

The swimming pool was behind the kitchen next to the gardener's cottage and laundry. We swam during the summer months about twice a week – the girls and boys on separate days. The schools nearby used it during the war as Sansome Walk Baths were too far from the shelters. If the siren went we had to go to the top passage in the orphanage as there was only one window there. Looking back I don't think we would have lived had there been a bomb as the building would have fallen on us, but we thought we were safe there.

When we first went into the orphanage the matron and master were very Victorian and very strict but as years went by other ones became a bit more human! The assistant matron was married there and our youngest sister was bridesmaid. She left but came back a couple of years later as the matron and master left suddenly. We were treated very harshly at this time as though it was a reform school. This was the one Christmas we had to go without our stocking. The assistant matron came back with her husband as matron and master. He was a Welshman and would sing for us at our Sunday evening service 'The Old Rugged Cross'.

We were allowed to have the radiogram on to hear important news like the abdication speech of Edward VIII, the Coronation of George VI and Queen Elizabeth and the outbreak of war on 3 September 1939 when Neville Chamberlain declared war on Nazi Germany.

During the war, the Scout hut in the grounds and the boys' playroom were used for concerts, dancing lessons and band practice. People came and gave us concerts. We performed our own concerts and pantomimes to raise money for the orphanage.

Some Saturdays we were allowed to go to the children's cinema and were given a box of sweets when we were there by the manager. We also went to the pantomime at the Theatre Royal.

We had the usual children's illnesses – measles, chicken pox when we were put in the sick room. One year we had an outbreak of mumps when nearly everyone got it. We only had two deaths through diphtheria while we were there.

We were proud of the orphanage and if children taunted us while we were out we used to say 'Grammar School Bulldogs, Secondary School Cats – when you see the orphanage please raise your hats!' We were taught to win for the orphanage.

Evacuees came to us from London, Birmingham and Coventry, also one from Poland. We gave up our beds for a whole school from London – I found out later they were billeted in the village we came from for the years of the war. We had a lot more freedom in these years, as we could go to a lot more things taking place outside our world. While working for two years after school we had one afternoon a week off when we could go to town or a walk. We did have a bicycle to use as well if we wanted to.

We did not realise it at the time but we were better off than a lot of children in the thirties as we were quite well cared for. We used to wonder why we had to go to the orphanage and not other children! We had a hard life but we had a lot of fun as well and were kitted out when it was time to leave, taken into the town and bought clothes for our life outside. We were found work to go to mostly in service for girls and gardening or the forces for boys. Some went to HMS *Ganges*. Some of the old boys were killed in the war.

I don't say were equipped for life but we did learn a lot about life that other children did not have the chance to – so our years were not wasted!

EDITH MARY JONES (1935–44)

I remember very clearly my first day, from waiting in the rector's study at Abberley in completely new clothes to going to bed that night. The ride in the car to Worcester was exciting enough to begin with, and then arriving at this huge castle! I walked up the imposing steps with my sisters to be met by the members of the committee just leaving, presumably after their monthly meeting. One member, complete with gold watch chain across his ample stomach, stopped to speak to us and said he hoped we would like living there. I said, 'Do you have fish for dinner because I don't like fish!' He laughed and gave me a penny! It must have been worse for my sisters than for me, as I was the youngest child there for a while. I was only five years old and was made a fuss of.

However, just about a month later another family came – the Monks – and Ethel was younger than me. The attention was switched to her and I was very upset, finally bursting into tears. I was very jealous, but eventually must have realised that this would get me nowhere and we became a pair for many years. It was a sort of love-hate relationship but we were always expected to be together by everyone. She was a 'biter' and was often fenced off in a corner of the playroom as a punishment for having bitten someone. The noise of so many people and the size of the rooms was a shock, and the dormitories with the rows of beds and the polished linoleum, is another vivid memory.

We all had numbers, mine was 89, and all our clothes were marked with this number. I can still recall many of the numbers matched to different girls. 104 was the highest number and that was Phyllis Coker. Later on when the number of inmates lessened we changed numbers and I became 54. All our clothes were made in the sewing room – where there was a sewing mistress, helped by ladies who came in daily, and several girls who had left school to do the mundane things like mending and sewing on buttons. I remember a very pleasant woman named Mrs Harris. She was a very gentle person and I often threaded needles for her. I remember going to her home to tea. I think she must have been there for many years.

It must have been an enormous job making summer dresses for us all. We seemed to have at least one new dress each summer – kept for best of course – worn to church with a panama hat with the orphanage badge on: a green and yellow badge with RAO on it. In the winter we wore gym-slips of navy blue serge; terrible things, as they rubbed on bare legs when we were small and not old enough to wear stockings. We had white blouses and a green and yellow striped tie and we looked quite smart. Navy blue warm coats and navy velour hats completed our outfits. Our shoes were rarely new of course, but I remember we all had new brown sandals every year. The cost must have been a headache to the committee. Later on the sewing room acquired a stocking machine and all the stockings and boys' socks were made on it.

We all had jobs to do, even the five-year-olds. I remember starting by shaking mats, and graduating to polishing door knobs and cutting up the week's supply of salt from huge blocks and filling salt cellars. Setting tables came next and cleaning cloakroom basins. It was many years before I scrubbed floors. In the early years passages were scrubbed every day except Sunday, but later we sprinkled them with disinfected sand and swept them and only scrubbed on Saturday. The playroom was scrubbed every Saturday too, and dormitories polished. Sometimes these jobs had to be done before school and sometimes after school – depending on the staff at the time. After leaving school of course we worked all day. A roster was made and we did several weeks in each job – kitchen help, laundry, scullery (washing dishes, preparing vegetables), sewing room, cleaning staff rooms and so on. The laundry was very heavy, hard work and took all day. Sheets had to be scrubbed and also boys' shirts. We had one small washing machine, but most things were hand washed in big wooden troughs, and ironing in the afternoon. All 'working girls' were allocated a certain number of boys' socks to darn which was a nightmare as I never seemed to get my quota finished for Sunday morning!

We were given one afternoon off during the week and half-a-crown pocket money, but any breakages had to be paid for, so sometimes we got nothing!

In my 'working' days we were allowed out to go to the pictures or even visit friends on our afternoon off, but we had to be at least two together.

Mr and Mrs Whitehead were the master and matron when we arrived in 1935. Mr Whitehead seemed a kindly old man, but Mrs Whitehead was a formidable figure with her white hair piled up on her head in Victorian fashion, I had very little contact with them and they are rather shadowy in my memory. I remember their Scottie dog much better!

We had school in the orphanage in the early days and Miss Pearson was my teacher – a very young, friendly and pleasant person. Mr Parry taught the big children. He was a loud boisterous man. He played the piano while we ate our meals quite often. I learnt to like Gilbert and Sullivan from him. He also organised concerts, and dressed up in female clothes at Christmas parties. I remember him with affection – and also his white Persian cat!

Miss Gossett was there for many years. Later she became Mrs Jenkins and Ethel and I were bridesmaids at her wedding. She came back as matron for a while several years later. Nellie (Bly) Butler was the cook in the early days and Margaret McGrath was in charge of the laundry.

Miss Williams, Miss Cooper and Miss Griffin were all there for many years. I can't remember the names of the couple who came as master and matron later on. Perhaps because they were not very popular and left under some sort of a cloud. They were not there very long and that was the only year that we didn't have Christmas stockings while they were with us.

Mr and Mrs Tyler came after them and were still there when I left. We had much more freedom while they were there and they organised a lot of leisure activities for us and really tried to make the whole place more 'homely'.

The girls' playroom was very large with lockers at one end and big cupboards down one side. There was a very large dolls house, but it was always used as a bookcase, and forms all around the walls. The windows were high up so that we couldn't see out, but it was always warm with central heating pipes all under the seats. We also had a large playground and in the summer spent most of our spare time out there.

Sometimes we were allowed garden plots – depending on the whim of staff at that time. We were not supposed to go into the gardens, but we often did and 'scrumped' fallen apples and plums in season.

My best friend for most of my years there was a girl called Doreen (Jenny) Jenkins. We played together and rarely fell out. We organised long-running games of our imagination: mostly that we were wealthy children and had our own ponies and bicycles etc.; we had so many kids to join in that the game went on for days – rather like present day soap operas! Then suddenly we would get bored with the whole thing and it would be back to cowboys and Indians or cops and robbers. Singing games were always popular and also skipping games. We rarely got bored as we could always drift away and join another group. Hide and seek in the fading light was very exciting and we got more daring and hid in the orchard or behind the swimming pool until someone came to call us in to bed.

In the playing fields there was always hockey in the winter and rounders in summer or watching cricket – only boys played cricket! We had long, long walks on Saturday and Sunday afternoons. We walked miles. Starting off in crocodiles, but being allowed to break ranks when we left the pavements behind. We went to Hallow and Crown East to gather primroses and violets in spring and blackberries in the autumn. We walked along the river both up and downstream, and to Powick and Rushwick the other way. We knew all the surrounds of Worcester and really enjoyed it, but I always knew I would be awake most of the night with aching legs – 'growing pains' I was told, with no pain killers and very little sympathy!

The swimming pool was one of the favourite places and how we enjoyed it; some people didn't swim of course, but for most of us, we couldn't be allowed in often enough. We always felt that the boys had more than their share of swimming, but they did have to clean it, and scrub the white painted bricks free of algae.

For my first two years of education we had lessons at the orphanage, and then went to St Clement's School, going to Christopher Whitehead's later on. I don't remember much about school at RAO except that I very quickly learnt to read. We had lessons under the big trees quite often in the summer, played games in the recreation room in the winter, and lined up for biscuits and milk in the morning playtime.

I enjoyed school and we seemed to be accepted by most other kids at the school, but let something be stolen and all eyes turned on us! After the war started, the evacuees were the suspects. At one time a whole school was evacuated to our school and we had lessons either in the morning or afternoon while they had the other session. We had dancing or singing or games in a nearby hall meanwhile.

Christopher Whitehead School was quite a walk away from home and we usually had a rush to get there after clearing tables and washing the dishes first. We were often late getting back after lunch and local people must have been used to seeing us red-faced and gasping rushing through St John's!

During the war anyone who could get home in ten minutes was expected to leave school and run home if the siren sounded. I can't remember it being necessary though. After school we had Girl Guides, and dancing classes, and a keep fit group. None of these activities were compulsory but most people took part. We often gave displays of both at fetes and village hall concerts and at intervals between football matches.

We got invitations to concerts and church activities and amateur theatricals. In fact, I think anywhere they wanted to fill up the hall! Not that we minded. We had several visits to the old Theatre Royal in Worcester, and of course, in the early years we often went to the St John's cinema on Saturday afternoons. After we had left school there was a brief period when we had lessons in the evenings, also violin and piano lessons, but whether the teachers moved away or gave up in despair I never knew!

In my early days the dining hall was a 'no talking' place. The noise of cutlery clashing with dishes drowned out any voices anyway. Long tables down the room, boys one side, girls the other and serving tables at the top. Later we had tables seating about six, and boys and girls were mixed. Then food was served by the big girl at the head of each table and each person took their strict turn to scrape the pudding dish!

All children up to seven wore bibs and then only girls wore pinafores over their clothes. No one was allowed in the dining hall without one. I often spent most of the dinner hour desperately searching for mine, having flung it down somewhere in my rush to get off to school! Grace was gabbled with one eye open to see what we were having, but if the presiding teacher wasn't satisfied we had to repeat it. We were always hungry and if you didn't like your food there was always someone else ready to eat it.

I found most of the food good, but stew with lumps of fat meat in it I could not swallow!

In the early years the menu was the same week after week but during the war years and after, we had whatever was available. Even during the war years we never seemed to be short of food, but I suppose we had less meat. We always had plenty of vegetables and fruit as the gardens grew everything and milk, eggs, and presumably bacon came from the farm. Pea soup on Tuesdays was the thing I hated most. It was thick and gluey and the peas would not go down! A big girl would be delegated to feed me and would often resort to holding my nose and pouring it down. I often missed my pudding then and sometimes got the soup again on the table at tea-time!

The only occasion I remember when there was nearly a riot was when we were given tripe for dinner. Hardly anyone could eat it and it was wrapped in hankies and pushed up knicker legs to be carried out and buried! Not many people had pudding that day. Every Saturday morning we were presented with a cup of Epsom Salts – regardless of the state of our bowels! We soon learned to hold our noses and pour it down.

Breakfast was usually bread and margarine and lumpy porridge. Dinner was main course and pudding; tea was bread and jam, with a rock bun on Sunday and when we were older bread and cheese for supper. Sometimes we had a boiled egg for breakfast and in later years we sometimes had bacon on toast. We occasionally had fruit with our tea, an apple or a couple of plums or sometimes a dish of raspberries if there was a glut.

The well remembered day when Americans came from a nearby camp with ice cream on Thanksgiving Day! We often got presents when the

Americans were there. Chocolate powder was mixed with milk and spread on bread as chocolate spread. It was delicious. The Americans again gave us parties at Christmas with food we had never tasted before.

Our Christmas always started early. Most of us had a little money in the 'Bank', given by our relatives when they came on visiting day. This was handed in, and the amount written down in a book by one of the staff. This was duly handed out for us to do Christmas shopping. Anyone without money was usually given a small amount at the beginning of December and one Saturday afternoon we set off for 'Woolies' (Woolworth's). Our money had to stretch a long way, but we usually managed to buy something for ourselves as well as our presents: mostly soap and hankies and sixpenny bottles of highly coloured scent. We had fun trying on the wire framed spectacles and hats, getting black looks from the assistants. I suppose a member of the staff was with us but it must have been a nightmare for them!

The sewing room was out of bounds to us for about three weeks before Christmas as presents were sorted by staff members and stockings filled and labelled. It was very exciting but must have been a lot of extra work. Stockings were filled from things sent by members of the public and I suppose accumulated over the year. A lot of them were second hand, but it didn't matter to us! Games or books were for the big Christmas tree present.

Christmas puddings were made early and we all got a stir, getting as much on our fingers as possible! Mincemeat and puddings cooking smell was wonderful.

People sent in their old Christmas cards throughout the year for us to cut up, but they would have been surprised if they had known what we did with them. They were shared between us and carefully put away in our lockers. When Christmas came they were taken out and sorted and on Christmas Eve we took them around the dormitory putting one on everyone's bed. Even your worst enemy had to receive one, but of course they got the dullest one we could find, commonly called a 'deague'. Some of the same cards were doing the rounds for years, with names crossed out and fresh ones written in. The ones you received were carefully put away to be sent on next year, with a few additions from the next share out.

The huge tree was brought into the dining hall a few days before Christmas and another one put in the entrance hall. Decorations were brought out and dining hall, passages and the playroom were festooned with everything that could be found. The boys brought in holly, ivy and mistletoe and put it up with shrieks and struggles! Carols were sung and excitement ran high. Some people went to midnight service but most of us were glad to go to bed early. The 'early birds' were up by 5 a.m. and sometimes staff members who slept nearby rushed in and confiscated stockings from noisy kids!

A traditional apple, orange, nuts and sweets and then quite an assortment of things, mostly small, but my first Christmas I had a Loch Ness Monster which was about a yard long. I had that hideous stuffed toy for several years. Diaries, games, pencils, jewellery: we were pleased with everything. Breakfast brought more presents beside each place. A little calendar from one of the city businesses and a new sixpence from one of the members of the committee.

Church came next and then dinner, the local doctor, Dr Bunting carved the meat – I can't remember what it was, but there was plenty of everything. Then came the puddings! The tradition was to bang spoons on the table and the noise was terrific!

In the afternoon we got presents from our families carried into the playroom in big laundry baskets. Parcels had been made up for people with no one to send to them, so everyone got something.

We 'dressed up' for tea, putting on necklaces, brooches, bracelets, in fact everything we possessed! Jelly and blancmange, cakes and biscuits – and of course crackers. Presents from the tree came next. Later on it was over to the 'Rec', and then the evening really started. Games and dancing, singing and 'turns'. It was all there and we enjoyed every minute of it. We stayed up until very late and the Boxing Day evening was much the same. New Year's Eve was another party night and we always saw the New Year in with 'Auld Lang Syne' to finish. We always had a party on the matron's birthday too, which was 6 January.

In later years we gave concerts around Christmas time and the last two years I was there we did very ambitious pantomimes which ran for a week. As many children as possible took part, but the main characters were usually played by friends of the RAO. Percy Huxter, an ex-Bertram Mills clown, was one of these and Sam Powell who was a youth organiser from Worcester. We enjoyed many evenings with him.

Once Christmas and New Year were over discipline and punishment were back to normal! We were supposed to have no talking in the dining hall and dormitories but in later years these rules were relaxed. Lining up and proceeding in an 'orderly fashion' was maintained – as of course it was in any school, but otherwise for girls; anyway, it was not too strict, except of course when the Carters were master and matron. I think Mr Carter had been a drill sergeant in the army or something similar. We had 'army drill' about twice a week. Numbering from the right and eyes left, we formed fours and left wheeled. We hadn't any rifles but did everything else! This was in preparation for marching to church. Instead of our usual erratic crocodile we swung our arms from the shoulder and stamped our feet to commands. I can't think what the regular church-goers must have thought. He also bought gym equipment and we spent many evenings with the vaulting horse and parallel bars.

Punishment was another matter. There was plenty of that. Boys were caned all the time, for serious matters in front of the whole assembly. I always felt sick at seeing this, but it always seemed much worse when girls were caned. It never happened to me, but I came near to it a few times. We were sent to stand outside the office and had to wait until the master or matron came along. The only time I had any physical punishment was in the early days when we still had school in the home. I had been talking (as usual) and was told to stand in the corner. Mr Parry, the senior schoolmaster, came in and spoke to me. I was dreaming away and didn't hear him. He took a ruler and smacked my bare legs. I got such a fright I wet myself, much to my shame and everyone else's amusement!

We wrote lines by the thousand, got sent to bed with no tea, stood on the forms in the playroom with hands on head. We often got in trouble for talking after lights out and one of the staff would creep up the stairs and then we were in trouble! Sometimes we had to get out of bed and stand in the corridor until we were told we could get back into bed. We didn't have dressing gowns or slippers so this was rather drastic on a winter's night. One night Miss Griffin didn't remember us and when they came up to bed about 11 p.m. we were all crouched shivering in the passage. I can't imagine why we didn't get back into bed.

The worst sort of punishment was by ridicule. There was plenty of that sort too. One poor boy who was rather retarded being made to stand in front of us without his trousers as he couldn't control his bowels. Another boy had a broom tied to his back because he had not done his work. I think that the boys had a much harder time than we did.

I did not take part in any of the night games on the flat roofs, but as my bed was next to the only window that let on to the roof I saw the comings and goings. We did explore when I was older, but only in daylight.

Every so often someone would run away – great excitement! All sorts of stories circulated. Two boys took the cook and her friend's bicycles! Two more got as far as Scotland before being found. We had several boxes of 'dressing up' clothes and these were sorted out for disguise by girls who were running away. They really looked far more conspicuous of course, and rarely got very far. The most we ever did ourselves was to sneak up to the corner shop to buy sweets.

My friend Jenny and I used to talk to the 'Stop me and buy one' ice cream man through the fence, and talked him into giving us one. In exchange we would take a photo of him. Needless to say we didn't have a film for the camera and had to keep putting him off. This was finally stopped when someone living in a house nearby rang the RAO and told them we were seeing him – although it was through six foot iron railings! This often happened as people were always watching to see we didn't step out of line.

The Air Ministry had a depot near the orphanage and we used to meet the workers getting off the train at Henwick Station and of course several of them said 'Hello' each morning. One man became very friendly and would often walk along with a group of us, chatting and asking questions. We thought he was very nice and looked forward to seeing him, but eventually someone told the headmaster. We were all called to the office and questioned and lectured, but no explanation was given to us. We were very innocent, and felt quite sad that our friendship could not continue. We were escorted to school for a week, but we never saw our friend again.

I remember polishing the dormitory linoleum by dragging each other up and down on a blanket.

In 1937 the Royal Train came through the cutting alongside the playing field and Queen Mary was standing by the window waving to us.

There was an old girls' and boys' reunion whilst I was there. We had to sleep and eat in the laundry for the weekend while the dormitories and playroom were taken over by these ladies all dressed up for the ball. They had once been like us!

I remember going to sleep to the strains of 'Jealousy' while a local Ballroom Dancing Competition team practised in the playroom below.

During the war the siren would go off during the night and we would hurry down with our clothes, which we had packed in a drawstring bag before going to bed. We sat or slept on mattresses in the corridors and had cocoa and biscuits. It was fun, except for hearing the bombs falling on Birmingham and Coventry. The only bombs falling close was one lunchtime when bombs were dropped on the Mecco factory nearby. I was in the playground and saw the plane and fell down with the shock of the blast. I believe several people were killed.

My worst memory was of being shut in a small cupboard by a big girl. She went away and left me there and I panicked and screamed and screamed.

Every year we had a month away from the orphanage. Everyone who had any relations was sent to stay with them, and other children were 'fostered' out. We all looked forward to the change – the staff most of all I suspect! Usually painting and repairs were done then and only a caretaker left there. One year our holiday with relations was cut short and we were all taken for two weeks to stay at a camp at Symonds Yat. I thought it was wonderful and consider that to be the happiest two weeks of my whole eleven years! We swam, and walked and had boats on the river. I think the whole thing was arranged by Sam Powell the youth organiser. He was there and saw that we really enjoyed ourselves.

When we were sixteen it was time to move out. We had no choice and mostly were sent into domestic service. One or two were sent to children's nurseries, but when my turn came someone was looking for a kitchen maid. Two of us were sent together to Holt Castle at Holt Heath. We were taken to Witts shop in Worcester and fitted out with two new sets of clothes. We were given a choice within reason but were fitted with corselets – whereas we had never even worn a bra until then. It was quite exciting.

Everyone got a present on leaving we were told, and there were rumours of bicycles and watches, but we got a bible and prayer book – which I still have.

We had plenty of training in work practices, but none in facing the outside world. We had had a few words about 'becoming a woman' at the start of menstruation and a deaconess from the cathedral had come one afternoon in our last year and shown a few pictures in a book of a baby in its mother's womb and a few words about 'keeping pure' – which left us very puzzled, but that was all. We asked no questions and got no answers.

I look back on the years at the RAO and remember mainly the happy times. I don't have any horror stories, and I'm sure in the long run we faired much better than we would have done if we had stayed in our small village.

Most of us would have grown into law-abiding adults and married and had families, although there would have been a few rebels.

KENNETH ROBERT KENDRICK (1936–41)

I had three different master-matrons during my six year stay at the orphanage, and I eventually became head prefect.

The first were Mr and Mrs Whitehead, who retired after thirty years' service. They were Victorian in their discipline and demonstrated no love or sentiment but gave harsh floggings.

Mr Parry and Miss Gossett were the second master and matron that I remember. Mr Parry was a cruel master, who seemed to delight in giving floggings. One's confidence always felt undermined by him, and he never gave praise to anybody. On the other hand, Miss Gossett was more of a kindly person. She would make a fuss of the smaller children and was understanding when children became ill.

Of Mr and Mrs Carter, I only remember that Mr Carter was an ex-Royal Marine PT instructor with a very loud voice, and although he shouted, he never used to flog.

On my first day I remember crying. I was ten years old. I could not understand what had happened to me after my mother had left the building. The building had a hollow and frightening aspect.

My first work duty was being a 'spud kid'. This meant that you prepared vegetables out in the dark kitchen yard from seven o'clock in the morning. As you got older (I was ten when a 'spud kid') you moved on to different work duties, such as scrubbing floors on hands and knees. Every Saturday and Wednesday the large dining hall was scrubbed. We all formed a row across the hall; about twenty children on hands and knees would work across the hall floor.

Mr Parry, the master, would sit on the stage and give the order to commence. Firstly, you would wet the floor with the water, apply the soap to the scrubbing brush, and scrub until he gave you the order to wipe. You would then move back to the next section. If you dragged your bucket instead of lifting it, you were beaten on the head. The dormitories also had wooden floor boards that had to be scrubbed. Later on in the years, they issued us with rubber kneel mats. The staff were known as 'officers' and they took control and made sure that discipline was maintained.

Boys and girls were strictly segregated – even brothers and sisters were not allowed to talk to each other, for fear of corporal punishment.

Between 1936 and 1939, a certain amount of bullying went on. Newcomers were known as 'fresh kids'; their heads were held down in the toilet and the chain pulled to flush it. Sometimes they would be thrown in at the deep end of the swimming pool, and often held under water. However, this did stop in the later years.

At mealtimes in the dining hall the older boys sat round the tables nearest to the stage. Next were tables for the very young girls and boys and furthest away from the stage were tables for the older girls.

The food during these years consisted of two squares of bread, margarine and a cup of cocoa with a little milk or sugar for breakfast; stew, rice and pea soup for lunch; and a cup of tea and two slices of bread with margarine at tea-time. There was a roast Sunday dinner, but never any second helpings. Grace was sung before and after each meal and no talking was allowed during eating. The tables were scrubbed, wooden topped and there were forms to sit on. If you were lucky you would sit at a table with a vase of flowers on – these were handy for emptying your glass of Epsom Salts into!

Christmas was the time of the year we really looked forward to. We could fill our bellies with good food. For the rest of the year, we lived in an atmosphere of strict discipline and sometimes attitudes that hardly differed from the Victorian regime of 1868 – the year this orphanage building was erected.

Only the boys were allowed to view the floggings that took place on the dining hall stage. Flogging took place regularly as part of discipline. I remember one boy, Roy Bishop, who came from Malvern. He was found helping himself to food in the cook's stores. Although he tried to hide in the sugar bin, he was caught. Mr Parry flogged him with a cane that had a brass end on, on his bare buttocks. His screams could be heard throughout the hollow building. In the dormitory that night we all took pity on him. He had to have medical treatment. However, the appalling nature of this incident leaked out, and Mr Parry was instantly dismissed. We all cheered from behind the railings when Mr Parry walked down the drive carrying his suitcase. No more floggings were ever given after this.

In the late 1930s the standard of education which we received was very poor. Lessons took place in the mornings and in the afternoons we would make rugs during the winter months and would go fruit picking or gardening on summer days. After 1939, we attended local schools for our education. A special classroom was provided for some of the backward orphanage children, but as time went on and improvements made, they joined the mainstream of the schools. Before then we were never allowed outside the orphanage gates. If we happened to acquire a few pennies, we would climb over the iron railings to go and buy a loaf of bread or some scratchings. These we would share out with our friends, but there was always the risk of punishment.

Those children over fourteen years old attended Holy Communion at 8 o'clock every Sunday morning. There was Sunday School in the afternoon and evening prayers at the orphanage. I was paid *7s. 6d.* by the vicar each month for pumping the organ.

The uniform when I entered the RAO was a black woollen suit with a hard collar, which we cleaned with monkey gland. We had a black and red striped tie, boots with hob nails, grey socks and a black cap with a red badge and the letters RAO on it. Overcoats were of all sorts and colours. After 1939 the uniform was changed to soft grey woollen suits, with a grey, yellow and green striped tie. We wore a grey cap with a yellow badge and the school initials. We also had navy blue mackintoshes. At the same time that the clothing improved, so did the food.

During Mr and Mrs Carter's service, I was made head prefect. I received five shillings per month and the other two prefects were given *2s. 6d.* As I was head prefect, I was excused quite a few duties, such as squad drill which took place in the recreation room, and cleaning duties. It was my job to march the boys to church in threes every Sunday, giving the orders 'quick march', 'halt' and so on. If you passed any member of staff in the corridor, you had to stand to attention, and let them go by. Mr Carter always treated me very fairly and taught me to read and write and spell. Alas, he was caught interfering with one of the older girls and instantly dismissed.

Many of the children had nicknames; mine was 'Marmite', because my mother used to send me a jar of Marmite every month. The word 'bootlacer' described using part of one's bootlace and toilet paper to make a cigarette. It was lit by a magnifying glass out of an old torch. One boy used up all his boot laces and used wire to do his boots with! He was punished when inspected.

The children who were too young for work duties were known as 'eat, sleep and play kids'; the use of this expression has remained with me to this day!

5

THE 1940s

The climax to the Second World War came with the dropping of the atomic bomb against Japan when Hiroshima and Nagasaki were laid to waste. No other act has altered the history of the world more than this. The story was too big for the newspapers of the day!

Those from the orphanage killed in the war were Alfred James Fudge who died in Normandy in 1944, who was twenty-eight; and Thomas Harvey Fogg who died in action in 1940 aboard HMS Glorious. *He was only eighteen years old.*

A Birmingham businessman and old boy of the RAO phoned me after seeing my advertisement in the Worcester News and Times. *He said that he couldn't watch the film* Oliver Twist *without bursting into tears, it reminded him so much of the orphanage. Then he proceeded to tell me about Freddie Mills who came to Worcester during the war. Several boys from the orphanage went to watch him box. At that time Freddie Mills was one of the greatest boxers in the world.*

The headmasters and matrons during this decade are as follows:

Mr and Mrs Carter 1940–42.
Mr and Mrs Tyler 1942–46.
Mr and Mrs Smith 1946–55.

JOHN BULLOCK (1938–43)

The journey from our home in Malvern Link although only seven miles away, was like travelling to the other side of the world. I was ten and my brother seven. My brother and I arrived at the orphanage accompanied by our father who departed very quickly or so it seemed at that time! We were allocated numbers which we kept for the duration of our time there. Mine was 21, my brother's was 5. We were handed over to a senior boy who was responsible for looking after us and generally showing us the ropes. The next few weeks I became so very homesick as the Malvern

Hills in the distance could be seen on clear days, our old home being at the foot of the Malverns.

Work duties were allocated almost as soon as we were admitted, although this was not so with my brother as he was a little younger than I was. I remember being detailed to potato peeling duties in the evenings after school hours. Then other duties consisted of scrubbing all the corridors, passages, floors and main entrance hall. These duties were all performed during the early morning before breakfast and school. Saturday mornings were spent scrubbing the floors of the recreation room and old school rooms, dining hall and in the summer months the swimming pool.

The main memory is of one headmaster, Mr Carter, an ex-PTI of the Royal Marines. He made life generally pretty grim. He had a Spartan attitude to everything and he was a very strict disciplinarian. I can recall the regular gymnasium sessions and I swear that some of the boys vaulted the box and horse with sheer fright, more so than a general ability to do so! All this changed when Mr Carter left us and Mr Tyler came. Life became by comparison quite pleasant.

Life in the orphanage was dominated by a certain amount of bullying by some of the senior boys, these positions being taken by more junior boys as the older boys left. I must have been guilty of bullying myself as I became more senior! There was however a great feeling and bond of comradeship amongst all the boys. The girls were strictly segregated. The only contact with girls on a routine basis was in the dining hall.

Discipline was very strict under Mr Carter but much more relaxed under Mr Tyler. Punishment was sometimes very physical in the form of extra sessions of PT and floor scrubbing as well as corporal punishment.

I can recall an occasion when scaffolding was in position during repairs. This gave access to the roof and to the girls' part of the building and full advantage of this was taken by both girls and boys!

We led a very full sporting life, including soccer, hockey, cricket, boxing, swimming and of course gymnastics. The orphanage boys were all outstanding at sporting activities as opposed to academics. We went to local schools and mixed with local children who were always referred to as 'outsiders'. The orphanage fielded their own teams in all the team sports and the local school teams were often made up of 50–80 per cent orphanage boys.

Life on the farm and in the gardens was mainly a happy period. This was because by the time I had left school at fourteen, Mr Tyler had become headmaster. We spent two years working in the gardens and smallholding under the supervision of the head gardener. I became a very close friend of him and his family and I continued to visit them for several years after I had left the orphanage. The work in the gardens was hard; all the ground under cultivation was dug by hand with spades. As many as a dozen or so boys with the gardeners would all work together on the same plot of ground, each taking a spit of ground across the plot one behind the other. No one could stop to rest unless everyone stopped at the same time. I always remember the sight of the spades hanging in the cowshed, the blades looking like burnished steel. There was a certain sense of pride in having a spade which was recognised as one's own. During the war years a lot of the fruit trees were cut down so that more ground was available to grow food and in turn this made more ground to be dug. By and large I have found the variety of jobs done during the two years in the gardens and small farm has stood me in good stead in later life.

I can only say this about religion as taught by the orphanage: it was simply rammed down our throats with it all being strictly compulsory, no freedom of choice whatsoever, with Bible classes, confirmation classes and Sunday School as well as Sunday morning and evening services. All this did for me was to make me a non-religious person.

Schooling at the orphanage was carried out on the premises until just prior to my brother and I entering. The result was almost without exception that orphanage boys were all a little backward in most subjects. The standards of teaching in the orphanage school must have been pretty low indeed. As I have already stated, what the orphanage boys lacked in the three Rs they made up for on the sports field.

Walking in crocodile I remember well, but we didn't walk, we marched like guardsmen or should I say marines. We marched to school, we marched to church, we marched back from school and believe me no outside children took the mickey; they didn't dare! All this marching and military bearing changed with the departure of Mr Carter. Under Mr Tyler we walked backwards and forwards to school as individuals.

During the real bad years we all dressed the same with short grey trousers and grey shirts or jerseys. Heads were all shaved. But this all changed for the better under Mr Tyler. I cannot remember details of dress but the older boys from fifteen or sixteen years old started to wear long trousers for the first time!

In one respect the orphanage equipped me for the outside world. I can

Orphanage gymnastics in the 1940s

sum this up quite easily by stating that when I joined the army as a volunteer in the closing months of World War II, I found the army life was like a holiday camp compared with life under Mr Carter!

As far as food goes I remember we were always hungry. From the day I entered to the day I left I was hungry. Slices of bread became a form of currency. Bread was always referred to in squares for a whole slice, half squares and half a half square. Pieces of bread were used as bartering agents for favours or exchanging for toys or sweets.

The food in general must have been wholesome and adequate but as my memory goes it was never enough. I recall the table arrangements: small boys, junior boys and senior boys. The small boys and junior boys dared not go for second helpings when asked to for fear of the senior boys afterwards, so it was always the senior boys who got the second helpings. The quality and variety was never varying: the same meals on the same day of each week, the only exceptions being the vegetables in season from the gardens. Like every other thing food improved with Mr Tyler becoming headmaster and I suppose at the end of the day the orphanage children were generally healthier and fitter than most outsiders during the periods of war time rationing.

GERALD BULLOCK (1938–47)

I can well recall that day, 8 October 1938, when having travelled from Malvern Link by train to Henwick Road Station, my father took my brother and me up the drive to what appeared to be a very large and rather ominous, though well kept building. We were met by the then headmaster, Mr Parry, and the matron, Miss Gossett. When our father left us I remember bursting into tears. We were put in the charge of an older boy who I think was called Wally Bird. Incidentally I have bumped into this person in later years, he was always a pleasant man who worked for the Metal Box Co. Ltd for many, many years.

The reason my brother and I entered the orphanage was the death of our mother. I was seven, and I stayed there until I was sixteen in August 1947.

During that period I remember many headmasters. After Mr Parry there followed Mr Carter, Mr Jenkins, Mr Tyler and Mr Smith. To my knowledge the last headmaster was Mr Hughes and then the orphanage closed down. Of the headmasters the one who stands out most in my memory is Mr Tyler who ran the establishment more like a boarding school than an orphanage. He was sports orientated and under the tuition we received from him we enjoyed great success in cricket, football, swimming and athletics, winning several trophies. Mr Smith, who succeeded Mr Tyler, was a very homely and caring man. The cook was a Miss Williams assisted by Miss Griffin and Miss Hughes.

When you became a junior boy you were given duties in the evenings and weekends. I remember my particular task was scrubbing the steps to the main doorway, six days a week – not Sundays! Also in summer evenings and at weekends we used to weed the gardens on our hands and knees.

One of our pranks was to sell produce from the orphanage gardens to people passing by. We had to choose our customers very carefully as some would report us to the headmaster! With the money from the sale of produce we would climb over the fence and run to the local bakery and buy stale cakes from the previous day. Incidentally, these cakes were kept specially for us! If other people asked for these cakes the owner of the shop would say, 'These are reserved for the orphanage children.' These cakes cost 1*d.* for four. We also used to buy loaves of bread, take the middle out and fill them up with scratchings from the local fish and chip shop.

We were made to go to bed at a certain time. No reading or talking was allowed. Some member of staff would be spying on us. Naturally we were spying on them also! One dormitory for the boys was next to a girls' dormitory with a door between always kept locked. We were very naughty and looked through the keyhole to see if we could see the girls undressing!

Bath night was always on Friday night, two in a bath with one of the staff in attendance.

On Sunday nights we had an evening service; this used to be known as our 'Home Service'. The matron or master took it and it was often attended by friends of the home, including committee members. This service I always enjoyed.

In the early days the dining room tables were long ones and you always sat at the same place. When the Tylers took over as master and matron they had individual tables with boys and girls mixed.

Discipline was very strict indeed. Various forms of punishment were administered. I certainly remember the cane being used many times and I am sure there was not one boy who did not have the cane at one time or another. Other forms of punishment were doing extra work such as scrubbing corridors or writing lines. On one particular occasion some new very large teapots were purchased. The handles at the top swivelled and one of the nuts holding the handle on the top came off. I was blamed and I had to scrub the dining room five times in one week hoping to find this nut. I never did find it! Another incident I recall was when I was given the punishment of scrubbing a corridor. Mrs Tyler came along and kicked the bucket over deliberately and said I had put it in her way. Next time she came along I said I would throw it over her if she threatened to kick it over again. For this I received the cane.

I was very keen on sport though not very good at it. During Mr and Mrs Tyler's stay at the orphanage they encouraged sport and we took it much more seriously than ever before. We played football and cricket on a regular basis competing against local schools and village teams.

We had our own swimming pool and we competed in the local Scout Championships, always doing well but usually finishing second. One year we won the cup and Mr and Mrs Tyler were so delighted we were treated to fish and chips. Our swimming coaches were Mr Cotterill and Mr Herbert who were both policemen. Mr Cotterill was a very dear friend to my wife and me for many years until his death.

There were Scout and Guide troops and we competed against other Scout troops in the area and had many successes. I remember being invited and attending several Scout camps with other troops outside the orphanage.

Children left school at fourteen years of age and for the next two years we helped in the gardens and with the care of the animals. We grew produce and milked our own cows. We also kept pigs and chickens, the tending of which was part of our job from fourteen until sixteen. Another of our duties was to look after the boilers which provided the orphanage with central heating and hot water. During this period I was taught to drive the tractor and how to plough, feed animals and milk the cows. The head gardener and stockman was a Mr Tong, a most likeable man who I believe came from Herefordshire. His knowledge of horticulture and agriculture was tremendous. We used to boil food for the pigs in an old copper and the grain we fetched from the local vinegar works on a truck which we pushed along right through the middle of the city of Worcester. The foreman of the vinegar works was a very kind man who used to give us sixpence. Incidentally, I see this man to this very day. We were paid five shillings a month for our gardening duties. As senior boys we were allowed into Worcester one Saturday afternoon a month, pay day!

We attended St Clement's Church every Sunday morning and Sunday School in the afternoon. A Mr Downie was the rector there and we found his services rather boring.

The first school I attended as an infant and junior was St Clement's Church School. The headmaster was a Mr Rabjohns. As a senior I went to Christopher Whitehead Secondary Modern School. As these were the war years very often we were called out to help local farms pick their crops for which we got paid.

Whenever we went outside the orphanage we had to walk in crocodile but this all changed about 1945 when we walked in smaller groups.

Generally grey was the colour of most of our clothes including Sunday best. If you were in the cricket team Mr and Mrs Tyler kitted you out with grey blazers and flannels.

Food was very basic, lots of bread and porridge. A rock cake was a Sunday treat. There was a boiled egg once a month. I used to swap a piece of bread for an egg. One of my duties as senior boy was stoking the boilers for domestic hot water and central heating. When I had finished this chore I went to the kitchen where the cook, Miss Williams, and one of the senior girls, Mary Jones, cooked me a Welsh rarebit. Really the food must have been more than adequate bearing in mind there was a war on.

Orphanage pantomime in the 1940s

Before facing the outside world we were encouraged to learn carpentry and other activities connecting with farming. I feel the discipline we received was good for us in teaching us to respect people and property.

During my time in the orphanage I remember the war years and the kindness of the American servicemen. On thinking back to the years I spent at the Royal Albert Orphanage I realise how fortunate I was.

Many years ago I had the great pleasure of attending the centenary of the foundation of the Royal Albert Orphanage when I met old boys and girls I had not seen for many years.

ELLA JEAN HARVEY (1943–49)

With reference to your letter in Tuesday's 'News and Times' regarding the Royal Albert Orphanage in Henwick Road – I was a child there with my sister Joan for six years from 1943 to 1949. I was eleven and my sister eight when we went in.

I don't remember much about my first day at the orphanage. I can't even remember who took us but we went by car. We went up the steps and then we were taken into the boardroom and Mrs Strangeman introduced us to the matron and then the matron rang a bell and Miss Griffin came along. Whenever a new child came into the orphanage the first thing they did was give you a bath and wash your hair and put you into orphanage clothes. When I went into the orphanage I had my hair down to my waist and it was blonde and curly. Well, the first thing they did was cut your hair. They took me to the playground and said to the girls, 'Got a brush, anybody want to brush the new girl's hair?' And they brushed it – all the girls had short hair. I had my long hair for about a month. Then we went into the dining hall for tea. We had bread and scrape and what I thought was cabbage. I said, 'Can you pass the cabbage down, please.' The kids laughed and said, 'It's lettuce!' They were in an uproar, they found it most amusing. I'd been in three homes before this one but I'd never seen lettuce. Well, the lettuce was something to put in with the bread and scrape.

I can give you names of all the staff at that time. The headmaster and matron were Mr and Mrs Tyler first, then after them Mr and Mrs Smith. The cook was Miss Williams. The mistresses who looked after us were Miss Wood, Miss Griffin, Miss Cooper, Miss Cattell, Miss Hughes (Cleo) and Miss Hill. The sewing mistress was Mrs Harris who became the matron after Mrs Smith died. Mr Cotterill (Rick) was our swimming instructor who also took us for PT.

While I was there, there were about a hundred children – boys and girls. We went out daily to school which was St Clement's, St John's or Christopher Whitehead School. I became very friendly with Mr Cotterill and his wife. Mrs Cotterill still lives in St John's. Mr Cotterill very kindly gave me away when I got married. He sadly died recently but I still keep in touch with Mrs Cotterill.

Pearl Milward was very good at acrobatics and ballet, but in March 1949 she was diagnosed with heart trouble. It must have come as a dreadful shock to her. She was a very poorly little girl and she was admitted to the Worcester Royal Infirmary. Pearl was removed from the Infirmary in August of that year at her mother's request. When she came back to the orphanage she was put in the corner of the dormitory. They bought her a radio – we didn't have one but Pearl was a special case as she was so ill. The orphanage was very kind and bought her this radio to pass the time for her. Pearl was a lovely girl. She died in September 1949 of heart trouble in Kidderminster District Hospital, when she was twelve years old.

We didn't have a radio downstairs for years. One of the kids would say, 'I heard something on the radio today,' and we all found it very new and exciting. After I left the orphanage I returned to help look after the little boys and it was while I was there that the news from the radio made a great effect on me. It was 6 January 1952 – the death of King George VI.

The weight of the saucepans we carried in the kitchen was enormous. One was 48 lbs cast iron which we filled with potatoes and other vegetables. The other was 24 lbs. That is probably the reason why several of us have had back trouble: me with my heart carrying such heavy weights. Two of us were meant to carry these saucepans but if nobody was around we had to do it ourselves. We don't think it did us any good, anyway!

I would help prepare the breakfast for the next day. I helped Miss Griffin do the bread and scrape, as we used to call it, for breakfast the next morning and I cut my hand a couple of times on that bread machine and I never had stitches in it – and I've still got the scar.

We had to do the vegetables the next day for dinner. We came home from school at dinnertime, some of the children were sent to lay the tables for dinner and some of us were in the scullery washing up the utensils that had been used during the morning. Then we had our dinner. Afterwards we would wash up and scrub the scullery and kitchen floor before we went back to school and half the time we were running down the road with dirty knees! It's true – we used to be late, but we hadn't got time to wash our knees because we were frightened of being late for school. You couldn't win!

At one time we had a cookery lesson at school – we were making a stew and cutting up carrots and I put a piece of carrot in my mouth as a joke. I got on very well with all the teachers at school and was a bit of a pet. She said, 'What are you eating, Ella?' and I replied 'Oh! a piece of raw carrot.' Then she said, 'You have a black star!' I didn't take any notice because all the other kids were saying, 'Well, we're eating raw carrots too.' So I never took any notice of it really. At the end of the day she said, 'Hands up those who think they've been good and we'll give them cakes.' So I put my hand up and she said, 'But Ella, you can't say you've been good, because you've got a black star!' So then I had to go to the orphanage and say I'd got a black star at school. Well, a black star meant five detentions and to go on the platform in front of the whole school at Christopher Whitehead. Back at the orphanage I got punished for it and received the cane.

In the morning, I don't know which day, the headmistress at Christopher Whitehead school used to read out the good stars and the black stars and she said, 'We've got one this week to spoil the record,

Ella Harris.' So I had to go on the platform in front of the whole school on stage. She said, 'Now what have you had a black star for?' and I said 'For eating a piece of raw carrot in school in the cookery lesson.' The headmistress cried, 'What did you say?' And I shouted, 'Eating a piece of raw carrot in the cookery lesson,' and the school was in an uproar. They laughed and laughed. They thought it was so stupid. I don't know if the mistress laughed but the other teachers laughed. They thought it was absolutely ridiculous! I don't remember getting the cane at school, but I do remember getting the cane for it at the orphanage. But that's life, isn't it?

Peggy Allison was the girl who chased the cook round the kitchen with a carving knife. Peggy and I were working in the kitchen with Miss Williams, the cook. We called her 'Ma Willie' behind her back. The teachers were all referred to as 'Ma'. I don't know what Miss Williams had said to Peggy but all of a sudden she got a knife and chased Miss Williams, who was a very fat lady. 'Go and get some help,' Miss Williams cried. But I just stood there killing myself laughing. I thought it was hilarious for Peggy. She was the tomboy of the lot, chasing Ma Willie round the table with a carving knife. Yes, it was really funny. I don't know what happened next. I suppose someone came in and stopped it, but all I can see is ginger-haired Peggy chasing Miss Williams round the table with a carving knife. What with me laughing and Ma Willie screaming – well, she was frightened, wasn't she! Peggy wasn't joking, she really meant it! She was very fiery. Peggy was my best friend.

During my time we had Christmas pantomimes in the main hall and PT displays in the orphanage grounds. On Christmas day we came down and had boiled eggs for breakfast which was quite a treat. Under the plate was a silver *6d.* which made us feel quite rich. At Christmas dinnertime after we had eaten our first course we would get hold of our spoons and start banging the table like mad, and saying, 'We want our pudding – we want our pudding.' Then the doctor brought it in all in flames.

But going back to the silver *6d.* The next day, Boxing Day, the Salvation Army came and played their tunes in the dining hall but we called them 'the mince-pie naggers'. They came for the mince pie and coffee and then handed their bag or plate round and we had to put our silver *6d.* or what money we had in their receptacle. That is all the money my sister Joan and I had all year. A lot of the children had their own money from relatives and they used to go and buy sweets on a Saturday. Joan and I were unlucky – we never had any money. The Salvation Army may do a good job in the world but they also took our silver *6d*!

Once we'd gone to bed and the lights were out and the staff had gone downstairs we would go into the bathroom and open the bathroom window and go down a slope on the roof. If you didn't do it you were called a coward and you all had to follow the leader. The leader was mostly Peggy Allison – she was a proper daredevil and you had to do it. Then you walked along a narrow ledge with the sides of the roof either side sloping upwards. When we walked past the boot yard it was a sheer drop and I was petrified.

After I left school I did six months parlour work, six months kitchen work, six months scullery work and six months laundry work. This was our two year stint before leaving the orphanage and going out into the world.

I went to bed one night very late after doing parlour work because the master and matron had supper very late – they had bacon and cooked meals. On going up to bed I thought I'd have a bath and got into the bathroom and Peggy Allison and Marion Brace were in the bath. They were not like our little baths of today, they were big baths. And I said, 'How long are you going to be, because I want a bath?' And they said, 'Oh! We've only just got in.' So I had a wash and got into bed. In our dormitory my bed was right by the door. All of a sudden Marion came out dressed in her nightie and she starts shouting, 'Roll up, roll up, sixpence to see the bare lady. Roll up, roll up, sixpence to see the bare lady!' Then all of a sudden the door opened and in walked Mr Smith the headmaster. Marion dived into bed. Peggy, I should think, was fifteen or sixteen at the time. She came out, waltzing around with not a stitch on, going from bed to bed, she couldn't understand why we were all as quiet as a mouse, we were killing ourselves under the bedclothes, and all at once she saw the headmaster and dived into bed. Then Mr Smith said, 'Good night, girls,' and turned the light out and that was that. We never did get punished for that, although once you had gone to bed you couldn't talk and we were very silent that night!

One night, when I was still going to Christopher Whitehead School, I was given some quicksilver mercury. I took mine to bed and in the next bed to me was Brenda. She and I were playing with the mercury, it was fascinating. We hadn't seen anything like it before and Miss Griffin caught us. We had to go downstairs and scrub all the passages along the girls' side and the sewing room late at night as our punishment for playing around with this quicksilver.

I remember coming home from school one day and I had to scrub the passages. It was a big passage to scrub and was red and black. I scrubbed it once and then I had to go and get Miss Griffin to examine it. She came and said, 'Scrub it again.' So I scrubbed it again. She came back the second time and said, 'Scrub it again.' I thought, well, I've done it properly so I took my time and just wiped it over. And she came back the third time and said, 'Scrub it again.' I waited a long time and just wiped it and it looked as if it had dried off slowly. I fetched her and she said 'Why didn't you do that in the first place?' It just shows you – she was in one of those moods!

Oh, I haven't mentioned the cabbage. Because half the time there were caterpillars in it! The cabbage wasn't washed very well. To this day I will not eat cabbage. I hate it and yet my sister Joan loves cabbage. She says it does her good. She'll save the cabbage water and drink it with her dinner. But my sister in those days was a little gannet, she would eat anything! She was always hungry!

They made brawn at the orphanage. Ugh! I wouldn't eat it if you gave me a thousand pounds today. I was supposed to eat it but half the time I would throw it behind the radiator. I didn't care that it stained the walls, because the boys used to have to clean the dining hall. Some of the kids would take newspapers into dinner and put the brawn between the news sheets! It's not like a soup or stew, it's very meaty and very fatty. Some boys would be prepared with paper in their pockets and put the brawn in the paper, into their pockets and then throw it down the loo afterwards. But we girls hadn't got pockets to do this. My sister would have anybody's brawn! Oh! I couldn't but I wasn't at the same table as she was. I really hated it.

When I became a working girl at fourteen I could have my dinner at any time. I would put mine in the Aga stove and say, 'I'll do this job and I'll do that job.' We were working in the kitchen all the time. And a bit later on when it was all dried up I would say, '1 haven't had my dinner!' And because it was too dried up it would be an excuse not to eat it. I don't know how I survived because I hated the food in the orphanage.

We had a new fire rope which was in the bathroom, so that if we had a fire you could escape via this rope. Peggy Allison dared us to drop her down into the yard and she would sneak back through the side entrance and up the stairs without being caught. She bet she could do it and we said she couldn't. So we let her down on the fire rope – it was like a tubing. She got down and undid herself and we rolled the thing up but when she got to the side door, it was locked for the first time! After a while she started chucking bits of coke up saying, 'Pss! Pss! Get me up, the door's locked.' And we said, 'We can't.' Because a thing like that is used for letting people down but not dragging them back up again. Anyway we dropped the thing down and she put it round her stomach and we pulled her back up. We eventually got her up and back into bed but somebody had heard the shouting and swearing from the Orphanage Lane, as we dragged her back up. They rang the orphanage to report this. The master and matron came up to the dormitory but we were all in bed pretending to be asleep. Sometimes they would come and shine a torch in your eyes to see if you were asleep. Peggy was really very funny, and was very nice too.

I remember the day Ethel Monk and Mary Jones left the orphanage to go into service. They were all dressed up in new clothes, because when you left you were provided with a rig-out and it came as a surprise to us that they came downstairs all dressed up, with their cases and they said, 'We are off for a new job.' Well, most if not all the girls went into service. It was cheap labour really. And that's all I remember. Ethel Monk and Mary Jones left the same day.

The thing I really hated was dancing lessons. I hated it. I was more interested in swimming and outdoor sports, but as far as dancing was concerned it wasn't my cup of tea – but you had to do it anyway!

Orphanage dancing display in the 1940s

We had a member of staff named Miss Tucker. She was taken to Powick Mental Asylum about midnight. They found she'd been shoplifting and she'd gone a bit funny. She used to be in charge of the laundry and could have been thirty or forty years old. I remember hearing the scuffling at night when they came to fetch her away. The next day we asked and they said, 'Oh! She's just gone.' They found her room full of shoplifted things, and food from the orphanage kitchen she'd put in her bedroom.

I still keep in touch with some of the teachers we had at Christopher Whitehead School. I was talking to one the other day and she said, 'The orphanage children were the best behaved children in the school.' Well, we were too frightened to do anything wrong at school because you only got punished when you got back to the orphanage. But it didn't do us any harm. Not really. I don't think so anyway. I was glad I was brought up in the orphanage.

JANET MARY WESTON (1945–47)

I can recall my first day at the Royal Albert Orphanage very well. I was overawed at the vastness of the impressive looking building that confronted my father and me as we turned into the driveway. However, as my two brothers were already there I looked forward to seeing them again after a long time. This took my mind off feeling nervous. I said goodbye to Dad who was upset at having to leave me there. I was just nine years old. However, it was a comfort to him to have us all under the same roof. Dad tried hard to keep us all together but the army insisted that after he had buried our mother who died unexpectedly, he went back into the army to be demobbed.

In those days the building was in much better condition than it is now. As I remember, the gardens were always neat and tidy. Now it always looks so shabby. I soon got into thc routine of daily life and made friends. My special friend was Heather Drew who I still see from time to time as she only lives round the corner from me. We were of course expected to do our share of the cleaning and were allocated our own patch of scrubbing the passages and common room which was rather long. We also had duties in the scullery. I well remember slicing the bread and buttering it up.

On my first evening there it was 'darning socks' time. I didn't know how to do it, got a reprimand from Miss and was promptly shown. Some of the socks had huge 'taties' in them which were skilfully mended by the older girls.

It was near Christmas when I first went there and the children were rehearsing for a pantomime so it all seemed very exciting. I didn't have a part because I was a new girl. Miss said I could stand very still at the back of the stage wearing a beautiful crinoline gown and curly wig. I was so thrilled.

I only have vague memories of the staff, their names escape me, but the reprimands and those awful lines, I do remember. Whatever we did wrong the punishment was 500 lines, or more! On reflection it put a common bond between us all because one could get into trouble for the slightest misdemeanour and groups of us would be sitting down writing out our lines. Some of the girls were headstrong and hated the orphanage life. This made for excitement and there would be the inevitable running away. They were always caught and brought back, and were sent to Coventry. No one dared to speak to them until it was allowed. We would all chatter on about it for days.

Life in the dormitories was great fun. After lights out, we listened for Miss to retire then played the game of 'Truth, Dare and Promise', and sometimes got caught. We would hear all sorts of noises from the attics which were not in use. One day it was found that someone had been hiding out up there. What great excitement and fear that created. It was said to be a German prisoner of war who had escaped from one of the camps. He had broken into the larder and stolen some food.

During the school summer holidays we were boarded out to families in the countryside. I went with my two brothers to Ivy House Farm, Bishampton. The lady of the house was a Mrs Corbett. She was a big plump lady who was very kind to all of us. What super food we had. The rats used to bite off the heads of the ducks. So duck was often on the menu. After the meagre rations at the orphanage I was always starving. Here we were really spoiled. What a pleasure it was to spend our days playing on the farm, in the fields, in the orchards and riding on the cart. I think it did us a lot of good to have such a fuss made of us all.

Walking in crocodile was a common practice. All I remember about it was that it was either very hot or freezing cold and the walks seemed to go on for ever.

The food was very mixed – what there was of it! I loved some of the puddings especially spotted dick, which was made in tall stone jars. The horror of all horrors was bread pudding which to me tasted very much like beer. It was always sloppy and looked awful. One day Miss caught the girl serving giving me a tiny portion. She was told not be so mean and give me more. A dishful! I had to eat it all up. Needless to say I was very sick afterwards.

Our clothes were the same. We always had our Sunday Best and to this day I keep a set of clothing to wear on special occasions, a good habit I think. We were lucky because we all looked smart for school and weekends. With the war on many people must have had to go without.

When it came to facing the world outside I found that living in the orphanage made me confident and independent which unfortunately did not go down too well when we were taken out of the orphanage to live with dad and a new step-mum.

Life in the common room was mostly okay but there could be arguments and even downright unpleasantness. A lot of children, especially girls, living under one roof breeds petty jealousies if one was made more of than another. I got into trouble many times because I was rather mature for my age at nine to eleven years so Miss could never make up her mind as to whether I should be a big girl or a little girl. The little girls were sent to bed very early and the big girls would go over to the building where we put on the shows and Christmas pantomime. There would be all sorts of treats going on. One day Miss decided I should go over with them but not to tell anyone. So what did I do? I went straight and told Beaky Griffin who was furious because she couldn't go. All hell let loose and did I get into trouble for that little indiscretion. Believe me, I really learnt to keep my mouth shut after that.

So instead I was made to stay behind on Saturday evenings to answer the front door. That used to terrify me because the little girls would be put to bed, the big girls would all be over in the hall with the Misses and I would be in the girls' half of the building by myself. Remember that it was wartime with mutterings of escaped prisoners all the time. My legs used to go to jelly if ever the door bell pealed. I was really frightened but had no choice but to do as I was told.

Another punishment, to my mind, was being thrown out to play on Saturday mornings in the middle of winter. Oh, the freezing cold! I hated it because the morning seemed to go on forever. Even now I won't hang about when the weather is very cold. On Saturday afternoons we were allowed to go into St John's to spend our pocket money. Of course everyone bought sweets. When we got back there would be much swapping going on. I remember there was a gym room and we girls loved to sneak in to play on the vaulting horse. If we got caught it would be the inevitable 500 lines of 'I must not . . .'

We also had a small swimming pool – what luxury for us in those days. I remember warm summer evenings having great fun in the outdoor pool. Then there was bonfire night – what excitement that created! I must not forget to mention the little romances that went on. All in greatest secrecy of course. Boys and girls were segregated except at mealtimes. If I remember rightly the girls used to sneak out after lights out. I don't know if any of them ever got caught.

Shortly before I left, a scheme was brought out to the effect that on Saturday afternoons students from the college in Henwick Road would collect us for a few hours to take us to tea. If I remember correctly we had an auntie and uncle each. This was a great treat in those austere years.

After two years Dad remarried and we went home. I think about the boys and girls often but a lot of the memories have faded!

MARIAN ANN BRACE (1945–52)

I'm sure it was a Saturday afternoon when I first went into the Royal Albert Orphanage. We were told we were going for a walk – no idea whatsoever that we were going into the orphanage. There were my two brothers and my twin sister, Stella. I was just ten years old.

Twins Marian and Stella Brace in 1945 (front row extreme right)

The impression I got of the building when I first saw it was very frightening. It looked like a huge castle in large grounds with a big sign saying the 'Royal Albert Orphanage'.

Work duties never really ended, because they didn't employ any domestic cleaners at all. The work and cleaning of the huge building with lots of rooms and long corridors was done by all the girls and boys. We were always scrubbing, on our hands and knees, always polishing and dusting. If it wasn't done properly we had to start all over again. The dormitories were huge with all these single iron beds. Every morning you had to strip your bed, turn your mattress, then make your own bed with all the sheets and blankets tucked neatly in at the corners much like they do in hospitals. The beds were checked by the mistress and if not made up to standard were stripped off and had to be made all over again. You were then reported to the master, and waited outside his office for the cane.

I always remember my first duty, it was to clean and polish all the girls' shoes in a little round building in the yard – it was called the 'Boot House'. But there were other duties to be done like laying the tables in the big dining hall. Boys sat at one end, girls the other. We were never allowed to sit on mixed tables. All vegetables had to be prepared the previous night. It was a large scullery, with one sink, a potato peeler and a bread slicer in a corner. In the other corner was a big fireplace. One of the older boys' duties was to keep it well stoked up with coke because it heated the water all over the building.

I remember the boy's name who used to do all the stoking up. It was David Allison but we always called him 'Clinkers' as a nickname. He also had a brother called Peter and a sister called Peggy who was quite a character; she was a tomboy and was always in trouble. Peggy was forever ripping her clothes, so they made her a dress of real tough grey material and made her wear that.

I seem to be jumping about a little bit but there were such a lot of things I want to tell you while they are fresh in my mind. We drank out of tin mugs which were always chipped and all the pots and pans were huge. I remember two huge pans being full of potatoes and two being full of porridge which was always cooked the night before on a great big Aga cooker. Then next morning it was heated up, no sugar in it and that was served up for breakfast with a big ladle. It took two girls to carry it.

Going back to the work duties again, the girls' playroom was very big. It had a wooden floor, which every Saturday morning had to be scrubbed.

There were so many of us for this duty. Each one of us had what we called a 'wag' (that was the width) and the whole length had to be scrubbed clean with no overlapping marks or else it had to be done again. The dormitories, playrooms, sewing room, passages, bathrooms, kitchen, scullery, laundry room and dining hall were also scrubbed clean by the boys and girls.

The main duties of the staff were to keep control of the children. A Miss Hughes was over the girls. I remember she lived in Kidderminster; she was a kind, portly sort of woman. She used to keep us in order and saw that all the work jobs were done properly, checked our clothes and shoes and generally gave us orders. Miss Edna Hill was over the boys. She lived in Upton-on-Severn. Then there was the lady in charge of the kitchen. I just can't think of her name, but she married one of the RAO boys.

One of the funny incidents I remember was one day we were all going swimming – girls only. Well, before I had a chance to take my clothes off, one of the girls pushed me in fully clothed. Well, the master came on the scene. I was trying to hide, but he spied me and said, 'Is there someone over there with their clothes on?' Of course all the girls were laughing. A Mr Cotterill taught us all to swim. We were taught on a piece of rope. It was put round our waist and we were pulled to the side, but if I remember nearly all the children could swim.

All I remember about the dormitory was rows and rows of beds each side with the gangway in the middle. There was the big dormitory and a little dormitory. Up to a certain age you were in the little dormitory. I always remember a little girl called Christine Anney. She was always in trouble for wetting the bed. The living room was called the girls' playroom. It was huge; there was a piano in the one corner and a few desks and chairs. At the one end were our own little lockers for all our personal bits and pieces. Not very big, but it was nice to have somewhere to keep your things a little private. In the middle of the room was a table tennis table, this was my favourite sport. The master often came and gave us a game though if any of us beat him, he didn't like it, but it passed many an hour away. The dining hall was in the middle of the building, a very big room with tables and chairs, boys up one end and girls the other, usually four to a table. A bell always rang for meals. A first bell to get ready, then a second bell to file into the hall for your meal. I always remember it was a big brass bell which always propped open the dining hall door.

Discipline was always very strict. Boys and girls could never mix. If you were caught together you were in serious trouble with the master. If we were caught doing anything wrong we had to write a hundred lines. I must not . . . whatever it was! Then another thing, we used to have to kneel on our chairs for an hour with our hands on our heads – that was very tiring. The girls and boys were always being caned for something they had done wrong. We always had to wait by the headmaster's office till he came and then he would take you inside and usually it was one on each hand.

Punishment was a very common thing in those days. If you did anything wrong you were punished simply by being barred from a film show which was shown every Saturday night in a building all on its own in the grounds. It was called the 'Rec'. It was a large room with a stage at the one end, where the pantomime was put on. We did our Saturday dancing lessons there and the Scouts and Cubs also used it. There was always some activity going on in there.

As I mentioned earlier there were plenty of sports activities. There was always table tennis. The boys played football and cricket. There was no tennis. The playgrounds were huge, surrounded by lovely gardens, beautifully kept by the gardener who lived round the back of the orphanage in a little bungalow. His name was Mr Tongue. There was another man who helped him. We used to organise a lot of our own games as well. Cubs, Brownies, Scouts and Girl Guides were very much part of orphanage life.

The older boys did quite a bit of the farming and gardening. They also fed the animals. The soft fruit was picked by the girls, to be made into jam in big kilner jars.

Church started off with Holy Communion. There was Matins at 11 o'clock, Sunday school in the afternoon, followed by Evensong. Our church was called St Clement's; it was a lovely church, not far to go just down the road. We were always in our Sunday best. In the summer the girls wore panama hats (you were lucky if one fitted properly) and in the winter a felt hat. We were all inspected from head to toe, then put into crocodile to walk to church. Sometimes we had our own Evensong in the dining hall which was quite nice, boys one side, girls the other. Then the master took the service and read the lesson. I always loved the hymn singing.

School was St Clement's for the infants and Christopher Whitehead for the seniors, but I do believe years ago, before my time, all the schooling was actually done inside the orphanage.

We walked in 'crocodile' everywhere we went, to church and sometimes on long Sunday walks, but always in a crocodile.

We wore a school uniform. All clothes were washed in the laundry and things were always handed down. Shoes were checked weekly for repair and were sent into St John's to be mended. I remember the shop; it's still there today under the name of Badhams.

The orphanage did very little to equip you to face the outside world. I still have my little brown case we were fitted out with together with one set of clothing which we were allowed to choose – our own coat, dress and shoes. I remember the day I left; it was sad really. I went to say goodbye to Mr Smith the headmaster. He shook my hand and his words to me were, 'We have been very proud of you.' This I shall always remember.

Food was very plain. We always had porridge. On a Sunday we had a piece of home cured bacon on a piece of fried bread. On very rare occasions we had a boiled egg. The stew always had lumps of fat in it, and I have always hated fat ever since.

On Christmas Day we used to wake up to the usual apple, orange and sweets! We had our Christmas tea in the big dining hall with lots of visitors who were friends of the master and matron. It was then that we were given our main present. I remember one year I had a table tennis bat. Another year I had a green backed plastic hair brush. I treasured the hair brush because it was my very own.

We had our own dancing classes. It was mainly ballet, some tap and some acrobatics. When we had learned our dances, in the summer months we used to go to various fetes and do the dancing on the green. This I loved mainly because we were able to wear a little makeup and curl our hair. Normally this was forbidden. The boys did gymnastics.

There were some sad times and happy times in the orphanage but I think of the happy times. It was very strict but did us no harm. In fact it taught us to respect our elders. I am now married with a lovely daughter and she often asks me to tell her about the days of the orphanage.

REUNION REMINISCENCES

These are the memories of nine ex-boys and girls from the late 1940s recalling some of their experiences as they toured the former Royal Albert Orphanage in Henwick Road, now the Worcester YMCA hostel, at a reunion recorded in the Worcester Evening News*:*

Headmaster 'Gaffer' Smith wielding his sawn off billiard cue and delivering blows across the hands of boys to leave two-inch wide weals.

Boys and girls receiving 'six of the best' after being kept waiting trembling for at least an hour in the corridor outside the head's office.

David Wilks well remembers receiving twenty-three blows with a stick and having blood seeping from the wounds for days. His 'crime' was failing to pick up stones in the playground.

Discipline was severe, corporal punishment frequent and the youngsters were compelled to undertake numerous hard and menial tasks.

Furious scrubbing every morning and evening as the boys and girls got on their hands and knees to wash their allotted sections of the floor throughout the orphanage.

The groans every month as the children were made to swallow a 'ghastly' green-coloured liquorice powder and also more regular doses of cod liver oil.

The noise of protesting stomachs as youngsters who had refused to eat their meals found them there at the next sitting and even the next day until they downed them. (Brawn was a particular horror.)

Fights behind closed doors as the new boys were 'broken in'.

The regimented plod of shoes along corridors as the youngsters were marched to assembly, outdoor recreation, church on Sundays, Scout and Guide groups, and to regular work in the fields and orchards of the orphanage where many crops were grown and chickens, pigs and cattle reared.

Some orphans occasionally made a run for it hopping on to passing trains at Henwick Halt. When they were eventually caught and brought back, they were put in 'solitary confinement' for weeks.

There were happier times:

The squeals of delight as the orphans plunged in the orphanage's outdoor swimming pool (since filled in) and learned to swim.

The banging of spoons on the tables as the huge annual Christmas pudding bathed in brandy flames arrived in the dining hall together with Christmas presents. Always the same gift each year for every boy and girl such as a table tennis bat or writing pad.

Giggles in the 'dorms' as the youngsters chatted after lights-out. Children went to bed at 8 o'clock and on light summer evenings they wore eye shades to help them sleep!

Counting of coins on the return from Sunday services at St Clement's Church; the offertory collecting bags emptied rather than filled up as they went along the rows of youngsters!

Escapades as boys shinned down the drainpipes to raid the kitchen, girls crept down secretly for bread and jam. Both risked strictly forbidden clandestine meetings. The two sexes were never allowed to mix. They had separate dormitory wings, separate halves of the dining hall, and even sat on opposite sides of St Clements Church.

Among the perks for the orphans were regular visits to the circus and cinemas and seaside day trips on Mark's coaches to Weston-Super-Mare.

Ilma Collins recalled: 'We made our own fun, we got punished and we worked hard but we were adequately fed and well clothed and illnesses were virtually non-existent.'

6

THE 1950s – EPILOGUE

As the 1920s brought us the Jazz Age after World War I, so the 1950s brought us Rock 'n' Roll after World War II with the music of Bill Haley and Elvis Presley.

This was the start of a new Elizabethan age. King George VI, called 'George the Good' died in 1952, and Queen Elizabeth II was crowned on 2 June 1953 amid scenes of magnificent pageantry.

The Daily Mail *called the 1950s a 'Golden Age'. Churches were full, motorways hadn't destroyed the countryside and towns. Trains ran throughout the land. There were no supermarkets, Seaside hotels were full in the summer. This was the last decade of traditional values.*

The Royal Albert Orphanage too had reached its watershed. When the decade began there were about seventy boys and girls on the roll but by the mid-1950s the state of the orphanage had become precarious, the number of children needing its care had dwindled to below twenty and the building had become too large to manage.

In its last days, Ilma Collins remembers going round the top floor attic of this huge building which was seldom used. It was spooky. Cobwebs swayed from the rafters, group photographs of children taken over nearly a hundred years hung from the walls. The corridors and dormitories echoed in silence. The place was full of ghosts.

In 1955 the Henwick building was closed down and the remaining children moved to Fort Royal House where they remained for a further ten years under the care of Mr Hughes and Mrs Harris.

With the arrival of the era of the foster parent, the orphanage became obsolete and the charity's cash reserves were used to convert Fort Royal House to flats for the elderly.

Adrian Christopher Porter was the last child admitted on 6 October 1965, being the 999th since the orphanage was founded in 1862.

The Admission and Discharge Book then closes with the words: 'After the last child had left the home ceased to operate as an orphanage. In

July 1966 a new trust deed was completed authorising the trustees to set up homes for elderly people in need, and to reserve a small fund to assist children in need. The main house at Fort Royal was converted into five self contained flats, a warden's flat and common rooms. In the grounds, an additional small piece was purchased and thereon was constructed a quadrangle comprising thirteen small bungalows suitable for married couples.

As one governor of a children's home once said to me, 'The problem of the nineteenth and twentieth centuries was children. The problem of the twenty-first century is old people!'

PART TWO

Princess Alice Orphanage
Birmingham

1

AN INNOCENT GROWS UP

I was born in Gloucester on 20 March 1935 – the last day of winter. The reason for Gloucester was that my mother wanted a hospital birth, whereas my sister Margaret had been born in our home, 'Brynderwyn' at Ledbury. My parents considered one of the three capitals: Worcester, Hereford or Gloucester, each sixteen miles away from Ledbury by train. In the end they decided I was to be born in a nursing home in Gloucester. The journey my mother took from Ledbury to Gloucester is no longer a railway, Dr Beeching saw to that in the 1960s!

Our home was in Woodleigh Road in Ledbury. As you turn in from Bye Street, my paternal grandparents lived at the black and white timbered cottage on the left hand side. Next to them lived my father's sister Lilian, her husband Walter and their daughter Barbara. We lived in the third house, 'Brynderwyn'. All houses were detached. Our grandparents' house was possibly Tudor but the other two houses were built in 1928. The gardens went back a very long way up Bye Street and our grandparents had a lovely cherry orchard.

My father's three brothers and two sisters had all been brought up at 22 New Street, Ledbury near the Talbot Hotel. It has recently been renamed 'Hamblin Cottage' by later residents. The four boys slept in one room and the two girls in another. When I was born Uncle Wilfrid, Auntie Tops and their daughter Susie lived at 22 New Street where he had a shoe repair business. Uncle Ernie, Auntie Em and their children Reginald, Kathleen, Ronald, Dorothy and Walter lived near the Woodleigh Road Railway Bridge. Auntie Lil and Uncle Walter had a general store and a barber's shop in the Homend, near the Ledbury Market House.

My father and mother met in the post office, where my father still worked, although at home he had a flourishing market garden business. My sister and I were very close. Indeed these were halcyon days but like all good things they were sadly going to come to an end. In April 1938 my father died after a long illness. The only things I remember about him were playing on the dining room table with the Hornby train set and me saying, 'I'll put the engine to bed in the shed!' The other time I remember was him falling off his bike and my mother ushering me out of the way. I was just over three years old. This was rather more painful for my sister Margaret as she was nearly three years older.

On 30 January 1938 my father wrote me a five page letter. He was only thirty-eight years old. I quote from part of his letter.

> My dear Alan, I have written a letter to Margaret, and now I must write one to you, although it seems beyond my power so to do, and although at this stage you are not old enough to comprehend the seriousness of the position, the time will soon come when you will be able to. For some time I have suffered with an internal complaint which is seriously affecting my eyes and the last week, it has got so much worse, that I want to write this letter to you while I can yet see to do it. It seems but yesterday that I went to the Nursing Home at Gloucester and there the nurse brought to show me a little sandy headed baby – a sweet little chap – and I was very happy. Since then my happiness has been marred by the trouble that has come to me, and I feel that anything may happen to me, and I want, while I am able to, to write to you and beg of you – should the worst happen – to look after your dear mummy and Margaret. I leave them both in your care knowing that you will not fail me. You are a dear little chap so loving, so manly that I know you won't fail. My work is hard with my failing sight, I dread the future but with the knowledge that your dear mummy has got you and Margaret, I feel more content, but what a hard time it will be for you all if I should be prevented from working for you. But you must make up for it when you grow up, and treasure your blessings, treasure and love your mummy – she is a lovely woman – far, far better than your daddy knew how to be. She will never fail you – never fail her. Now I must close, my task is done. My God bless you all, and guard you, may you all be happy and please think of your poor daddy sometimes. My fondest love, dear little man, Your Ever Loving Daddy'.

I've always warmed to his courage that he should think of other people when he was going through such a difficult time himself.

Life was not good for the Hamblin family. My father died in 1938, His father in 1939 and his mother in 1940, all in April. I have very fond memories of my Grandad and Granny Hamblin. Grandad was a kindly bearded gentleman and I remember sitting on his lap eating his bread and milk. Granny was a small stout woman and had bright red hair even when she was old. They are all buried in the family plot between the two chapels, ten paces behind the statue of a girl. Their monument has always been a sacred place since my mother first took me there many, many moons ago. Jews turn to the wailing wall in Jerusalem, Christians to their altars, Muslims to Mecca, but I always turn to the monument of my ancestors ten paces behind the statue of the girl in the Ledbury cemetery.

Soon after my father's death my mother rented out the Ledbury home and moved to Worcester where she got a job in the post office there, and acquired a house in McIntyre Road.

While my mother was getting back on her feet we were for some months billeted out. My sister went to live with my mother's brother Percy, his wife Addie and their two children Ruth and Philip. I went to live with two of her friends, Ivy and Olive Thomas in Malvern. My father had sent a postcard to Ivy, when she lived in Cheltenham. The card is dated 20 March 1935 – the day I was born.

> Dear Ivy, A boy this morning. Everything OK. Mildred would like to see you tomorrow, *Thursday* night if you could possibly manage it. If you can't let me know and I'll fix a night for you next week. She can have *one* visitor a night. Time 7 till 8 p.m. Address Clarence Street. Just outside GWR Station. Go straight on by market, bear to right and first turn on left. Let me know as I shall have to fit them in as best I can. Yours Arthur.

I have always referred to Ivy and Olive as my aunts. Ivy was born in 1900 and Olive in 1902. They were school friends of my mother's. Olive was a school teacher but Ivy looked after this Edwardian mansion. I remember their kitchen. On the high shelves were arranged a collection of the most enormous saucepans. One thing I just couldn't stand was their front room which was full of flowers – it was much like the hot house in Kew Gardens! To this day I don't like flowers and plants inside a house. Ivy and Olive were a lovely couple and were very kind to me. They had a black Labrador called Scamp. I used to pull his tail and he never hurt me. My uncle Bert was rather keen on Ivy when he was a young man. They went to the same church but one day he heard her telling off a load of children. This put him off her! So he went and married someone else. But Auntie Ivy was very good to me.

My sister and I also spent a great deal of time in these early years with our maternal grandparents. It was my grandmother who taught me to read, tie my shoe laces and tell the time. Their bungalow was lit by gaslight. In their kitchen was the most lethal meat hook, must have been over a foot high with hundreds of bills pushed down on it. On the side were the flat irons heated on the gas stove.

The one thing I remember about living in the house in McIntyre Road, Worcester was a small woman who was looking after us at the time forcing me to eat an egg. I hated eggs and I was sick. I was never to eat an egg again!

My mother took my sister and me to the Bromyard Road Methodist Church on a Sunday. I remember colouring and drawing as most parents give children to do during the long hour's service. The only thing I recall from those days is the Methodist Minister who I guess was a bit of a 'hell-fire' preacher. He looked down at me, or seemed so to do, as I continued drawing, pointed his finger and shouted, 'You sinner.' I ducked down behind the seat in fear!

We lived in the house in McIntyre Road for only a short time, then we moved to Nelson Road. We both went to the school in St John's. My sister being nearly three years older was in a higher class. I occasionally met her in the playground. White tape crossed the windows in these early days of the war. Sometimes the whole school walked towards the air raid shelters. Whilst sitting on the school floor during a lesson I wondered how I could design a large raised pond and tried to solve the problem of how to stop the water from sinking into the ground. I never came to any conclusion – it was still a problem!

Whether it was for a day or a week, I don't know but my mother took my sister and me to the seaside town of Weston-Super-Mare in the summer of 1939 just before the start of the war. I can still picture the double-decker buses going along the front. I remember crying when I hit my head on the door of an ice cream shop in Weston-Super-Mare.

In 1941 we were travelling back from Malvern with my mother, sister and grandparents. At Henwick Railway Station, my grandfather and sister had already alighted. I put one foot out to get down from the train and the train started off! My mother quickly pulled me into the train and I was in a terrible state. Whether she was able to close the door as well I don't know. When we eventually arrived at Foregate Street Station my mother and grandmother dragged me up to the guard of the train. I don't think they got much joy there. Then we walked up to the engine driver where they shouted their wrath at him. He replied by 'F–ing' and 'B–ing' through the clouds of steam and smoke!

We had a very dear lady to look after us – I think she must have been quite young, perhaps about twenty. She was delightful; her name was Nancy. My mother had whitewashed the coal cellar which we used as a shelter. Margaret and I were down there on beds with Nancy and her boyfriend. My mother was at work. Nancy's boyfriend was in his soldier's uniform, he was a brilliant artist and drew a beautiful badge of his regiment. The air raid siren went, and then there was heard the roar of aircraft engines, to which Nancy's boyfriend said, 'Jerry overhead!'

I dreamt a lot and one dream was about me walking over the earth which was on fire, the world was all in flames!

Two things I recall in my relationship with my mother. I said to her, 'There is a tiger under the bed.' 'No,' she replied. 'You must have been dreaming.' But I was convinced it was real! Once I crept up to her bedroom and saw my mother kneeling by the side of the bed. She was praying. This made a very great impression on me.

Another couple lived with us for a time at Nelson Road with their pretty daughter Patricia. One day when the three of us were returning from school after buying a quarter of a pound of sweets for threepence three-farthings I tapped Patricia on the knuckles with a ruler. My sister told me off. It was a friendly tap but I was in for more trouble. Patricia told her dad and he beat me up – he punched me all round my body. I didn't like him and didn't tell my mother, but soon they left.

The three of us had survived for four years but in May 1942 it was decided that my sister and I were to go into an orphanage. I found this unbelievable as we had so many relatives. My mother was the sixth of seven children and my father was the sixth of six children. But that was how it was. We had no choice in the matter! I believed we were old enough to look after ourselves. The worst years were over. We didn't need to go to the orphanage. I was seven and my sister was nearly ten. We could have done the shopping and helped our mother with the chores. This is not politically correct and I would probably be in a minority of one regarding childcare in 1942 or in this twenty-first century! – but it would have saved Margaret and me from four years of misery.

The night before we were to go to the orphanage we were at our grandparents in Malvern. Our clothes were being marked. I still have a hairbrush with my name on written in blue ink by my grandmother. It's still in a case in the loft somewhere! We dreaded the next day but even though I was scared it was much worse for my sister. She was older and knew more what was happening.

2

PRINCESS ALICE ORPHANAGE

So this horrendous day dawned, 29 May 1942. It was a Friday, the day we went into the Princess Alice Orphanage – part of the charity now called 'Action For Children' – some six miles outside the centre of Birmingham. We travelled with Mother from Worcester on the 144 double-decker Midland Red bus. When we arrived at the PAO the governor introduced himself to us; he was a very friendly Irishman called Mr Harold Roycroft. He was a good man but he laughed out louder the more I cried. In fact I cried more that day than most women do in a lifetime! To me everything was grey: Mr Roycroft was grey, the children were grey, the buildings were grey, the grass was grey – this was hell! It was the most miserable day of my life up to that point.

I remember asking my mother how long we'd be there. Possibly in a

Princess Alice Orphanage, Birmingham. The orphanage is now demolished and a Tesco supermarket stands on the site

state of panic she said, 'Three weeks' – it was to be four years! Then before Mother left she said, 'Well, Margaret can look after Alan.' But Mr Roycroft replied, 'The orphanage is separated into boys and girls.' In fact brothers and sisters were never to meet! Margaret went to live in E.J. House and I went to Beatrice. This was the final indignity. As my sister said, 'We lost our father, we lost our home, we lost our mother and finally we lost each other.'

The first boy I met in Beatrice House was John Christian. He was ten years old and was playing with his trains. He was to remain friends with me till this day. I found at night I couldn't reach the light when I wanted to use the toilet. I was much too small! The first thing I remember doing – following my mother. I knelt down by my bed alone in the dormitory and asked whoever my mother prayed to to take me away from this terrible place.

That same day up in Lancashire a little girl called Shirley Anne Bloomfield entered the orphanage in Edgworth. She was to grow up to be the famous film star Shirley Anne Field. Years later I was to work with her brother Guy, at Harpenden in Hertfordshire.

During its hundred year history the Royal Albert Orphanage in Worcester hosted 999 children. Since 1869 over 27,000 had passed through the National Children's Home and Orphanage before me. The Princess Alice Orphanage was only one of forty branches of this Methodist institution. In fact PAO was originally for children of Methodist parents but I don't think this was the case in 1942, even though my mother was a Methodist. Princess Alice Orphanage was founded by industrialist Mr Samuel Jevons on 19 September 1882. He promised to give £10,000 to build the orphanage if the Wesleyan Methodist Conference could give another £10,000.

The Royal Albert Orphanage in Worcester, some old boys claimed, was 32 acres whereas the Princess Alice Orphanage in Birmingham was 320 acres. PAO was on the corner of Jockey Road and went right down Chester Road. The chapel with a high clock tower was one end of the orphanage, which was one side of a huge square of grass. Opposite the chapel was the hospital built in 1933. On the left-hand side were the boys' houses: Marsh, Seymour, Meriden, Beatrice and Wand. On the right-hand side were the girls' houses: Shaftesbury, Copeley, Icknield, Jevons and E.J. On the left of the chapel was the Brampton Hall and on the right the sisters' dining hall. There was a baker's, and the laundry and swimming pool were behind the girls' houses. In the corner of the field between the boys houses and Jockey Road stood a huge water tower.

The boys and girls were looked after by two ladies dressed in a blue uniform – they were called ‘sisters’. During my years at Beatrice House, I was looked after by at least half a dozen of these ladies. They included Sister Mary Foxhall, Sister Monica Seward, Sister Lilian Sincock, Sister Olive Matthews, and Sister Jean Curtis. We had one sister in training. She must have been between eighteen and twenty years old and was dressed in grey. She was a ‘grey sister’ and her name was Sister Rose Richards. I’ve never been so afraid of anybody as much as I was of Sister Mary Foxhall – even the other sisters were afraid of her! She was a real toughie and I’d seen her in her time punch a boy on his nose when he was rude to her. Yet she was known to be just and fair, which was true. She wouldn’t, however, tell off the bullies. It was alleged she felt that bullying would toughen up the person who was being bullied! The sisters were known as ‘weenies’ and a song was made up by the boys and girls about them. The hymn ‘There’s a light upon the mountain’ was changed to:

There’s a light up in the bedroom
And the weenies coming up
And she’ll give you all a whacking
If you do not hurry up.

Gloria Dawn, who I was to fall in love with in later years, lived in Copeley House and she knew more words to this song. Gloria emigrated to Australia with lots of other boys and girls from the National Children’s Home in January 1950 and broke my heart. My wife and I had the pleasure forty years later of meeting Gloria in Australia. Sadly she died a few years ago.

The sisters were very strict but I suppose they had to be, with two women looking after thirty boys. We were encouraged to write home to our parents and we always started our letters: ‘Dear Mummy, I hope you are well and happy.’ The sisters ate their meals off white linen table cloths. Our meals were eaten off bare whitewood scrubbed tables. However, when visitors visited the orphanage, white cloths were placed over the tables!

In 1943 when I went to the cinema in Birmingham to see the film *The Wizard of Oz* I instantly identified my mother as the good fairy played by the American Edwardian theatre actress Billie Burke and the wicked witch of the west was definitely Sister Mary Foxhall! I felt very much under her power. In fact in those days the sisters were very hard on the young grey sisters in training. It was the custom that they wouldn’t talk to these new young sisters for six months to show if they had 'stickability'.

When I think of the work we children had to do my memory is almost a blank – nothing like so good as the children who were at the Royal Albert Orphanage, Worcester. One thing I do remember was sweeping up the leaves outside Beatrice House. By the time Sister Mary Foxhall had come to inspect my work the leaves had all blown back by the wind. 'That isn't very good,' she said, 'Do it again.' I did it again and again and the result was still the same! One of my first chores was sitting in a circle with the other boys round a large tub in the kitchen peeling the potatoes and other vegetables ready for dinner. Meanwhile two of the older boys Tony and Bob Badger watched us as they puffed away on their cigarettes. They rolled their own. I remember them relighting their fags by the gas stove flame. One day I helped clean the governor's car with two other boys. I remember saying, 'I will write a book one day.' I wonder whether this is it!

Sister Olive Matthews once wrote of her memories of walking round Sutton Park. She said, 'Spring is well on its way, the garden is full of snowdrops and crocuses and bulbs are springing up everywhere. I do love the spring; it always makes me think of Princess Alice and Sutton Park.' However Sutton Park also held dark secrets as I will reveal.

During the last war it was the custom at Princess Alice Orphanage to go wooding and this meant a five or ten mile walk on Saturdays. The sun beat down on us as we passed the German prisoners of war, stripped to the waist and bronzed by the heat, working on the road, watched over by a couple of English soldiers armed with rifles. This was sometimes followed by a Sunday walk. On this particular occasion we were all decked out in our Sunday best, blue blazers and grey shorts (only boys of fourteen years of age and over wore long trousers). Off we set, thirty of us from Beatrice House, accompanied by Sister Mary Foxhall or was it Sister Monica Seward? Whilst at Princess Alice I was very friendly with two boys, Wally Day and Don Parr, and it was Don who featured largely – to put it mildly – on this particular walk. Through Sutton Park and round the lakes we walked, often tired out.

I was not with Don when his fracas took place – I only saw him on the walk back. What happened was this: Don was challenged by red-haired Fred Vowles to jump across a bog. 'I bet you can't jump that!' laughed Fred. 'Oh, yes I can,' said Don. And with one leap he landed in the swamp. Fred's face changed from laughter to fear and as one can understand, he ran off and Don was left to his own devices with no one there to help him. Gradually he sank lower and lower into the bog. He knew that if he didn't do something soon he would very quickly disappear beneath the mud. By this time Don had sunk down to his waist and feeling absolutely desperate clutched at a very slender branch – would it hold his weight? He knew he had no choice and gradually he heaved himself out of the mire. Once he was out the branch broke and he kissed and kissed that little branch for saving his life.

The end of the story is one of irony. As you can guess the sister was not very pleased having a boy of hers walking home covered almost from head to toe in mud. Back at the Beatrice House Don received his punishment. He was sent to bed without his tea for messing up his Sunday best! But Don, humorist as ever, was not really put out. 'I'd have much rather been sent to bed without tea than lose my life!' Don later emigrated to Australia at the same time as Gloria Dawn. He always wanted to be a missionary and became a Methodist minister in Australia.

The dining room was below the younger boys' dormitory which contained fourteen iron beds, seven each side with a corridor in the middle. The dining room looked out onto the playing field and Jockey Road. One morning during breakfast, one of the boys pointed to the perennial stains on the ceiling. Whether they had been there since 1882 who knows! They were urine stains where the chamber pots in the dormitory had been spilt and come through the ceiling. However many times the ceiling was whitewashed the stains still showed through. The boys laughingly stared at each of the fourteen stains. Starting at one end they pointed to where the boys slept: 'That belongs to Fatty Foxworth, Hank Wall, Drayton Byrd, Don Parr, Jack Bull, Wally Day, Nelson Fraser . . .' and so on to where the beds were placed in the dormitory.

As I sat there in the dining room my mind always thought of escape. Where could I run to as I looked across the playing field to Jockey Road? There was really nowhere to go. If I crossed the Channel that would be no good – it was occupied by the Nazi jackboot. All seemed hopeless!

The dayroom was below the older boys' dormitory which also contained fourteen beds. The two oldest boys slept in the small room, which made a total of thirty boys. The dayroom looked out on the massive grass square and faced the girls' houses. In the dayroom were housed thirty tall lockers for all the boys' belongings. Inside each locker were placed big black bibles, in large print of 1611 Authorised Version, in almost mint condition. I guess they were seldom used!

When we went to bed we all wore white nightshirts. The sheets were starched cotton and very comfortable – they were cleaned weekly at the laundry. One night we in the younger dormitory were invited to go into the older boys' dormitory. We each got into other boys' beds. There Frank Brown who was a wonderful storyteller started on his story. He said, 'There were two men who had gone to an island but after some days had not returned. Worried about their fate two of the friends started off on this adventure to find them . . .' Frank was interrupted by the sister who came up and chastised us. I never did find out how the story ended!

Soon after I went to the PAO I was caught in the allotments. I didn't know I was out of bounds; I just followed the other boys. For the first time in my life I was caned – I couldn't understand it, I little knew what was happening. Joe Brassington who was the orphanage steward held out a stick about an inch in diameter and said, 'Hold out your hands'; I received one stroke and then had to hold my other hand for a whack. I screamed and screamed. I was only seven. But Mr Brassington was not amused. 'If you don't stop crying,' he said, 'I'll cane you a lot more.' Fortunately he didn't – he was a giant of a man. Many years later I was to see Joe Brassington again. 'Hello Alan,' he said. I looked down at a red-faced plump little man!

I remember looking at the magazine *Picture Post*; it must have been 1943, I was only eight years old. Its centre spread frightened the living daylights out of me. It showed the German army doing the goosestep. The headline read, 'They are coming over here.' In the corner was a diagram – it showed the number of the Germany army as ten men but the British army was only half-a-man. I really thought we were going to be slaves of the Nazis! Adolf Hitler was the 'bogey man' of the time. The sisters used to tell us, 'We pray to Jesus, but the German children pray to Hitler!'

When the air raid siren went there would be a stampede as all thirty of us in Beatrice House would gather our bedding and charge downstairs. There would be a flurry of sheets, pillows, blankets and mattresses and boys descending below. We slept under the tables in the dining room and dayroom till the all clear went. In the day time we listened to the radio and the older boys would tell us to be quiet as the news came on the air. Then the news came through, 'Today 32 allied planes have been shot down and 165 German.' It went something like that! We all cheered but it was obviously British propaganda! Next door at Meriden House a bomb knocked off the chimney; the bomb landed in the woods and made a huge crater.

Sport was very much part of the life of the orphanage. Cricket, football and athletics were held on the field facing Jockey Road. The boys' houses played cricket and football against each other. I remember at cricket half the Beatrice House team were out for under 10 runs! One boy after another would put on his cricket pads, walk out from Beatrice House and walk back after being given out, and so it went on. The orphanage had a very good football team and we played against other schools and institutions. Two of the older Beatrice boys were in the team.

The orphanage had a large farm. As I mentioned there were 320 acres of it. Wheat was grown and harvested and we had a very good baker's run by Mr Salt who was an old PAO boy. The farm contained many cows and milk was delivered every morning to the various houses. Over three hundred children had to be fed. I remember the tall galvanised milk churns each enough for thirty starving boys standing outside the front door! John Coombes was the eldest boy in Beatrice House and he worked on the farm. He was seventeen years old. One amusing incident always makes me smile. It was when a big horse galloped around the field near to Beatrice House, farting as it went. The horse made a very loud noise!

On Sundays and weekdays over three hundred of us, aged from seven to seventeen, assembled outside our respective houses, the boys on one side of the massive square dressed in blue blazers and grey shorts, the girls on the other side of the grass square wearing blue gym-slips, white blouses and black stockings. Then together at a given order we converged on the chapel in a column of twos, oldest in the front, youngest at the rear accompanied by the sisters in true military style. For two hours every Saturday morning we were instructed (all three hundred of us!) in the art of hymn singing by the small, aged, fiery, red-haired Sister Jessie Drayton. Armed with a wooden ruler which descended on the pulpit in ever increasing taps, she would shout, 'NO – NO – NO – NO – NO!' Sister Jessie had even trained the children in hymn singing through the Great War of 1914–1918. As you can guess we got to know the Methodist Hymn Book pretty well. I guess the most sung hymn then was 'I vow to thee my country'. In those days of harsh discipline I still look back in amazement at the graffiti written in the hymn books. Beside one number (say 12) someone had written, 'Turn to 568'; after turning to 568, we were invited to turn to 891. After pouring through some fifty or sixty hymns we came to the climax, which usually read, 'Nosey Parker!' or 'Ivy Willard loves Adam Dean!'

Audrey Wilson was a marvellous soprano and often sang at Sunday services. Her breast heaved in and out in unison to the music almost breaking the buttons on her dress as she sang the anthem 'O for the Wings of a Dove'! We had orchestras and other singers from Birmingham and we would try and stop laughing at funny high notes. It is very difficult to try and stop laughing in church! The boys sat on the left and girls on the right facing the front of the chapel. Could it be that the girls were more blessed than the boys – because in the parable of the sheep and goats, the sheep on his right inherit eternal life, whereas the goats on his left went away into eternal punishment!

We went to church three times on a Sunday. Morning service at 11 a.m., Sunday School at 3 p.m. and evening service at 6.30 p.m. I remember the lovely colourful texts I brought back from Sunday School. Sadly like most of my things they have gone the way of all flesh. The choir processed up the aisle during the first hymn and recessed in the last hymn. The choir boys sat on the left in the choir stalls and the girls on the right. The girls wore black gowns, white tabs and black hats. The boys wore black gowns. My sister Margaret sang in the choir, though I didn't know this at the time.

During one service I pondered the meaning of life. What was it all about? What were we here for? Coloured no doubt by the war, I came up with the conclusion that in this life we are being trained – then when we die we are to fight for St Michael and his angels against

Princess Alice Orphanage, Birmingham. Interior of Chapel

Satan and his angels to finally overcome evil in the universe, just as the Allies were fighting against the evil of the Nazis.

We had very well meaning clergy at the Sunday Services who said, 'When you go home, boys and girls, look up your bibles and read this story again.' As I've already mentioned we had large bound black copies of the Authorised Version in our lockers – possibly there from when the orphanage was founded in 1882. I doubted very much whether the boys in Beatrice, or the boys and girls in the other nine houses, would consult the 'Good Book'. The only piece of scripture the boys in Beatrice knew was found in 2 Kings, chapter 18, verse 27!

Rev. John Litten, principal of the National Children's Home and Orphanage, was a constant visitor. He had written the service book we used in chapel. Another minister who came from NCHO head office in Highbury Park, London N5 was the Rev. Cecil Walpole. Rev. George Parkinson was also on the executive of the NCHO and he would come and give us recitations on Charles Dickens (especially *A Christmas Carol*) – he was a marvellous speaker and a lovely man. The only sermon I ever remember – the rest went over my head – was a preacher who said the most terrible words in the English language were 'Too late'. How true is remorse when we look back at our lives and see the wrong decisions we have made but time has passed us by! (Though the worthy cleric was obviously talking about eternal salvation.) Of the stories and children's addresses I did understand, the most well known parable was the one about a bad apple and how that one bad apple can infect all the other apples in a barrel. So one bad person can have the same effect on the life of the world.

The hour long church services can be too long and too much for a child's bladder and this was the case with Gloria Dawn. She desperately wanted to go to the toilet but in the end found she was wetting herself. But this wasn't the end of the story. The pews we sat on were heavily varnished and in Gloria's case her urine had removed the varnish from the pew and left a big hole. Every Sunday afterwards Gloria was reminded of this when she saw the hole in the varnish. The girls from Copeley House where Gloria lived were much amused and treated her terribly. From then on they teased her and called her 'wet knickers'.

I always felt safe in church – it was a sanctuary. Here we were free from bullying. Then there was an extra bonus. The services were very uplifting, the singing was tremendous under the direction of Sister Jessie. It was like going to a Cathedral Choral Evensong every Sunday.

Every morning Monday to Friday before school we assembled outside the houses where we attended a fifteen-minute service in the chapel. Then we went to Green Lane Junior School by the Midland Red double decker bus. On the bus we would sing:

This time next year where shall I be
Not in this old misery!

The boys and girls referred to Princess Alice Orphanage as Princess Alice Prison! Two things I remember at Green Lane School. One was sitting cross-legged on the floor in a circle with the other children looking up Miss Townrow's skirts! Miss Townrow was a very pretty teacher. The other time was in assembly when the headmistress Miss James rang the bell and made the announcement that the Allies had gained victory over Italy. This was 1943. The boys of eleven years of age and older went to Boldmere Secondary Modern School. At ten years of age as there was an extra intake I went up to Boldmere School in September 1945. I was always ill and John Christian who was my senior by three years kindly walked me back to the orphanage. I was sick all the way!

On 30 September 1942 the secretary of the National Children's Home and Orphanage, Highbury Park, London N5 wrote to Mrs Couch, of The Lindens, Harborne, Birmingham 32. Phyllis Couch and her husband Ray had befriended me and had taken me to their church and into Birmingham. They were extremely kind people. In his long letter the NCHO secretary said, 'I am so glad that you were able to see Alan Hamblin. You may like to know that he was born on 20 March 1935. He is fatherless and the mother has to go out to work, and sometimes is on night duty, and as she was unable to find anyone suitable to look after her children she asked the Home to care for Alan and his older sister Margaret, who is also at the Princess Alice Orphanage.' Phyllis and Ray Couch took me out to tea and the shops and sometimes to the shows in Birmingham. It was all so marvellous. As I mentioned they were very kind but in some ways, with the greatest respect, as I was very fond of them both, I wish they hadn't bothered as I always had to return to the orphanage in the end!

When Mother visited us she always took us into the centre of Birmingham. One day we decided to go to a restaurant we had visited many times before only to find it bombed. This was a common experience of the war, that there were great gaps where buildings had once stood. One of our favourite shops was the large department store

John Lewis. How I enjoyed watching the change machines as they buzzed along the wires.

Quite often on a Saturday morning (the two-hour hymn singing came to an end when Sister Jessie retired) we went to the pictures in Sutton Coldfield or Birmingham. We couldn't wait till the next Saturday to see how the exciting serial finished up. Christmas pantomimes were my favourites; how magical they were and still are!

My memory about food is not so good as the boys and girls in the Royal Albert Orphanage, Worcester. I know we had a huge variety – beef, lamb, pork, toad in the hole, haddock and plenty of rabbit. I know we were always hungry. Once I bought a huge bag of buns from the local baker's for one penny and walked round the field opposite Jockey Road eating them all – I felt very fat afterwards! Another time I went to the local cafe, just outside the orphanage gates on Chester Road, where I sat down for beans on toast for nine pence! One thing I will give Sister Mary Foxhall credit for, she never forced me to eat an egg. She respected my mother's recommendation. In the dining room we sat on stools and the tables were bare white wood. After breakfast one of the boys would bring in a large wooden bowl which contained extra scraps of bread. After the meal we had to put our hands on top of our heads.

Fête days were held once a year on the huge green square of the orphanage when hundreds and hundreds of visitors would come. There would be many stalls and bowling for the pig. The event was always opened by a famous person. All proceeds went to the orphanage. We were happy to show the visitors around.

In those days of the war there were numerous butterflies of all colours, but mostly cabbage whites. On the playing field opposite Jockey Road we would chase the butterflies with our jackets open to try and catch them. We never did, they were much too fast.

One boy I remember falling from a tree; he suffered in hospital from lockjaw. Another boy cut his thumb in the laundry – I believe he cut it off – and went running around the orphanage in agony. He was very tall, in short trousers as he wasn't old enough to wear long trousers. Sybil Sankey died in 1944; she was only fourteen years old. She died from double pneumonia after sitting on the wet grass. The girls from the orphanage were allowed to attend her funeral but we boys had to go for a very long walk instead.

The older boys in Beatrice House decided one day to have a 'willie competition', to see who had got the biggest! We dared not refuse to go in for it or we would have got a hiding. They got a tape measure and we had to have our penis measured. One and a quarter inches, one and half inches, two inches, I heard mentioned. Who won the competition I don't know!

One of the common practices of the boys was to look through the keyhole of the upstairs lavatory after the sister had bolted the door. They would run away laughing. Boys will be boys!

I would lie down on a seat looking up at the sun and dreaming of Utopia – of a world where no one suffered: a world not controlled by the survival of the fittest – sadly I didn't come to any conclusion!

I wet the bed, for how long I don't know, but again I wasn't chastised by Sister Mary Foxhall. What I had to do was put the sheets into a large metal bucket, the one with holes in for draining a mop, then carry the bucket across the huge square of grass over to behind the girls' houses to the laundry. However on my way past the girls' houses I saw two girls running around the playground with their gym slips tucked into their navy blue knickers. They too had obviously wet the bed and were now performing their punishment. In the summer they were OK but this was winter and their arms and legs were blue and numb with the cold. The girls were from Jevons House which was looked after by Sister Ethel Bonsey who was known as being one of the hardest of the sisters. Yet she was a local preacher and told the most beautiful children's addresses in chapel. She was a great storyteller!

As I said I was treated very well by Sister Mary Foxhall for wetting the bed but up in Edgworth, Lancashire it was alleged that the film star Shirley Anne Field wet the bed as a small girl. As a punishment she had to stand in the corner with her wet sheets over her head for some considerable time.

I have always been interested in dates and tried to think of the year in which things happened. I remember holding a nickel threepenny piece and thinking it is this year's – it was 1943 and very shiny! Then I was walking past the Brampton Hall and saying to myself, it is 1944. We are all controlled by time and retrospect about things!

They were tough days; boys were always fighting. If you had teeth you were a cissy! One afternoon I saw the boys running towards the Chester Road. There the older boys were lining up the columns. The total orphanage must have been there – some 150 boys. We were marched up to the quarry where we confronted some hundred or so boys from Kingstanding all lined up in the distance holding their flags. We called them Kingstandingites and were to fight them. We younger ones were pushed into the front and advanced. We threw stones and stones hailed around our heads. I thought this is ridiculous and went back to the orphanage. Later I saw some boys returning with cut heads, blood smeared – the result of the stone fight.

Some boys ran away – it was alleged the longest some boys were away from the orphanage was three months. They lived by stealing and travelled in goods trains. Some boys went as far as Scotland!

Wally Day and Don Parr asked me to run away with them. So after breakfast we walked round the houses outside the orphanage and stole bread and milk from the doorsteps – much to our shame – to help feed us for the day. Then we walked to Sutton Coldfield and stole things from Woolworths. We heard one of the ladies shout, 'Stop those boys!' but we were off! Along the street we were met by a policeman. 'Why aren't you at school?' he asked. Wally Day who was our spokesman replied, 'Our mother is ill and we have done the shopping and are taking these things home to her.' The policeman seemed OK with Wally's reply and wished our mother well. We went to a quarry to eat the bread and drink the milk and had fun sliding down the quarry. We also ate a large tin of fruit which we had stolen. We had remembered to steal a tin opener and spoons! I was amazed that day how many men were around on the streets of Sutton Coldfield. Why weren't they fighting at the front? I never did find the answer. Later at evening time we decided to go back to the orphanage. We were met by the governor Mr Roycroft who drove us back in his car. There was no chastisement but the following day at school they wanted to know why we had played truant.

Wally Day's older brother John asked me to go with him and visit a friend of his outside the orphanage. However when we got there he said, 'They are on holiday,' and decided to break in. Several things were taken, including jam and food. Some time later, whether I had spoken out of turn or not, the police were called in. At eight years old I went in front of a deputation of eight Birmingham police chiefs encrusted with gold braid who sat behind a desk asking me questions. I think their verdict was, 'You were easily led.' Unfortunately for John Day he was eventually sent to Borstal.

I was nearly always in hospital suffering with acidosis and by the time I was better after several weeks I had to learn to walk again. In those days I was quite depressed but the sisters in the hospital were very kind. It is a marvellous thing to wake up in the morning and know you're going to be looked after! On the radio one day in hospital, it was possibly 1943, I heard the most glorious sound that seemed to chase all the gloom of mine away. Over the air came the song:

There'll be blue birds over
The White Cliffs of Dover
Tomorrow just you wait and see . . .

Never has music so enraptured my soul. Whether it was Vera Lynn or Anne Shelton or someone else it was a very young voice and it was absolutely marvellous. I always think a woman's singing voice has the edge over a man's.

In the hospital in those days were boys and girls who were suffering from scarlet fever, diphtheria, mumps, measles (English and German), chickenpox and whooping cough. I had chickenpox and I remember it so well as I had my eighth birthday there. The only trouble was all my birthday presents were burnt once I had seen them! I remember thinking how ridiculous that was. I had a few postage stamps and I wondered how one little stamp could spread disease!

We were very naughty and would put a tin by the side of our beds in hospital with a few coppers in. When visitors came to visit the orphanage they would pass us and say, 'Poor little chap,' and put a few coins in the tin. Much to my embarrassment I made quite a few shillings!

In those days we had toothpaste – Gibbs Dentifrice in tins. We rubbed our toothbrush over a hard paste.

People may feel sorry for orphans who have lost one or both parents but in many ways children are much tougher emotionally than adults. One should feel a great sense of sadness for the widow or widower, who has lost half of themselves.

During the whole time I was at PAO I never saw another boy's relatives come to Beatrice House. But I guessed they had a mother or father. I guess much less than one per cent of children ever lose both parents. My mother was the only one who visited.

With the healthy revolution of the 1930s and all the keep fit clubs, it was the custom to be outside and this was the case with us. It seemed to be a sin to be inside! In the coldest weather we would be outside crying because of the cold. Older boys, say twelve or fourteen years of age, would come and rub our hands to try and keep us warm. We always had 'chaps'.

The orphanage had an indoor swimming pool behind the girls' houses. Many competitions were held between the various boys' and girls' houses. I once went there in my costume and was chucked in the deep end. Here I am to tell the tale but I was scared of water then and still am today.

Many Eisteddfods were held in the orphanage. All sorts of arts and crafts were competed for by the boys and girls. Mrs Roycroft, the governor's wife, was very much part of this.

My main dream or nightmare in those days was with wolves. Why this was I don't know. I would see their red eyes and would be so afraid. I was always running away from them but never quite made it!

Welshman Trevor Thomas, who was a brilliant man, took over as governor from Harold Roycroft in the summer of 1945. Mr Roycroft went to be governor of the Harrogate branch of NCHO. Mr Thomas was extremely strict and would lecture us after assembly, in church. He would say, 'What did you say, laddie?' and laddie would have to reply from the nave of the chapel! He came from the approved school of the NCHO in Penarth.

We at Beatrice House once went on strike. We went around the orphanage banging on pots and pans and didn't do any work. Why we took this line of militancy I don't know! About this time Sister Rose Richards was punched in the nose by a boy and he made her nose bleed. Neither the punching of Sister Rose nor the strike would have taken place in Sister Mary Foxhall's day but she had retired by then. Regarding these two incidents we had a visit from Mr Thomas. The rest of us were in the dining room and he took the ringleaders out in the hall and caned them. We heard their screams!

But Trevor Thomas thought Beatrice House had done well on Christmas Day when we came second in the table decoration competition for the main dinner held in Brampton Hall. What he didn't realise was that we had won in 1942, 1943 and 1944! Christmas was a lovely time in the orphanage. We could do nothing wrong for those two days.

Beatrice House was blacklisted because of our strike and we weren't allowed to go to the American Services parties. Boys who went from the other houses said they were chucking sweets away on the road because they had so many. We really did lose out!

Gloria Dawn once had her photograph taken with the Hollywood film star Vivian Blaine who visited the orphanage during the war. Vivian is known for her part in *Guys and Dolls* with Marlon Brando, Jean Simmons and Frank Sinatra which was made in the mid-1950s. Gloria stood by Vivian Blaine eating an ice cream. Gloria was twelve, Vivian about twenty-four. The photograph was signed by Vivian Blaine. I would have loved a copy.

On VE Day on 8 May 1945 we danced around a bonfire dressed up as cowboys and Indians. It seemed unnatural that peace had come. After all war was the natural state of affairs! About that time we went to see a film at the cinema in Birmingham. The tune 'O God our help in ages past' was the theme music of the film about a family who lived through the war. After the film was over the screen showed portraits of generals, admirals and marshals of the three services of all the Allies, three pictures at a time. It went on for ages. Every time the portraits changed we all cheered. These men had conquered the world in our eyes – especially Churchill, Montgomery and Eisenhower – they were like gods!

Before the General Election of 1945 the streets of Birmingham were painted with the words 'Labour for Victory' in huge white letters. This was a complete irony, when in everyone's eyes Churchill had won the war.

I received so many presents at Christmas 1945 that I didn't write one thank-you letter – it was all too much, I'm ashamed to say. I even had the help of the house girl. She was very nice. House girls were orphanage girls who were fourteen years old and came to help the sisters.

At the orphanage up in Edgworth, Lancashire a fellow girl inmate said that little Shirley Anne Field would walk up and down the dormitory in her nightdress saying, 'When I grow up I'm going to become a film star.' Many, many years later I mentioned this to Shirley Anne at an 'Action For Children' Reunion and she said, 'And I did, didn't I?'

Throughout our time at the Princess Alice Orphanage, Margaret and I received weekly parcels from our mother. Inside was a letter and a gift all wrapped up in brown paper and string and sealed with sealing wax. They were always much appreciated.

In 1944 the government brought in the Curtis Report – it was to change everything. No longer were boys and girls to be separated – they were to be mixed in small groups of ten or twelve. We boys used to bath and shower, sometimes two in a bath, and the boys were discussing the Curtis Report and said, 'Well now we will be able to bathe with the girls!' Also in the Curtis Report the school leaving age went up to fifteen which meant I'd have to stay a further year in the orphanage – I wasn't happy!

3

HOLIDAYS

My mother wrote to the National Children's Home and Orphanage on 31 March 1942 asking, 'Could Margaret and Alan come to me or relatives for holidays?' The answer came back from NCHO on 2 April 1942 with a positive answer, 'You or anyone whom you nominate can have Margaret and Alan for summer holidays.'

However, this was not to be the case. NCHO were economical with the truth as we were not allowed to go home for our holidays in the summer of 1942. Presumably we hadn't been there long enough. My sister and I were devastated as we were very close to our mother. NCHO's action was very cruel.

Summer 1942 we had to spend at Princess Alice Orphanage but the summers of 1943, 1944 and 1945 thankfully we spent with our mother and relatives. These years seem almost to be rolled into one with the odd exceptions. Our six weeks' holiday in these years were spent either with my mother's parents at their bungalow in Malvern, with my mother's sister Phyllis, her brother-in-law, Newton and our cousins David, Dorothy and Eunice at their farm in Bringsty, Worcester, or with my father's sister Lilian and her husband Walter and our cousin Barbara at Ledbury. They were all a little surprised to hear me talking with a Birmingham accent! When my mother wasn't working we lived with her at her home in Worcester and for a time in 1945 we went to visit my mother's friends in Canterbury.

Our grandparents lived in a beautiful bungalow at the base of the Malvern Hills. To reach it we had to walk up a very steep hill. As we climbed the hill, on each side of the path hung pear trees, and apple trees of all types and plum trees both Victoria and Pershore which we could pick on our way up. Near the bungalow at the top of the hill were planted 'Lloyd George' raspberries, gooseberries, blackcurrants, strawberries and many vegetables.

My grandfather, Sardius Hancock, was in many ways my hero. He was very short of stature, slightly balding, had a moustache, took size 6 in shoes, and was seventy when I was born. When staying with our grandparents it was wonderful to wake up to the sound of the cock crowing at their bungalow. My grandfather kept hens and was always upset when foxes would bite through the chicken wire and kill the hens. I would follow him around his large grounds and then into the undercroft of the bungalow where he kept his feed and all the fruit lined up on shelves.

He would tell me about David Lloyd George and Winston Churchill whom he knew before the Great War 1914–18. In those days Lloyd George was to bring in a 'Great Land Reform Campaign' but this never took place because of the outbreak of the Great War. My grandfather was one of Lloyd George's 100 speakers. He never did get into Parliament at Westminster but fought the West Worcestershire seat in the General Election of 1922 against the Chancellor of the Exchequer, Stanley Baldwin, who received 11,193 votes for the Conservatives and my grandfather (Sardius Hancock) 5,749 votes for the Liberals. My grandfather said, 'Lloyd George destroyed the Liberal Party.'

Oliver Cromwell, so my grandfather thought, was the greatest man who had ever lived. He also thought a lot of Gladstone. He had a birthday book and he was very proud of the entry of his great-uncle John who wrote in it with his birth of 1794. His great-uncle told him he could remember the Battle of Trafalgar in 1805. I saw for myself the lovely copperplate writing of 'John Hancock 1794' in his birthday book.

On my grandparents' sideboard was a picture of my grandfather's younger brother all dressed up in robes. He was a lovely man with a bushy white beard who had a quite eccentric wife. Years later I had lunch with Great Uncle Gideon and Great Aunt Catherine and she said, 'When you are choosing a husband or wife it is like picking up a stick from a bunch, make sure you pick up the right stick!' Great-uncle Gideon was the proprietor of a drapery store in Salisbury. He eventually became Lord Mayor of Salisbury, and opened the New Harnham Bridge over the River Avon, in Salisbury, on Wednesday 8 March 1933.

A framed document hung on my grandparents' wall in their lounge. It contained the medals of my Uncle Wilfred. He was a rifleman in the King's Royal Rifle Corps and was killed on 3 September 1916, a month after his twenty-first birthday, at Guillemont in the Battle of the Somme. He was one of 750,000 men who never came back. At the start of the war he worked at the Government Offices in Coventry, where people passed the 'white feather' as a sign of cowardice to men who had not joined up for service. This, so my mother told me, was the reason why he joined up.

His older brother Ralph had a broken leg which caused him to be on leave in 1916 when he heard of the death of his brother Wilfred. This upset him greatly as Wilfred had been given a white feather and Ralph did not consider that his brother was cut out for fighting. Uncle Ralph, a lieutenant in the Worcesters, returned to the front once his leg was better. He was taking his men over the top of the trenches in no-mans-land, when he was shot from a tank. His body was never found and my grandmother thought he would turn up. Married only two years, his death in 1917 left a young widow and a child not a year old. His daughter Joan, born in 1916, was the apple of my grandparents' eyes they were always talking about her. Sadly Joan has since died.

My grandmother had five sons. As I've mentioned, Ralph and Wilfred were killed and Bertram came back from the war terribly gassed. Her eldest son was Clive and her youngest Percy. She never went to a Remembrance Service as she was too upset to go. I remember her saying to me that if only women were in charge of the world it would be a much better place.

In the late 1880s my grandmother was a dressmaker and I once asked her why women didn't wear trousers. She said to me, 'Well, a man's body goes straight down, whereas a woman's body goes in and out with their hips – therefore trousers don't hang well on them.'

On Sundays my grandparents invited the ministers who had conducted the morning's service at Somers Park Methodist Church in Malvern, back for lunch. It would be marvellous listening to their conversations – I was always fascinated by what adults said. In those days children were seen but not heard but I was quite prepared to listen! They were all so articulate and full of wisdom. Every mealtime my grandfather would have the open family Bible by his side. The signatures of the Hancock ancestors went back to 1720. He would always read a portion from the Bible before we ate.

The two most memorable people my grandfather brought back from the church at Somers Park were American servicemen. I believe in the war there were eight American hospitals in Malvern. From the top of the Malvern Hills all the American hospitals looked white. Major Lovain, who was a chaplain, was a very jolly fellow. I thought he was like a man from the moon – he was so different to us in accent and clothes. He always came laden with goodies. His uniform was absolutely magnificent.

Major Lovain was from Georgia and many years later invited my mother to the United States but I don't think she ever went. One Sunday Major Lovain brought back with him a young tall lieutenant from the American army. He was twenty-one years old and was 6 feet 4 inches tall. I remember he broke his violin string when he was with us. He was a brilliant violinist – he was in fact the great-grandson of the famous Czech composer Dvorak!

My sister related to me an incident which I recall happening at our grandparents' bungalow when we were there. Margaret writes, 'Do you remember the time in the war, when we were asleep, and we heard this clumping up the stone steps outside the bungalow? I know Mum thought the Germans had landed and it was their hob-nailed boots clattering up the steps. It turned out to be a big horse which had got out of its field and it was the horse shoes that were clumping up and down the steps!'

From my grandparents' kitchen-dining room we looked down over the half an acre of ground, with all the fruit trees in bloom – it was a wonderful sight. There was only one snag: with fruit trees come wasps and during the war there were millions and millions of more wasps than there are today! In fact I believe it was the cold winter of 1947 that vastly reduced the population of the wasps and butterflies. One lunchtime we had eaten our first course in peace and were about to start on our pudding. It was a lovely plum pie, made in a dish with a funnel in the middle. Instantly through the window came a squadron of wasps, in several formations – I should say at least a hundred of them. They flew around and around our heads. There were as many wasps as plum stones around the edge of my fruit bowl. 'Eat up your pudding, Alan, never mind the wasps!' said my mother. But I was terrified of being stung in the mouth as I ate my plums. I only wished my grandparents and mother would kill more of them. They could kill a wasp in mid-flight by flicking them! Fortunately I never did get stung.

My grandparents had a lovely ginger female cat called 'Tit'. Every night my grandfather would put Tit on his shoulders and carry her down the steep path of his grounds to a shed where she spent the night.

I always consider the quarrying of the Malvern Hills as one of the saddest things done in nature. During the war the North Hill was all exposed stone; it has now grown over since the quarrying has stopped but still has a very dangerous drop. For some reason there were nearly always fires on the hills during the war – why this was I never did find out. As far as I know no houses were damaged.

I remember listening to the radio alone in my grandparents' front room, it was the summer of 1944. In those days there was a five minute slot for charities to advertise their product. The programme was called 'This Week's Good Cause Appeal'. This particular week it was on behalf of the National Children's Home and Orphanage. I pricked up my ears! Listening to it I found it was all 1944 'Political Spin'. The National Children's Home and Orphanage they painted was absolutely perfect, nothing like the real thing. It was a complete whitewash! But that's politics for you!

Our visits to our uncle's farm during those war years of 1943, 1944 and 1945 were some of the most memorable. The farm was in Bringsty, Worcester, miles from anywhere and in the distance you could see the Malvern Hills. My cousin Eunice said, 'It was a glorious sight.' My mother's older sister Phyllis had travelled out to Canada in 1929 on her own to marry my Uncle Newton. They had three children, David born in 1930, Dorothy in 1931 and Eunice in 1936. In 1939 they returned to England for a holiday but never went back. My uncle was full of remorse in his retirement. 'If I had stayed in Canada I would be a multi-millionaire,' he would say. In fact when he first went to Canada in 1922 he had worked for a very old farmer who in his youth had fought with General Custer!

My uncle was always very modem in his approach to farming, something he had inherited from working in Canada. He had a herd of some two dozen cows. They were black and white, British Friesian, and were milked mechanically. At milk time in the cattle shed a large saucer of milk would be put out for the wild farm cats. We could never catch them. There must have been six to a dozen of them living in the huge barns.

I always found it fascinating when we travelled by horse and cart watching the horse's mane go up and down and from side to side as it pulled us along. We spent many happy hours with our cousins in the cornfields and on the combine harvester at harvest time. There was no indoor toilet, but one in a little wooden hut at the bottom of the garden. I believe my uncle buried the contents! At the time my uncle had a German prisoner of war working with him called Hans. I don't believe my uncle knew any German and I don't think Hans knew any English but they got on OK.

My Uncle Newton and Auntie Phyllis were a good couple and went to the Methodist Church in Bromyard. Again it was fascinating at mealtimes listening to their conversations. My aunt once said to my uncle, 'You love the cows more than you love me!', as my uncle was often talking about Buttercup and Daisy and others of his cows. Years later I mentioned this to my cousin, Dorothy and said how your mother would share a joke with your father saying, 'You love the cows more than you love me!' My cousin replied, 'She wasn't joking!' Husbands and wives say things to each other through familiarity but I don't think they wish to really hurt.

We slept at the farm for several nights during these years. The farmhouse was very old, possibly Tudor, and the door handles were catches. It was a very picturesque black and white property. One night they put me to bed, possibly through lack of room, with my cousin Eunice who was a year younger than me. In the morning I woke up alone in bed. I said to my mother, 'Where is Eunice?' My mother replied, 'You were on top of her, squashing her, so we took Eunice out!'

Several days we spent with our Auntie Lil and Uncle Walter and cousin Barbara in Ledbury. Auntie Lil was my father's older sister. Ledbury is a lovely market town and it was always a pleasure to be there with my sister. In many ways we had returned home! My aunt had a general stores in the Homend and we would sleep above the shop. Also upstairs there was a lovely lounge. Behind the shop downstairs was the dining room where we would eat our meals.

Here in Ledbury we would visit Miss Minnett who had a sweet shop next to the cinema. Our Uncle Wilfred, Auntie Tops and cousin Susie we always looked forward to seeing at the Hamblin shoe shop, near the Talbot Hotel in New Street. I remember my Uncle Wilfred made me a white and leather football. We would go to Daisy Cottage and visit Uncle Ernie, Auntie Em, and cousins Kathleen and Dorothy. Cousins Ronald and Walter were away fighting in the army, cousin Reginald fighting the Japanese. Sadly he died in September 1944 during a sea voyage between two Japanese camps; they had been on the water for three weeks. He was twenty-nine years old, and he died from lack of food and beri-beri, a disease which accompanies malnutrition, and was buried at sea. He had been captured at Singapore in 1942 and nothing more was heard until after VJ Day when the Red Cross gave what information they knew.

I would love listening to the conversations between my Uncle Walter and my Auntie Lil, pulling politics to bits, discussing the latest news of the war and putting the world to rights. There was a water pump out in the yard and in a separate building on the other side of the passage was my uncle's barber's shop. My aunt would tell me about her older sister Beatrice who lived with her husband and six children down in Bournemouth. We never saw my cousins Barbara, Eileen, Lilian, Charles, Daphne and Sylvia during the war years but met up with them years later. Our thirteen Hamblin cousins were at least a decade older than me, my father being the youngest of six. Auntie Lil would go on to tell me about her older brother Archibald who had died in the Great War. He was killed when our country was very short of men, and he had no choice of regiment. He was put in the King's Shropshire Labour Corps and was in France for six months. A Ledbury man was with him whilst he sat on a biscuit tin writing a letter to his mother and a bomb from German plane killed him on 9 September 1917 aged twenty-five years. The Ledbury men buried him. Uncle Archibald and cousin Reginald's names are inscribed in the plaque in the Ledbury Parish Church and also on the war memorial opposite the market house.

It was whilst we were staying with my mother in Worcester in the summer of 1945 that I was listening to the radio in bed. Never had I heard such an embarrassing speech as that made by Winston Churchill after his defeat by Labour. His words went something like this: 'What I have done for you people during the war; you treat me like this, and put in a load of Bolsheviks!' This is putting it mildly, this is the cleaned up version, it was much worse than this! I couldn't believe it as his words came over the radio. He certainly didn't take it with good grace.

My mother, Margaret and I must have spent a week in Canterbury in the August of 1945. We went to stay with Mr and Mrs Hopper and their four children who had recently returned to Canterbury after being evacuated to Worcester during the war. My mother met the Hoppers at the Methodist Church in Bromyard Road, Worcester. They were bakers by trade.

Here on their long drive I learnt to ride a bike after practising for some time. Mr and Mrs Hopper's youngest daughter learnt one day and I learnt the next. Years later their eldest daughter married the son of the holiday giant, Fred Pontin. I went to their fabulous wedding, lavishly held in the Trocadero Hotel, Piccadilly, London. We had seven courses at dinner followed by cigars and speeches which went on for a very long time. I remember going to the cloakroom and one of the hotel staff in his uniform brushed me down and I gave him half a crown. That was all I had in my pocket! Later there was a three course meal followed by dancing. I was dancing with the bride in the evening but left in time to catch the last train back to Harpenden. This was in 1958.

I was ill in bed, in the Hoppers' home in Canterbury in early August of 1945. As I listened to the radio I heard that the Allies had dropped an atomic bomb on Hiroshima, Japan on 6 August 1945 on a population of 375,000 people. To my mind this was cheating! We later went to Dover where I saw marooned sunken war ships in the harbour.

I remember on the day before we were due to go back to the orphanage after six weeks' holiday I was crying in the bathroom of my grandparents' bungalow in Malvern. I can't remember whether it was 1943, 1944 or 1945. When I came out of the bathroom my mother asked, 'Why are you crying?' I knew that adults would not understand the truth that I didn't want to go back to the orphanage, so I said, 'I have hurt my toe.'

4

EXODUS

My sister was sent to the children's home at Alverstoke, part of the National Children's Home, the other side from Portsmouth Harbour, in October 1945. Margaret went to Alverstoke because she was ill with asthma. They thought the seaside air on the south coast would do her good. When we had gone to the PAO in 1942 Margaret was well, and it was me that was ill with acidosis. Margaret was to join a mixed family of only ten children in Hudson House, Alverstoke. Amongst the children were Ann and Valerie Pretty.

One day I was in the Beatrice House kitchen. This was in January 1946 and Sister Rose Richards came in and said, 'I have good news, Alan, you are to go to Alverstoke to be with your sister.' At the same time through the window came a great light – the kitchen was nearly always in darkness. A voice through the light seemed to say, 'You thought I'd forgotten you but I have answered your prayer!' I was blinded and dazzled by this light. All this time Sister Rose from behind me kept repeating, 'Isn't it good news, Alan. Isn't it good news?' I was in two minds. Though I was very grateful I turned towards the light and said to myself, 'But why has it taken so long – why did I have to wait four long years!'

I was angry yet grateful all at the same time! It had been to me four years of hell and yet never once had I thought of suicide. Puberty had yet to take place with me. I believe adults are more vulnerable to suicide once puberty has taken place. In the days of innocence there is no such thought. At puberty when the hormones start rushing through the body it makes us emotionally weaker. Therefore I believe puberty makes adults emotionally weaker than children. As William Wordsworth said, 'The child is father to the man.'

People say there is no certainty in life apart from death! I would say the other certainty in this life is prayer. Archbishop William Temple who was Archbishop of Canterbury from 1942 to 1944 said, 'When you pray coincidences seem to happen. When you don't pray coincidences don't seem to happen.' I'm sure he was right.

I feel I was touched by that same wonderful power we read about in the 'Good Book'. It was a miracle. I should have had to stay at Princess Alice Orphanage till 1950 – instead I left in 1946. When I look back at my long life I think the greatest virtue we human beings possess is a sense of forgiveness and charity towards others.

For the four years I was in Beatrice House I felt I was like a small white dove living in a large birds' cage, an aviary where the biggest birds, the eagles, the hawks, and the vultures were fighting each other in the centre of the cage. I would shelter at the edge. Then when Thursday 31 January 1946 arrived the gates opened and I flew up high into the deep blue sky! When I arrived at the Princess Alice Orphanage all those years ago everything was grey. Now I looked down and everything was full of light, there were reds, oranges, yellows, greens, blues, indigos and violets – all the colours of the rainbow. I flew around the orphanage three times looking down at the children, the houses, the clock tower, the chapel and the hospital all bathed in colour and then I flew south!